D0700215

AGENCY AND ETHICS

The Politics of
Military Intervention

Anthony F. Lang Jr.

STATE UNIVERSITY OF NEW YORK PRESS

Published by
State University of New York Press, Albany

© 2002 State University of New York

All rights reserved

Printed in the United States of America

No part of this book may be used or reproduced in any manner whatsoever
without written permission. No part of this book may be stored in a retrieval
system or transmitted in any form or by any means including electronic,
electrostatic, magnetic tape, mechanical, photocopying, recording, or
otherwise without the prior permission in writing of the publisher.

For information, address State University of New York Press,
90 State Street, Suite 700, Albany, NY 12207

Production by Cathleen Collins
Marketing by Michael Campochiaro

Library of Congress Cataloging in Publication Data

Lang, Anthony F., 1968–
    Agency and ethics : the politics of military intervention / Anthony F.
Lang, Jr.
        p. cm.—(SUNY series in global politics)
    Includes bibliographical references and index.
    ISBN 0–7914–5135–6 (alk. paper)—ISBN 0–7914–5136–4 (pb : alk. paper)
        1. Intervention (International law)—Moral and ethical aspects.
    2. Humanitarian assistance.   I. Title.   II. Series.

    KZ6368 .L36 2001
    341.5'84—dc21   00–054789

10 9 8 7 6 5 4 3 2 1

Contents

Preface

In May 1798, the French government sent Napoleon Bonaparte with a large army and armada to conquer Egypt. Intervening in Egypt was not a new French policy; it had been suggested by the philosopher Leibnez in the seventeenth century in order to undermine the power of the Dutch. In 1798, however, the enemy was now England. While invading England herself was not possible, striking at perfidious Albion through Egypt and India seemed more sensible.

The intervention, however, was not only about power politics. A report from the French consul in Ottoman Egypt in 1797 justified the expedition in more humanitarian terms: "He declared that the hour was ripe for intervention, that the Egyptian people, victims of oppressive and corrupt government, would welcome it, that Turkey, the suzerain Power, would rejoice over the downfall of the Mamlukes, unruly subjects and bitter adversaries (Elgood 1931, 50). Spreading the ideals of the French Revolution meant freeing those unfairly oppressed by backward and uncivilized rulers.

A further normative reason for the intervention had to do with knowledge. The French believed that after their revolution they would be able to provide the world with the reason and knowledge of the *philosophes*. Part of that process meant uncovering the lost wisdom of ancient civilizations, like Egypt. So, accompanying Napoleon and his army was a second army of sorts, a group of scholars and artists whose role was to make a record of the vast store of Egyptian antiquities. As the army fought the ruling Mamlukes, the scholars accompanying them made sketches, measured distances, and wrote journals.

So, while power politics certainly played a role in the decision to intervene, normative reasons remained central. Indeed, throughout the course of the intervention, these normative reasons continued to play an important role in the explanations given to the Egyptians, French soldiers, and French citizens.

Two records of this expedition give us a unique picture of it, a picture that remains relevant to this day. The first comes from Dominique Vivant Denon whose work *Voyage dans la Basseet la Haute Égypte* rivaled only the *Description d'Égypte* in its popularity. Vivant Denon chose to accompany one of the generals whose task it was to pursue the Mamluke leader, Mourat-Bey, into southern Egypt. In the course of this pursuit, Vivant Denon was able to record ancient temples, the mores of the people, and even the weather and topography, both in pictures and words. His work has recently been republished as part of the French government's celebration/remembrance of 200 years of interactions between Egypt and France (Vivant Denon 1998).

This record of the Napoleonic expedition to Egypt has much to teach us about military intervention. Even though it was written by a scholar whose primary aim was not political or military conquest, his comments on these elements are revealing. Vivant Denon does not hide his pride in being a Frenchmen, and has no compunction in celebrating the intervention as a demonstration of France's Enlightened approach to the world. As the ships set sail, he sees in them "la splendeur de la France, de sa force, de ses moynes." Nor is this expedition only for the aristocracy; as France represents now the "rights of man," those gathered on the shore to send off the expedition include "individus dus de toutes les classes de la société" (Vivant Denon 1801/1998, 37). The glory of France exists not only on the departure, but displays itself in the midst of the intervention as well. As the troops pursuing Mourat-Bey come upon the glory of Thebes, they burst into spontaneous applause. For Vivant Denon this reaction reveals that which makes France unique—that its troops had such a sensitivity to art and beauty they would applaud while in the midst of a military campaign (194). And, not only can they appreciate beauty, the soldiers are also sensitive to the humanitarian needs of a native population oppressed by the ruling Turkish class, caring for children left behind in their villages (207).

So, on one level, the military intervention in Egypt represented not simply power politics (although that certainly prompted the intervention), but a larger task of somehow presenting France to the world. Vivant Denon's book became one of the best-selling books describing the expedition and was translated into a number of other languages soon after its publication in French. But presenting France to the world was not the only fact of the intervention. It also disrupted the life of Egyptians, socially, economically, and politically. Vivant Denon observes how the presence of troops had a profound influence on the lives of those living in Egypt. He describes how the French army, the model of efficiency, created its own society and economy when it took over a town or village (211). Perhaps more importantly, he describes how the presence of the French army caused disruptions in the systems of tribal authority which existed in Egypt (81), to say nothing of the fact that the French created their own government in Cairo, run by a French general who had converted to Islam. The second text that provides insights into this intervention comes from a different perspective, that of an Egyptian. Abd al-Rahman al-Jabarti, a Muslim scholar of Ottoman Egypt, provided three different accounts of the French intervention. His most famous is the *Tarikh muddat al-Faransis bi Misr*, or *Chronicle of the French Occupation*, written in the midst of the intervention. It describes the French attempt to win over the Muslim population. More importantly, however, it describes the Muslim revolt of mid-October 1798. While that particular uprising failed to change French policy, it did provide a "harbinger for future Franco-Egyptian relations" (Tignor 1993, 9). Those relations were characterized by the local population resisting the French presence at every turn. While the French eventually left Egypt in 1801 for a number of reasons, one of the most important was undoubtedly the resistance offered by Egyptians as described by al-Jabarti.

The normative impulses that lead to and sustain an intervention, and the resistances and conflicts generated by those normative impulses, can be found in almost every intervention since that time. The attempt to accomplish a set of normative aims and the assertion of the identity of the intervening power can be seen in interventions as old as the French in Egypt and as new as the Americans in Somalia. This book is an attempt to describe and explain these elements of military intervention. It seeks to do so by explaining why interventions, even humanitarian interventions, seem to fail more often than they succeed. Not only that, it is an attempt to put those elements in a larger context—to use them to understand what is "the political." Not politics, although the political certainly informs and structures politics, as this book will demonstrate in one particular realm. No, this book is about the political, that "constitutive, quasi-transcendental setting or matrix of political life" (Dallmayr 1996, 193), a distinct realm, one that differs from the economic, the social, the family, and the religious. While the political impacts and is impacted by each of these other areas of human existence, it cannot be reduced to any of them. The political inhabits a particular space in the ambit of human life. In supposing that one can speak of the political as a separate realm, I follow the lead of political theorists like Claude Lefort, who seek to "look for signs of the political in areas where its existence usually goes unnoticed or is denied, and a willingness to recognize and identify those signs" (Lefort 1988, 1). While Lefort's search takes him to the intersection of politics with the social, my search moves elsewhere to the realm of interstate politics, or what is more commonly called international relations.

In this book, I focus on the normative and the political, both of which are manifestly displayed in a military intervention. Normative does not mean ethically good on every register; rather, normative are those actions that either regulate behavior or construct identities. In the terms of Aristotle, the normative characterizes almost every action, for every human action is designed to accomplish some good, or *telos*. The political is the world of conflict and competition. It is a realm in which identities are asserted, contested, sometimes dissolved and remade, but always in a state of agonistic tension. But it is conflict of a particular type, a stylized conflict. It occurs within the confines of a structure, whether it be a parliament, an international organization, a labor-management negotiation, a church council, or a student council. What distinguishes politics from a brawl is that it is structured by certain rules, the most important of which is that the players are granted some form of agency. Their status may not be completely equal (although they usually have some formal equality), but they must be given some form of agency, the ability to speak and act as individuals. The rules that structure their contest will define this agency in certain ways, but it will always assume that it exists.

With these two notions in mind, the ethical and the political, I intend in this book to explore a particular political phenomenon, military intervention. More specifically, I will demonstrate that these aspects lead to the failure of intervention. I recognize that studies of military intervention do not usually focus on questions as broad and deep as those I have raised. This book differs from most studies of intervention in that it does not seek to extract "lessons" that can improve intervention in the future, nor does it seek to establish an explanation for intervention based on its frequency. Instead, it employs a deductive framework to analyze a political phenomenon. Simultaneously, it will use this phenomenon to explore and expand this deductive framework.

This book also seeks to combine the empirical and the normative. For one of the banes of modern social science is the inability to see beyond the simple dichotomy of a world divided into is and ought. Especially in politics, where what is is constantly being reshaped to create what ought to be, such distinctions create sterile analyses. The pursuit of objectivity and elimination of bias will be part of this analysis, but the refusal to confront normative conclusions will not. For, in the end, I argue that military intervention is a politically and morally flawed policy. This conclusion is not based on my "subjective feelings," but on my analysis of what constitutes the political.

In the pages that follow, I explore three twentieth-century military interventions to elucidate these notions of identity, conflict, agency, and ethics. By exploring what may seem to be highly theoretical concepts, I intend to provide answers to some of the more pressing practical dilemmas of international politics.

Acknowledgments

This book, like any other, is the product of many helping hands. While those I mention here played an obvious role, others I have inadvertently forgotten have been just as instrumental.

When this book, in a much different form, began as a dissertation, friends at Johns Hopkins University were extremely generous in discussing its ideas or reading chapters: David Bernell, Martha Bishai, Stephan Cornellis, Douglas Dow, James Marino, Char Miller, Carol Pech, Jason Phillips, and Ward Thomas. Conversations and debates with Jim Marino and Char Miller have been exceptionally helpful, as has been their friendship. Friends at other institutions who have read or discussed the ideas include Matthew Slaughter and Kenneth Scheve.

Academics at Johns Hopkins and elsewhere have played a key role in sparking my interest in these ideas and helping to bring them to fruition: Thomas Berger, William Connolly, Benjamin Ginsberg, Siba Grovugui, Cynthia Weber, and Alexander Wendt all read sections and commented on them. Four individuals in particular deserve mention. David Campbell's seminars prompted many of the questions raised here and his ideas continue to challenge my thinking. Nicholas Onuf, whom I met through a symposium on international relations theory, was kind enough to read large sections of the theoretical chapters and make exceedingly useful comments. His willingness to read the work of someone not his own student and his hospitality in Florida reassured me that scholars of international relations can "construct" a world that stretches beyond institutional boundaries. Richard Flathman piqued my interest in one of the two political theorists whose work informs this essay, Hannah Arendt. His reading of this book *qua* dissertation greatly improved its theoretical rigor and analytic clarity. Even more so, his patience with a student of international relations assuaged many of my concerns upon venturing into the realms of political philosophy. Steven David played an invaluable role in this work.

He introduced me to the classical realist scholarship that informs much of this essay, and his readings of my work forced me to clarify my tortured prose, reminding me that a study of international politics must not only speak to fellow academics but a wider audience as well. And while he remains skeptical of conclusions that veer toward the moralistic, he is a realist who understands the moral concerns of everyday citizens. His example as a scholar, department chair, and policy analyst exemplify the highest standards of the profession of political science, standards that I can only hope to someday match.

Once this work left the dissertation stage, it was helped along by many others. As an assistant professor at the American University in Cairo (AUC), I found an atmosphere supportive of my research and amenable to the interchange of ideas. I was given grants to do research at archives in London, Paris, and Washington, DC, for which I thank the university administration and the Political Science Department. Members of the university community who were helpful in discussing ideas and reading sections of the manuscript include Jean Allain, Liz Cooper, Bahgat Korany, John Murray, and Kurt Mills. Two colleagues at AUC deserve special mention: Tim Sullivan, now University Provost, has been an extremely supportive mentor. His example as a teacher, scholar, and administrator convinced me that professors can only succeed if they recognize the importance of their students. Bill Demars, a fellow assistant professor, has been willing to discuss the ideas presented here, and many others, with a rigor and enthusiasm that I have failed to find elsewhere. His friendship helped sustain both me and this book throughout the four years I spent in Egypt.

In my current position at the Carnegie Council on Ethics and International Affairs, I have found further support. Jenny Ruzow, Joel Rosenthal, Christian Barry and Paige Arthur have read sections of this book and greatly improved its contents. Eva Becker, the Vice President of the Council, was instrumental in providing the support I needed to put the finishing touches on the manuscript.

My students have been the best critics of this work. Students in my classes on Ethics and International Affairs at The Johns Hopkins University and The American University in Cairo demanded explanations of how norms could possibly play any role in a world they see as shaped by power politics. The idealism and enthusiasm of students in the Model United Nations and Model Arab League Programs at AUC have given me hope that we will come up with new ways to solve international dilemmas, even though this work may seem to say otherwise.

Finally there is my family. My parents, siblings, and in-laws have given me the support and love that makes it possible to write a book and remain sane. My parents in particular have taught me what morality means by their words and actions. My brother Jim Lang played a particularly important role in reading and commenting on sections of the book.

My wife, Nicki Wilkins, has played the most important role in bringing this book to its completion. She has read much of what is written here and, more importantly, listened to me discuss, develop, and complain about it. Her ideas on ethics and politics have challenged me to rethink many of my assumptions and conclusions. This work is as much hers as it is mine, and it is to her that I dedicate it with much love and appreciation.

CHAPTER ONE

Introduction

Humanitarian intervention is not working. From Somalia to Bosnia to Rwanda to Kosovo to East Timor, the attempt by states to address complex humanitarian emergencies by means of military force has not been successful. The trauma of these failures has been further compounded by the often genuine moral urge that accompanies the decision to intervene. While it is probably impossible to act in a purely altruistic manner, many interventions have been undertaken by states with very limited national interests in the regions at stake. A genuine dilemma thus arises—why are actions based on morality producing such immoral results? Why does political conflict seem to consistently interfere in attempts to provide aid, end ethnic conflict, or restore democracy?

This book is an attempt to answer this question. My answer begins with a deductive interpretation of military intervention which is then explored through three case studies: the American and British intervention in Bolshevik Russia in 1918; the British, French, and Israeli intervention in Egypt in 1956; and the American and United Nations intervention in Somalia in 1992–3. These three interventions are rarely categorized together. Their goals range from humanitarian to geostrategic, and the states involved range from great to medium powers. But they share one key feature: they all failed in their professed goals, with the troops in each case being ignominiously recalled. My explanation of these failures does not fall into the typical "lessons of intervention" category, however. *In essence, these interventions, along with many others, fail because of a conflict between political agents who embody and enact divergent normative visions of international and domestic order.* In other words, the failure of intervention results not from an amoral or immoral power politics, but from an excess of normative politics.

What exactly is a normative conflict? These three interventions produced conflict on numerous levels. The failure of the British and American

1

intervention resulted from conflicts between the two allies, conflicts between the White forces and the allies, conflicts within the democratic systems of both Great Britain and the United States, conflicts between allied soldiers and the political leaderships, and conflicts between the intervening soldiers and the Russian peoples. The failure of the British and French intervention resulted from conflicts between the British and French and the Israelis, conflicts between the three intervenors and the Americans, conflicts between the intervenors and the government of Egypt, and conflicts between soldiers and Egyptian citizens. The failure of the American and United Nations troops in Somalia resulted from the conflicts between the United States forces and the United Nations (UN), conflicts between aid workers and soldiers, and conflicts between the Somali leaders and American forces. In all three cases, the conflicts that caused these interventions to fail did not exist in any one place; they were both domestic and international.

These conflicts have been explained by an inequality in power in the international system, by an inadequate attention to alliance politics, or by a failure to understand the politics of the target state. One explanation that has not been offered, however, focuses on norms, or rules and ideas about how the world should function. Admittedly, when viewed in hindsight, the motivations for the Russian and Egyptian interventions hardly seem concerned with normative issues. And there is no shortage of attempts to argue that the intervention in Somalia had no normative grounding but was simply an imperial adventure to secure access to oil in the Persian Gulf. Nevertheless, in reading the documents from each intervention, one is struck by the continued reference to moral norms as the justification for action. Woodrow Wilson believed that the norms of the American political system, liberal democracy and capitalism, were preferable to the norms embodied in communism. Anthony Eden and Guy Mollet believed that the norm of colonialism retained some moral purpose, especially when compared to the "radical" policies of Gamal abd al-Nasser. And George Bush believed that feeding Somalis and protecting them from warlords was a norm worthy of the United States.

But how can norms cause conflict? They cause conflict because in the competitive world of international politics, agents—primarily states—employ their histories and ideals in order to secure for themselves a prominent position in the international system. This form of conflict, one that results from the way states narrate themselves, is the primary reason for the failure of intervention. For, as I will demonstrate later in this chapter, narration is an important part of the ways in which states act. It is the link between a state's history, its ideals, and its actions that leads to the failure of intervention.

As the last case study will demonstrate, however, states are not the only agents in world politics. The UN, while formally composed of its member states, has become an agent in its own right. Moreover, it also narrates its agency, as the proliferation of publications both by and about the organization reveal. The fact that many of the arguments I use to explain state agency can also apply to the UN makes this analysis relevant not only to the "Westphalian system" of sovereign states but to whatever political agents will emerge in the next global order. In a point I return to in the conclusion, changing the type of agent will not necessarily eliminate the conflicts I am identifying. Instead, we need to reconsider the concept of agency itself in order to ameliorate these conflicts, a task I undertake in a cursory way in the conclusion. Nevertheless, as a realist, I also believe that these normative conflicts will continue because they grow out of the very nature of politics itself.

THE CONCEPT OF INTERVENTION

Intervention is a commonly practiced, but also badly defined, international action. One leading publicist of international law has argued that almost any action a state undertakes to influence another state could be considered intervention (Henkin 1993, 869). Borrowing from the standard international law definition, intervention can be defined as a violation of the sovereignty of one state by another (Oppenheim 1948, 272–87). In this book, I focus more particularly on military intervention. For the purposes of this book, military intervention is defined in the following manner:

> Military intervention is the use of armed troops to effect a change in the political system of a sovereign state without prior permission and without declaring war.

The term "armed troops" distinguishes this action from the use of air power alone to force change in a political system, or what some have called coercive diplomacy (see George 1991). The lack of a declaration of war also distinguishes intervention from war. This definition does not cover all cases. I have chosen it, however, because it seems to conform to the types of military action undertaken by great powers in the twentieth century that will become more common in the twent-first century. Military intervention as defined here also seems to raise a great deal of political controversy in democratic societies such as the United States, a further reason for my definition.

In other words, I have presented a definition of intervention designed not to test the entire world of possible interventions. Rather, I have chosen this definition to explore a particularly troublesome, but also important and ubiquitous type of political action. This approach may not please positivist-empiricist political scientists, in that it does not seek to capture the "reality" of intervention. But, as this book will make clear, intervention does not conform to a single reality but instead is the subject of highly contested interpretations. If this contestation is the case, then it seems more fruitful to explain the reasons for my definition than suppose it conforms to an observable reality. Moreover, this approach does not detract from whatever truth may arise from my analysis. Truth cannot be confined to the positivist-empiricist approach. Rather, I would argue that the truths to be found in this book include greater understandings of politics and ethics, understandings that can help guide United States foreign policy and international politics into the twenty-first century.

Others have grappled with intervention, resulting in a rapidly proliferating body of work. Some respond to current United States dilemmas of humanitarian intervention (Damrosch 1991; Harriss 1995; Hehir 1995; Smith 1997; Weiss and Minear 1993; Weiss 1999). Other works address non-United States interventions, such as the French literature on *le droit d'ingérence* (Salamé 1996; Landrin 1998; Zorgbibe 1994). There also exists a more theoretical body of work on intervention (Bull 1984; Debrix 1999; Feste 1991; Finnemore 1996; Forbes and Hoffman 1993; Lyons and Mastanduno 1995; Teson 1989; Vincent 1979; Weber 1995; Wheeler 2000).

To review the entire body of works on military intervention is beyond the means of this book, and probably beyond the attention of the reader. These works have created the background to this study and will be quoted and addressed when necessary. But because this book is using intervention to explore deeper questions of ethics and politics, this chapter will provide an explanation of some basic concepts. In order to understand my thesis that the failure of intervention results from the conflicts between political agents engendered by their pursuit of normative goals, both "normative goals" and "political agents" require further explanation.

ETHICS, NORMS, AND INTERVENTIONS

This book does not argue that all interventions are motivated by morally good aims. Rather it seeks to locate in an intervention its normative components. As recently defined by Peter Katzenstein, norms:

> describe the collective expectations for the proper behavior of actors of a given identity. In some situations, norms operate like rules that define the identity of an actor, thus having "constitutive effects" that specify what actions will cause relevant others

to recognize a particular identity. In other situations norms operate as standards that specify the proper enactment of an already defined identity. In such instances norms have "regulative" effects that specify standards of proper behavior. Norms thus either define (or constitute) identities or prescribe (or regulate) behavior, or they do both. (Katzenstein 1996, 5)

As Katzenstein notes, norms both constitute identities and regulate behavior. The practice of intervention demonstrates both of these aspects of norms, as the historical chapters will demonstrate. Briefly, an intervention constitutes a state's identity in that the reasons for intervening are often closely linked with the state's history and values. Especially because interventions seek to create political order in a society, the order to be created is often modeled on the intervening state's conceptions of politics. Interventions also display the regulative power of norms. In an intervention, states seek to justify their actions according to some larger norm of behavior shared in the international system. Whether that norm is creating democracy, guiding young nations to political maturity, or saving lives, an intervention will be justified according to certain standards of behavior.

Three different bodies of literature address the normative elements of international politics. The first can be called "positivist constructivists." These approaches have sought to demonstrate the importance of ideas or norms in international politics, usually contesting the neorealist/neoliberal premise that ideas do not play the same role as power and wealth in explaining international politics (Adler and Barnett 1998; Barnett 1998; Bierstecker and Weber 1996; Finnemore 1996; Goldstein and Keohane 1989; Katzenstein 1996). Instead, these constructivists believe that norms and ideas not only help explain the outcomes of international interactions, they even help explain the very identities of those engaged in such interactions. The second group of writers who have addressed the question of norms can be called "legal constructivists." The two leading theorists here are Friedrich Kratochwil (1989) and Nicholas Onuf (1989, 1998). Their arguments develop the idea that norms construct the world around us by creating the rules that make social and political interaction possible. Following philosophers of language such as Ludwig Wittgenstein and John Searle, Onuf and Kratochwil have demonstrated that norms are not simply entities that prompt actions (as is the case with positivist constructivists), but are the sinews that hold together the social and political body. These writers have focused on international law as the place where such rules are most apparent, but their works are not limited to law alone. The last group of writers can be called ethicists. These writers address questions of international politics through the lenses of well-known moral and ethical traditions of thought. This group of theorists remains more on the margins because of their often explicit rejection of either positivist or legal modes of analysis, the two most common in the study of world politics. Journals such as *Ethics and International Affairs* and *Millennium* have given a voice to some of these works, albeit from very different angles. Theorists such as Charles Beitz (1979, 1985), Chris Brown (1992), David Campbell (1993), Stanley Hoffman (1981), Andrew Linklatter (1990), Terry Nardin (1983, 1992, 1996), Joel Rosenthal (1991, 1995), Michael Walzer (1992), and Daniel Warner (1991) have addressed questions of ethics from a variety of perspectives.

This book builds upon all three of these modes of writing about norms. The positivist constructivists have provided the discipline with a way to think about norms as constituting both behavior and identities. I am hesitant, however, to fully embrace the positivist tenor of some of these works that seek to "trace" the role of norms in specific decisions or foreign policies. As the remainder of this chapter will demonstrate, I see norms not as a factor along with wealth and power, but as the very basis of how we think and act politically. The legal construtivists have also been influential in the ideas developed here, mainly in their focus on language and the way in which it structures our political universe. And, the ethicists have brought to bear the great moral traditions of philosophy on pressing questions of global politics. Both the legal and ethical traditions, however, tend to focus on how norms can lead to greater forms of cooperation and peaceful coexistence. This book seeks to demonstrate how norms also create conflict. In fact, this differentiation from the legal constructivists' focus on positive modes of cooperation has led me to a greater awareness of the insights of realist theory. While all these works have been instrumental in defining the issues and clarifying concepts, they often fall victim to the problem raised by E. H. Carr in his prescient work on realism, that is, international politics founded solely on a utopian morality will ultimately lead to conflict and chaos. Only an international political system that is founded on both power and morality can successfully provide peace and justice in the international system (Carr 1939). This book demonstrates the truth of Carr's insight. Indeed it conforms to the more general realist argument that morality without an understanding of politics will lead to conflict. Rienhold Niebuhr argued that international politics cannot conform to the same moral rules as personal conduct because political leaders cannot act without considering the consequences (Niebuhr 1932). George Kennan castigated American diplomacy for its excess focus on idealistic and moralistic conduct of foreign affairs (Kennan 1950). And Hans J. Morgenthau sought to infuse his political realism with an awareness of both power and morality (Morgenthau 1986; Russell 1990).

Recent work in international relations theory has continued this trend of finding in realism a normative element. Arguing that realists are not advocates of amoral *realpolitik*, theorists such as Alastair Murray (1997) and Roger Spegele (1996) have found in the realist approach a normatively based guide to both understanding and acting in the international realm. While this book copies neither one of these two theorists, it is written in the spirit of both; that is, it seeks to find a middle ground between the excessive moralism of an idealistic approach and the amoral cynicism of a power politics approach. This book follows in the path of these realists who understood that international politics is about both politics and ethics. They also understood, and I hope this book will demonstrate, that ethics when unconstrained in the international arena will lead to the exact opposite of what such norms demand.

I present in this book three norms that motivate military intervention: liberalism, colonialism, and humanitarianism. The three terms are not always considered as "norms" because of their negative valences, especially colonialism. Nevertheless, they are norms because they justify and explain political action in moral terms. They regulate behavior and constitute identities.

Liberalism means an attempt to create a political system in the target state organized around the concepts of democracy, rule of law, and protection of individual rights. In an intervention, though, liberalism also has an international aspect; that is, a liberal intervention does not only reform the target society, it also turns the state into a member of a liberal world order and seeks to promote principles of self-determination and respect for international law. Both the domestic and international variants of liberalism are evident in all three interventions, but they are particularly apparent in the American interventions in Russia and Somalia.

Colonialism revolves around a feeling of responsibility. As with the liberal norm, the colonial has two manifestations, a domestic and an international. Domestically, it reflects a belief that the target state exhibits a certain "barbarism" that makes it incapable of ruling itself. This requires an intervening power that does not necessarily teach liberal values but basic administrative skills. Internationally, the colonial meaning of intervention manifests itself in the belief that the intervening power has a responsibility to protect other areas from the possible rapacious attitudes of the target state. Thus the intervention is intended not only to protect the people from themselves, but also to protect other vulnerable populations from the control of the "barbaric" target state. While there are elements of colonialism in all three interventions, it is most apparent in the British intervention in Russia and Egypt, the French intervention in Egypt, and the UN intervention in Somalia.

Finally, the humanitarian norm is the easiest to understand. It is the attempt to provide physical aid to individuals and communities that have been deprived of such goods either because of a natural or human made disaster. This norm played a role in all three interventions, but, obviously, it was most apparent in the United States and UN intervention in Somalia.

THE POLITICS OF AGENCY

Understanding the role of norms in an intervention can only take us so far. A more comprehensive understanding requires a focus on politics. Politics can be defined in a diverse number of ways including the distribution of goods and values, the competition for influence or power, or the pursuit of public policies. But any definition of politics requires a political agent. What are political agents? In international relations theory, agency has recently found a place through the works of sociologically inclined theorists such as Alexander Wendt (1987, 1992, 1994, 1998). But these works, due to their sociological basis, have not addressed the political nature of agency. While the remainder of this section will explore the concept of political agency in more detail, briefly it can be defined as the status of individuals in a public space that gives them the ability to engage each other. That status is partly legal, partly moral, and partly ontological—all of which add up to it being fundamentally political. The engagements that define political agency can be both conflictual and cooperative, but they are always competitive. While political theorists who have explored this concept traditionally focused on the individual person in a political community, this book will shift that focus to the nation states, international organizations, and other political agents who compete at the global level.

The outcome of these engagements is the creation and destruction of other agents, of the rules and institutions that shape these engagements, and of the public space itself. In other words, the process of agents interacting with each other creates the structures upon which later engagements depend. Even in competitions that seem to have no structure, such as war, there exists institutions that structure competition; rules and laws of war, which differentiate between civilians and soldiers make even violent competitions possible. The competitions of politics tend to both create and destroy the space of politics, the institutions necessary to continue the contest. But the institutions themselves are necessary. Furthermore, the institutions are both physical spaces, such as parliaments and international organizations, and ideas, such as international law and political ideologies. The space of politics is created not only by the walls of a building but by the decisions of men and women.

The remainder of this chapter explores the concept of political agency especially as it pertains to international politics. As anyone familiar with the work of Hannah Arendt will recognize, these formulations of political agency are borrowed from her. Using Arendt, this chapter explores the distinctive nature of political agency. Because Arendt's work was not written with state agency in mind, I then turn to the work of Hans Morgenthau to link her works with international politics. The concluding chapter uses these two theorists to more fully explore the questions and dilemmas raised in the narrative sections of the book.

Hannah Arendt's work has generated both acclaim and hostility. Her book *Eichman in Jerusalem* (1964) based on her attendance at the trial of the Nazi bureaucrat Adolph Eichman made her a number of enemies in the American and international Jewish community, in that she challenged conventional notions of guilt and responsibility for the Holocaust, resulting in her famous argument that Eichman's trial demonstrates the "banality of evil." One of her articles on segregation in the American south, in which she argued that the use of federal troops may not have been justified to fix what she called an essentially "social" as opposed to a "political" question, also raised a storm of controversy in the intellectual community (Arendt 1959).[1] While some feminist thinkers have appropriated her work, it has also been criticized for her separation of the political and the social (Rich 1979; Honig 1995). These divergent interpretations of her work have made Arendt both a highly controversial but also intellectually stimulating figure.

But her work has not only created controversy. Her book *The Origins of Totalitarianism* (1968) linked questions of anti-Semitism, nationalism, and totalitarian politics in a critical essay that continues to challenge to this day. In *Between Past and Future* (1968) and *The Human Condition* (1958) she utilized Greek and Roman political philosophy to interpret social and political action in the modern world. As a German immigrant to the United States, she sought to understand a country that she considered to be unique in the history of the world; her book *On Revolution* (1963) compared the American and French revolutions and argued that the former helped create a stable governance system while the later did not. But she also did not hesitate to criticize the American system, especially in her reflections on violence and politics (1972). Her relationships with German political philosophers such as Martin Heidegger and Karl Jaspers generated some of her most important insights into the relationships between history, politics, and ethics (1968; also Kohler and Suner, 1992, Young-Bruehl 1982). Her corpus of works has generated a large body of literature, which seeks to follow her advice to "think what we are doing" (Arendt 1958, 5).[2]

The work on which I draw to develop a theory of agency is Arendt's *The Human Condition*. Like many of her works, this book uses ancient notions of politics to confront current politics. The focus of the work is the *via activa*, or that aspect of human life concerned with doing rather than thinking.[3] She divides human action into three realms: labor, work, and action. Labor is that which we do to stay alive, the daily activities that provide food, clothes, and shelter. Work is that which results in goods that outlive us, that is, creations of buildings, art, and crafts that are not consumed but remain after individual human lives pass away. Because labor creates goods that we consume, it is only through work that the material objectivity of human existence is created.

The final category is action. Action is the most important realm in terms of politics, for action is that human activity in which human persons reveal themselves in moments of interactions with others. It is the way in which we assert who we are, in which we create ourselves by presenting ourselves in public. Politics, on the constructed stage of a parliament or town meeting, provides the paradigmatic instance of moments in which the human person can be revealed. Arendt develops this concept of action in an engagement with Greek and Roman philosophers who sought to define the realm of the political. That realm, combining a Homeric agonal spirit with an Aristotelian notion of speech as the quintessentially human characteristic, results in a public space that allows for competition and conflict.

According to Arendt, the public realm is the place where persons distinguish themselves, the arena in which "everybody had to constantly distinguish himself from all others, to show through unique deeds or achievements that he was best of all" (1958, 41). Indeed, it is this ability to act publicly that defines the human person:

> A life without speech and without action, on the other hand— and this is the only way of life that in earnest has renounced all appearance and all vanity in the biblical sense of the word—is literally dead to the world; it has ceased to be a human life because it is no longer lived among men. . . . With word and deed we insert ourselves into the human world and this insertion is like a second birth, in which we confirm and take upon ourselves the naked fact of our original physical appearance. (1958, 176)

Public political action puts us into the world and reveals the "who" of our existence in a way that no other practice can.

Furthermore, since Arendt believes that political action is a public presentation of the self, there must be a community to whom this presentation is made. She notes that action occurs within a "web of human relationships," a place composed both of other people acting and speaking and of the "common world" that surrounds and anchors human interaction: ". . . most words and deeds are about some worldly objective reality in addition to being a disclosure of the acting and speaking self" (1958, 182).[4] Politics thus requires a public realm, one composed of fellow humans with an agreed upon equality, not one of merit but one of agency.

Political action is not like labor, something to be consumed and instantly removed from existence. It is closer to work in that it creates permanent spaces that will outlive individual human lives. But while work creates physical structures, action creates the institutions, structures, and spaces that guide political action such as constitutions, treaties, philosophies, or histories. The Greek *polis* provides a model. Viewing the lawmaker not as a political actor, but as a maker or founder, the Greeks envisioned the task of the founder as central to their political life:

> In their opinion, the lawmaker was like the builder of the city wall, someone who had to do and finish his work before political activity could begin. . . . To them, the laws, like the wall around the city, were not results of action but products of making. Before men could act, a definite space had to be secured and a structure built where all subsequent actions could take place, the space being the public realm of the *polis* and its structure the law. (1958, 194)

This passage seems to indicate that, for Arendt, politics exists in a space between the physical place of the city and the ideational space of the law. Yet she goes on to argue that the Greek *polis* was not simply the physical space of politics:

> The *polis*, properly speaking, is not the city-state in its physical location; it is the organization of the people as it arises out of acting and speaking together, and its true space lies between people living together for this purpose, no matter where they happen to be. "Wherever you go, you will be a *polis*": these famous words became not merely the watchword of Greek colonization, they expressed the conviction that action and speech create a space between the participants which can find its proper location almost any time and anywhere. (1958, 198).

The space of politics, then, is not only a physical space, but more importantly an arena where talking and acting together create a realm for appearance. It is in this common space that the public presentation of the self occurs.

Arendt moves from conceiving of political action as occurring within a web of human relations to action within a *polis*, a *polis* that has the same intangible quality as the web, yet simultaneously has a more concrete meaning. But Arendt's understanding of political action does not simply rest within this web of meaning. In presenting her idea of political action she stresses its unpredictability, and its similarity to a miracle—something one cannot expect and cannot contain. Action tends to go beyond the boundaries within which we attempt to contain it:

> Action, moreover, no matter what its specific content, always establishes relationships and therefore has an inherent tendency to force open all limitations and cut across all boundaries. Limitations and boundaries exist within human affairs, but they never offer a framework that can reliably withstand the onslaught with which each new generation must assert itself. (1958, 190–1)

Political action has a tendency to go beyond the borders we impose on it, precisely because of its unpredictability. While the *polis* is an attempt to create a physical space for political action, that action simultaneously forces itself beyond those boundaries.

Ultimately, action does not just create spaces and institutions for politics, it creates the agents themselves. It is here that Arendt's work moves to the ontological realm. For in her argument, humans exist as fragmented, alienated, and acquisitive entities until they engage in political action. Once they appear on the public stage, either through words or deeds, human agents become a definitive "who" as opposed to a "what." But how does action reveal the essence of the agent?

For Arendt, action reveals being through narration. Only when stories are told about the great actions that persons engage in can these actions contribute to the revealing of who they are. According to Paul Ricouer, "The political enterprise, in [Arendt's] sense, is the highest attempt to 'immortalize' ourselves" (Ricouer 1990, 151). In acting and narrating, persons are revealed. Selya Benhabib finds in Arendt's work two modes of political agency, what she calls the agonal and the narrative:

> [W]hereas action in the agonal model is described through terms such as "revelation of who one is" and "the making manifest of what is interior," action in the narrative model is characterized through the "telling of a story" and "the weaving of a web of narratives." Whereas in the first model action appears to make manifest or to reveal an antecedent essence, the "who one is," action in the second model suggests that "the who one is" emerges in the process of doing the deed and telling the story. Whereas action in the first model is a process of discovery, action in the

second model is a process of invention. In contemporary terms, we may say that the first model of action is essentialist while the second is constructivist. (Benhabib 1996, 125–6)

Benhabib uncovers in Arendt an alternative to the agonal politics of the Greeks. Instead of securely constructed individuals contesting each other in a competitive atmosphere, we find in Benhabib's reading of Arendt a theory of political agency that relies on the history of an event. The meaning we give to a political action comes not just from the intention of the agent, but from the interpretation of that agent and his action. As Arendt herself says:

> Although everybody started his life by inserting himself into the human world through action and speech, nobody is the author or producer of his own life story. In other words, the stories, the results of speech and action reveal an agent, but this agent is not an author or producer. Somebody began it and is its subject in the twofold sense of the word, namely, its actor and sufferer, but nobody is its author. (Arendt 1958, 184)

The narrative model of action forces us to reconsider political history as well:

> The meaning of a committed act is revealed only when the action itself has come to an end and become a story susceptible to narration. Insofar as any "mastering" of the past is possible, it consists in relating what has happened; but such narration, too, which shapes history, solves no problems and assuages no suffering; it does not master anything once and for all. (Arendt 1968, 21)

For Arendt, action does not exist just in the moment of doing; it is as much, or rather more, in the narration of the event. In one of her essays, Arendt provides us with a powerful critique of history, arguing that modern history has become a means of limiting political freedom and action by adopting a deterministic outlook (Arendt 1968). Political action requires not only a historical actor, but also a historian and an audience (Hansen 1993, 18). For only in the telling of the event does it acquire meaning, the meaning that makes such events politically relevant.

Benhabib's exploration of Arendt's thought not only links it to narration, it also demonstrates how political agency can lead to the creation of an associational political space. But the public good is not usually associated with state agency or foreign policy. In fact, the more agonal contest between states at the international level does not give much hope for a dialogue that might lead to public policies that are good for the whole. Does this lack of a public good mean that Arendt's theory of political agency is ultimately one that will simply reinforce and reinscribe the power politics of the international system?

Perhaps. But I prefer to look to an alternative reading of Arendt, one that accepts the lack of an explicit articulation of a public good but can still lead to a democratic engagement. In her attempts to find a place for Arendt in feminist political theory, Bonnie Honig articulates this aspect of Arendt's work most clearly. Honig argues that Arendt "theorizes a democratic politics built not on already existing identities or shared experiences but on contingent sites of principled coalescence and shared practices of citizenship" (Honig 1995, 3). In other words, Arendt does not assume that political actors assert their identities in certainty and confidence. Instead, only when they act do they take on an identity, and not an identity that is fixed but one that is fluid and changing with each political engagement.

> When they act, Arendt's actors are reborn. . . . Their momentary engagement in action in the public realm engenders identities that are lodged forever in the stories told of their heroic performances by the spectators who witness them. Prior to or apart from action, this self has no identity; it is fragmented, discontinuous, indistinct, and most certainly uninteresting. (Honig 1995b, 140)

Honig's formulation thus moves Arendt's argument from an ontological to a normative one. For she presents an Arendt who is not simply identifying a politics of contest and competition, but a politics that, when it does not rest on stable identities, can lead to a more democratic engagement of agents. Not every theorist follows Honig here; Benhabib argues that Arendt theorizes an "agonal" politics as opposed to a more associative one (Benhabib 1996).

Honig's move is the key to understanding the politics of international agency and the reasons for the failure of military intervention. For when states, who are the primary political agents of the international system, engage each other with settled notions of what they are—either as guardians of an ideology, standard bearers of an ethnicity, or saviors of the world—they will engage in an agonal politics that leads to the reaffirmation of anti-democratic international structures. But, if they engage each other cognizant of their unstable and constantly shifting identities, if they see the politics of military intervention as a means not just to solve a problem but as a moment in which they create themselves and those with whom they interact, if they treat their identities not with certainty but with flexibility, perhaps the conflicts generated by a military intervention will lead not to hostility but to new forms of global governance. Articulating a political agency for the state which is open, contestable, and, ultimately, more democratic, is one of the tasks to which this book is dedicated.

THE POLITICS OF STATE AGENCY

Before exploring how this understanding of political agency can make the global system more democratic, it is important to step back and ask a more fundamental question: Can the nation state exist qua political agent in the way of Arendtian individuals? Can the theories and ideas that she explores in relation to the human person interacting within a political community have any relevance for the interactions of nation states?[5] Action, understood in the Arendtian sense, constitutes the bulk of what we call international politics. States contest each other in a continuum ranging from war to diplomacy. They present themselves and engage in contests. These contests can lead to more permanent political institutions. International organizations, treaties, regional organizations, and international public law are some of the lasting contributions that the actions of states have left behind. A quote from Arendt, in which states are replaced for persons, captures this element of international politics:

> the public realm itself, the *polis* [international system], was permeated by a fiercely agonal spirit, where everybody [state] had constantly to distinguish himself [itself] from all others, to show through unique deeds or achievements that he [it] was the best of all (*eien aristeuein*). The public realm, in other words, was reserved for individuality; it was the only place where men [states] could show who they really and inexchangeably were. (Arendt 1958, 41)

But is there room for the kind of democratic agency that Benhabib or Honig draws from Arendt? Can we find in state agency the means by which to reconceive global politics while admitting that states will remain predominant actors? This section will suggest how such a move is possible (although rare) in international politics by drawing on an unexpected source: the political realism of Hans Morgenthau. At the end of this chapter, I compare this theory of state agency to realism and neorealism, which I argue are distinct from the theory articulated here. Nevertheless, it is in Morgenthau's writing on diplomacy and the national purpose (not national interest) that we see how state agency can arise from narration and can possibly lead to a more democratic engagement.

Although rarely considered in tandem, these two theorists dealt with a number of overlapping themes: nationalism, imperialism, American exceptionalism, the relation of history and politics, and the relation of politics and ethics. Moreover, as two German Jewish immigrants to the United States, their political concerns about the role of the United States, Israel, and Germany in the global political system inspired them in ways that demonstrated their ability to apply theoretical insights to political practices.[6] They also knew each other personally and sustained a mutually supportive friendship (Young-Bruehl 1982). But they also differ from each other in important ways. Morgenthau's more Hegelian conception of the state[7] stands in stark contrast to Arendt's emphasis on republicanism and citizenship. And Morgenthau's understanding of power (Morgenthau 1986) contrasts sharply with Arendt's (1972). My reading of these two theorists together here should not be seen as an attempt to force them into the same framework. Rather, I see in the combination of their ideas on political agency a valuable means by which to challenge conventional notions of politics in International Relations.

Morgenthau's work provides important insights into two basic aspects of state agency, representation and the national purpose. I have thus far implicitly assumed that state agency is unproblematic. In fact, this assumption is common in both the discipline of international relations and in popular descriptions of world politics. International law has traditionally been structured around a mode of discourse in which states are the agents of world politics, even when the concerns of states may override those of individual persons (Henkin 1993; Corbett 1951). According to this understanding, political action on the world stage takes place among states, not persons. The underlying assumption here is that the state, a legal institution, somehow represents the community. The fact that the discipline is called inter*nation*al relations further reveals that states are generally assumed to represent nations. But what does this representation mean? And how does it operate when states act?

In answering these questions, the most logical step is to look to the formal representatives of the community. Moreover, since Arendt's theory addresses persons it makes sense to begin with them. These representatives not only represent the interests of the citizens of a state, they also represent the state to the representatives, and thus citizens, of other states. The concept of the representative in international relations is an issue to which Morgenthau devoted his attention.[8] Morgenthau's theory of international relations demands that there be political representatives, diplomats, who can bring all the resources of the nation-state to play on the world stage (Lang 2000). In *Politics Among Nations,* Morgenthau lists various aspects that compose the political power of the nation-state: geography, industrial capacity, population, and natural resources. But while these elements make up the power of the state, it is the diplomat who enacts them:

Of all the factors that make for the power of a nation, the most important, however usable, is the quality of diplomacy. All the other factors that determine national power are, as it were, the raw material out of which the power of the nation is fashioned. The quality of a nation's diplomacy combines those different factors into an integrated whole, gives them direction and weight, and awakens their slumbering potentialities by giving them the breath of actual power. . . . It is the art of bringing the different elements of the national power to bear with maximum effect upon those points in the international situation that concerns the national interest most directly. (Morgenthau 1986, 158–9)

The representative or diplomat embodies the state in moments of agency. Even more importantly, Morgenthau's conception of state agency implies that only in those moments of diplomatic (or military) action does the state really come into existence. Otherwise it only exists in potential; the representative must actualize the power of the state.[9]

Thus we see in Morgenthau's idea of state agency a means by which the state may present itself to the world. In those moments when the diplomat or soldier presents the various elements of national power, it is, in fact, the state that is being presented. But is the state constituted solely by these potential elements? Does the state as an agent only exist as an element of power that is wielded as a club against other states similarly presenting themselves? Here Morgenthau's conception of the national *purpose* helps us understand state agency. The national purpose is, more so than the national interest or the factors of power, that which gives agency to the state in the Arendtian sense of the term. And, more importantly for my argument, the national purpose gives to state agency an essentially normative character.

Like many of the classical realists, Morgenthau was sensitive to history, and in an important, and often neglected, work, *The Purpose of American Politics* (1960), he explores the idea of the national purpose as providing the historically grounded meaning without which a state cannot conduct its foreign policy. Focusing on the historical record of the United States, Morgenthau argues that the ideas of freedom and equality became the central political ideas that motivated political action both within the United States and toward other countries. The national purpose is a complex philosophical concept that enables meaningful political action. It derives from the historical record of the nation-state, allowing it to express deep ideological commitments.

In order to comprehend the reality of the national purpose, it is not necessary to listen to the ideologies of nationalism. It is only necessary to consult the evidence of history as our minds reflect it. We know that a real nation worthy of our remembrances has contributed to the affairs of men more than the successful defense and promotion of its national interest. . . . In order to be worthy of our lasting sympathy a nation must pursue its interests for the sake of a transcendent purpose that gives meaning to the day-by-day operations of its foreign policy. (Morgenthau 1960, 8)

The national purpose gives meaning to political action. It is this national purpose that analysts must comprehend if they are to truly comprehend foreign policy decisions and actions.[10]

Combining our understanding of the way the diplomat represents the state with our understanding of the national purpose produces a theory of state agency. The diplomat does not just combine the elements of national power in his presentation of the state; more importantly, he represents the national purpose, the historical record of the state, a historical record that embodies the political and ethical ideals of the community. Moreover, and more specifically in relation to the topic of this book, a military intervention is a moment in a nation's history when the national purpose becomes both extremely important and also highly contested. It becomes important because the intervening state attempts to accomplish its reforms and provide colonial guidance through its own national values and historical traditions. As we examine the discourse of an intervention, not just the public discourse but the private memos and reflections of those deciding that action and those effecting it, we see that the justifications and explanations rely heavily on the moral values leaders think their state is to embody, moral values that derive from the political history of the state. Furthermore, while this may occur in war and other international actions, it is particularly relevant in an intervention precisely because there is an attempt to create a functioning political system where all they see is anarchy and chaos. Thus the model of their own society and political system plays the role not only of justifying their action to their own constituents, but it also becomes the model upon which this new system is created. Morgenthau's national purpose, then, provides us with a useful tool to understand the political and ethical aspects of intervention.[11]

The combination of Morgenthau and Arendt concerning the question of intervention produces some hitherto unexplored understandings. The self that is presented in international politics is the state. The state is embodied and represented in the diplomat/soldier. The diplomat/soldier does not just embody the physical elements of power, but the moral and historical as well. In sum, the self that is presented and revealed in international politics is an historical and ethical community that strives to express this history and ethic in its relations with others. Through their interpretations and ideas, states create the spaces of politics within which they act. More importantly for a theory of agency that relies on narration, states are the final interpreters of international political action. The space of politics in which states interact with each other, perhaps constituted by accretions of historical interaction and basic legal principles, is in the end the province of the states themselves. Thus the ways in which states choose to interpret their actions will be the most decisive in the creation of politics. The language game of international politics is constituted and controlled by state interpretations.[12]

State agency depends on the ability of representatives to embody the national purpose of their communities. That national purpose represents the narrative quality of political agency that Arendt has identified. Do other agents exist in the international system with a similar form of agency, one linked with narration? Other agents certainly exist, if by agency we mean the ability to engage other agents in the public sphere. But how many exist with formal representatives and with the ability to narrate for themselves a history that gives them a normative purpose? Does, for example, an international organization like the United Nations have this capacity?

The UN is, of course, reducible to its member states. Especially in that part of the organization which can be said to "intervene," that is, the Security Council, the agency of its member states predominates. The Security Council, however, is not the only organ of the UN involved in an intervention. The Secretary General's Office also plays a key role in both the decisions to intervene and the implementation of these decisions. Unlike a state, the Secretary General is not an executive agent capable of acting on his or her own. Rather, the Secretary General is quintessentially a representative, both of the institution and of the member states. He or she must, in other words, act as a representative of the institution and, in doing so, embody its normative purpose by means of narration. In Chapter 5, I demonstrate how the UN as an institution has narrated itself a form of agency in its writings on different interventions, both successes and failures.

While *The Human Condition* presents an Arendt who finds in agonal competition a means of sustaining democratic politics, and while my reading of her alongside of Morgenthau has led to a framework in which she might seem to advocate a realist world of power politics, Arendt's work in a wider sense does not conform so easily with this image. In particular there exists a tension in my reading of Arendt and Morgenthau as supportive of a similar theory of state agency. Arendt's critiques of imperialism and totalitarianism make her an unlikely ally of a theory that interprets world politics as a competitive process in which the most powerful dominate (Arendt 1968). One might interpret this tension as a conflict between the general approaches of Morgenthau and Arendt, with Morgenthau envisioning the nation-state as the highest form of politics and Arendt seeing political action on a more local scale as the highest fulfillment of politics (Arendt 1963).

But in fact, both Morgenthau and Arendt were ambivalent about the nation-state. Morgenthau, while arguing that international politics is about nations and not persons, also expressed concern about the dangers of nationalism and sought, through diplomacy, to moderate some of the excesses of competitive nationalities. And Arendt, while seeking to construct a common world in which ideology and nationality were not the determining aspects of political life, also argued that a theory of human rights that is not tied to particular national communities risks the creation of stateless persons, that is, refugees, who are more easily excluded from the human world and thus more easily persecuted (Arendt 1968, 300–2).[13]

Thus there is not just a tension between Morgenthau and Arendt, but a tension within the works of both concerning states, nations, and political agency. The theory of agency developed here provides a starting point from which to examine the historical instances of intervention in the next three chapters. But those historical chapters also reveal the tensions between state agents and individuals that interventions create. Moreover, it is this same conflict between the person and the state that, I believe, created strains within the works of Morgenthau and Arendt. In other words, the next three chapters, while beginning with a framework that assumes state agents act in a competitive atmosphere, will simultaneously extract a set of problematic elements from that framework. In the concluding chapter, I return to those tensions, summarizing them from the historical chapters. I then return to Morgenthau and Arendt and use the ambiguities in their works to develop a critique of intervention and, in the process, state agency. Thus Morgenthau and Arendt provide both a framework for analysis and also a means by which to critique this framework.

REALISM, CONSTRUCTIVISM, AND STATE AGENCY

Thus far, I have proposed a theory of state agency that draws primarily on political philosophy. Using the work of Arendt and Morgenthau, I have demonstrated how political agency can be understood on the international level. And while I have used Morgenthau to transfer Arendt's arguments to the international level, I have yet to turn toward the literature in International Relations theory. Are there any overlaps between the theory of state agency I have proposed here and International Relations theory?

Realism

My argument may appear to some as a version of realism. States are the primary actors and they engage in a competition. Their competition is not absolute, as liberal theorists argue, but relative; that is, states are more concerned with their power in relation to what others have and not in increasing the wealth or security of everyone (Grieco 1993). Arendtian agonal politics may seem strikingly similar to the neorealism of Kenneth Waltz.

Despite the similarities, an Arendtian theory of state agency differs in some fundamental ways from realist IR theory. In both realist and neorealist theories states pursue power. In most of these theories, power becomes an object, something that can be accumulated and even measured. Arendt's notions of power are quite different from the realist conception. For Arendt, power only exists when persons act together in the public realm. Thus, power is not a "quantity" that states accumulate but is, rather, a result of actions undertaken by groups (Arendt 1972). Furthermore, an Arendtian idea of state agency does not assume states pursue power (although it also does not deny that they seek power), but that they seek something else, a sense of presence, a position in relation to others. For example, Canada may not have the same sheer power as the United States, but it has chosen not to compete with its southern neighbor. Instead, Canada finds its presence on the international stage defined in other ways, in its tradition of support for UN peacekeeping operations and funding of international agencies.

Another difference between my approach and realism concerns the ends of foreign policy. Certain classical realist authors do consider goals outside of security as constituting state action. According to Raymond Aron, states pursue security, wealth, and glory (Aron 1966). Arnold Wolfers argued that states pursue "milieu goals," or an attempt to shape the international system along certain broad ideological lines (Wolfers 1962). Morgenthau argues that "prestige" is a primary goal of state actions. But for Morgenthau, Wolfers, and Aron, these goals are purely instrumental ones— means by which the state can accomplish a particular end (Markey 1998).

Following Arendt, I would argue that political action does pursue some specific action, but, importantly, its most important purpose is to create the space for further action. Arendt's theory of political agency is, despite her indebtedness to Aristotle, distinctly anti-teleological. As Dana

Villa has argued, to reduce Arendt's theory of political action to one that remains tied to the creation of a particular type of political community or consensus is to undermine Arendt's more Nietzchean elements (Villa 1996). Arendt's political agency does not present a goal for political action. Its only concern is for the creation of spaces in which political agency can continue, in which the freedom to act is guaranteed (Arendt 1968).

In other words, Morgenthau's national purpose and Arendt's agonal politics reveal a set of concerns different than the traditional realist emphasis on security. For if Morgenthau is correct, states pursue not security but the accomplishment of certain moral aims. Realists have certainly exhibited a certain level of skepticism when it comes to moral claims at the international level (Cohen 1985). At the same time, classical realists like Morgenthau can be read as representatives of a more chastened form of morality (Rosenthal 1991). For realists like Morgenthau, a state may not act in ways that conform to individual norms of morality, but it does in fact pursue a set of normative goals in its foreign policy. The national purpose provides a tool by which to understand these goals as linked to the community's history and values. States seek to convince others that their ways of life are normatively positive. Intervention is perhaps the most obvious way in which it makes that pronouncement, for it attempts not just to lead by example, but recreate what it sees as its own moral goods in an "empty" space.

But as the Arendtian exegesis demonstrates, it also seeks to present itself in competition with others. The combination of the national purpose and agonal politics leads to a framework in which states seek to impose moral goals, but in competition with other states. Intervention demonstrates both of these tendencies, and, as the next three chapters demonstrate, it is an action in which they are seen in the clearest light. This book, then, does not just provide insight into the practice and meaning of intervention; it also provides insight into the more general question of state agency. For the practice of intervention demonstrates more general tendencies of the international realm, tendencies that more often lead to conflict than cooperation.

Constructivism

Constructivism, on the other hand, overlaps with the argument being made here in some interesting ways. Constructivist theory posits that the interests, and even identities, of states are not presumed givens but are constructed through the process of interaction with other states and international organizations. The structures, especially institutions, within which states find themselves "teach" norms to states (Finnemore 1996; Adler 1998). Rather than the realist claim that interests, identities, and norms are irrelevant to international relations, constructivists have argued that such factors are essential to explaining such relations. Martha Finnemore has put the constructivist claims to work in her analysis of intervention. She argues that an often neglected explanation of an intervention is the normative idea that lies behind it. In particular, she explores how nineteenth-century interventions were, in part, prompted by changing European notions of who counts as "human." Using the case of the British intervention in the Greek civil war, Finnemore demonstrates that the idea of what counts as a legitimate person to be protected plays a key role in the decision to intervene.

I have addressed, albeit briefly, the ways in which this book overlaps with some versions of constructivism concerning questions of norms. My theory of state agency, however, while accepting the importance of norms in explaining international relations, differs from the constructivist argument in two important ways. First, while I do not presume along with some neorealist accounts that norms play no role in international relations, I do believe that the norms that states embody and pursue in their foreign and security policies are more the product of their own particular histories than they are learned from international organizations. Adler, for example, argues that states "learn" from international organizations the proper norms of conduct. The theory developed here, on the other hand, assumes that the norms that states seek to pursue arise from their of interpretations of their national histories.

Second, the theory of state agency developed here does not presume these states act in peaceful cooperation. Some neorealist critiques of the constructivist project have emphasized the inherently conflictual nature of international relations (Mearshimer 1994/5). While I agree that conflict rather than cooperation is the norm in international politics, I also would not side with Mearshimer and others who develop this critique into an overall dismissal of the norms literature. Instead, I do think that norms matter, but I also think norms can lead to conflict.

The theory of state agency in this book differs in important ways from some of the mainstream works in International Relations theory. In contrast to realism and neorealism, this theory does not presume that states only seek power or security. Instead, it posits that one of the goals of political interaction is the pursuit of norms that result from national histories. In opposition to constructivists, who also emphasize the importance of norms, this work seeks to highlight the way in which normative visions of states are not learned from international organizations but are the result of historical interpretations of states' own national histories, interpretations that are controlled by state leaders and representatives. Finally, unlike constructivists, this argument posits that norms can lead to conflict more often than they lead to cooperation.

METHOD

Because of the use of political philosophy, the approach employed in this text does not conform to the more prominent social science methods. This is not to say, however, that the analysis is totally removed from some elements of traditional social science. First, the research design of the argument is roughly the same as that of a comparative case study. I begin with a deductive theoretical framework that is then explored through three case studies. Case studies do not demonstrate the validity of a theory by means of frequency, but rather explanation. Relying on narratives that can emphasize key elements of a theory, case studies should not be read as establishing probability. They present, rather, illustrations of the important aspects of a theory.[14] The approach utilized in this book is closest to Alexander George's "structured, focused comparison" (George 1979). George argues that case study research can provide important theoretical insights, if the cases chosen are organized around a logic that can lead to theory development. This requires that the cases be presented with a particular focus on those elements that contribute to the larger theory.

A case study approach also requires that the cases chosen conform to a logic inherent to the argument. In this book, the three cases have been chosen for a number of different and overlapping reasons. First, the cases are all from the twentieth century. More importantly, they represent three different eras of this century. If one assumes that the bipolar Cold War system is the most important systemic construction of the twentieth century, this argument examines a pre-Cold War case, a Cold War case, and a post-Cold War case. The cases thus represent different systemic moments in the history of international politics.

The cases can also be seen as representing different ideological types of intervention, with ideology here meaning the set of beliefs about political reality that shape political action, both domestically and internationally. The British and American intervention in Russia in 1918 represents a Wilsonian idealism and liberalism.[15] It also reflects a realist conception of power politics, especially in Winston Churchill's arguments about the necessity of keeping a balance of power in Europe. The Anglo-French-Israeli intervention in Egypt in 1956 reflects the last gasp of colonialist world politics, especially from the perspective of the British and French. The Israeli motivations were more traditionally realist, arising from security concerns on their border with Egypt. And, the United States intervention in Somalia in 1992 reflects a humanitarian ideology, coupled with a multilateral conception of how to act in the international system. Thus, the three case studies reflect not only different structural features of the international system, they also reflect the varying ideological features of different international agents.

The theory also provides a causal explanation of political reality. But the notion of causation in this book is not the simple covering law of social science positivism (Hempel 1965). Causation is a complicated concept, especially when it is applied to human interactions. In what sense can a political event "cause" another event? We are so accustomed to this word that to highlight its complexities may seem niggardly. But, it is important to emphasize that causation can have a range of meanings. Rather than seek to explain my understanding of the term, I will simply note that while I use the term in its ordinary sense, I am hesitant to embrace many of the positivist connotations that accompany it. Why this is the case will, hopefully, become clear as the book progresses.

Third, the theory presented here is falsifiable. Falsification is one of the central requirements of most social science theorizing, for it allows the reader to "test" the analysis made. Again, I am hesitant to embrace all the valences that this term has in the world of positivist social science. But, the argument I present can be disproved. I do not believe that "testing" its results through a larger statistical survey can capture the important elements of the theory, but I do think it is open to contestation. In fact, drawing as it does on political philosophy, I would argue that the theory presented here is perhaps better contested through the dialogue and debate that characterizes political philosophy. This would mean that rather than statistical tests, the theory should be subjected to critical analysis that would seek to establish whether or not alternative conceptions of the political are more accurate.

While the argument does use case studies, has some notion of causality, and is open to faslifiability, other aspects of it do not lend themselves to traditional social science analysis. The most important is the distinction between analyzing events and processes. Interventions are not decisions but processes. To interpret intervention as a process rather than a decision locates it within a narrative context. Analyses of intervention that treat it as an event tend to focus only on leaders and their initial decisions. Seeing intervention as a process rather than a decision means focusing on not only the leaders' decisions, but on the diplomats' attempts to convince allies and enemies of the wisdom of the intervention, on soldiers' attempts to translate decisions into actions, on victims' attempts to deal with the imposition of an alternative set of political arrangements, and on historians' attempts to give meaning to an intervention after it has taken place. When these various elements of the process come to light, intervention takes on a new meaning, one that reveals why it so often fails. For these different players in an intervention provide alternative meanings, all of which contribute to what we understand as an intervention. Of course, no analysis can include every individual person's perspective on an intervention. Instead, the goal is to highlight those individuals who have the most important roles in deciding on, implementing, and interpreting an intervention. When these perspectives are explored, new insights on intervention arise.

Another important difference between the method employed here and more traditional social science concerns the importance I place on narrative. The theory of agency developed above depends in important ways on narration, or the writing of history (Campbell 1998). In what ways does this theory actually effect the method I employ? For, like any political analyst, I am constrained by the documents that I use to make my argument. The linguistic construction of international relations is largely parasitic on this understanding of state agency, as the previous section explains. To understand aspects of international politics like intervention, then, it appears that we, as analysts, must participate in this understanding. It is important to note that state representatives believe that in their political and ethical actions they are embodying the state agency of the community they represent. Thus the interpretations on which we focus are those of state representatives, especially at those moments in which they act in the name of the community. For it is at these moments that the political and ethical ideas that make possible state actions like intervention become the most clear.

But state representatives do not completely control the narration of an intervention. Also important is the debate that surrounds interpretations. That is, while the interpretations of agents create a certain set of meanings for a political action, these actions change their meanings depending on the context in which the interpretation is made, the later interpretations of that action, and disagreements and debates to which those later interpretations give rise. Practically, this debate exists in two main places: in the actual political debates over an action that take place in most political communities, but especially in democracies; and in the historical records of political action, which either become debates themselves or add to political debates. The interpretive strategy, then, revolves around the interpretations of those undertaking the intervention. In the concluding chapter, I offer a critique of this strategy; nevertheless, the link between history, ethics and intervention makes a focus on the intervening state central to the understanding of meaning. The language game that provides the political context for intervention is generated and sustained by states. Moreover, it is one focused on the moral norms that justify state action, what Morgenthau called the national purpose. But that national purpose must be deployed in a competitive atmosphere with other states, leading to the conflicts to which interventions give rise.

CONCLUSION

In this chapter, I have combined Arendt's notions of agonal agency with Morgenthau's conceptions of national purpose to develop a theory of international political agency. From Morgenthau's concept of the national purpose, I argued that state agency relies on the construction of a specific national history, one that both constructs and reinforces a particular national ethos. That ethos then gives rise to actions like intervention, in which the state agent attempts to reveal itself by revealing its historical, national purpose. Arendt's alternative model of political agency, the narrative, leads us to reconsider not the state agent, but the national history that gives the state agent its purpose. Morgenthau's idea of national purpose depends very much on the conflation of the state and the nation; indeed, much of the literature in international relations conflates these two terms.[16] The state as an agent in international politics is very much a representative of the nation. But perhaps it is time to consider ways in which state agency can move beyond, or at least exist along with, histories and moral purposes other than those of a single nation. That is, perhaps the public revelation of the state in the international realm can be a public revelation of something other than the history of a particular national community; or, more accurately, the history of a national community that certain members of that community wish to valorize.

What would the alternative be? It might consist of international action that does not triumph a glorified national history, but one cognizant of injustices and injuries that have been committed in that community and which are now being mirrored in the community that is to be the target of intervention. For example, rather than debate the possibility of intervening in the Balkans because of the belief that the United States is the only superpower capable of such action, instead such action might spring from a recognition that the United States went through (and is still going through according to some) a period of deep and decisive ethnic or racial conflict. Based on this similar history, leaders could present their action not as a triumph of national power and purpose, but as an empathetic response to a history too similar to be ignored. Similarly, interventions in Africa to provide food aid need not be based on the assertion of French or American national pride, but might instead result from the recognition that French colonial policy and American military aid during the Cold War led to some of the consequences we see today.

Recent work in international relations theory has begun to address this link between history and state agency. David Campbell's recent work on ethics and international relations theory does so in the context of how the United States should respond to the crisis in Bosnia. Campbell argues that the construction of states as agents has led to a conceptual framework in world politics in which human tragedies are ignored until they impinge on the prerogatives of state agents. There is also a tendency to fit complex political and social conflicts into a state-centered framework. Thus the civil war in Bosnia did not see a sustained humanitarian intervention until five years after the conflict. Moreover, the solution proposed revolved around forcing individuals into ethnically pure states, accomplishing what the Serb aggressors had intended all along (Drakulic 1994). Campbell looks to the theoretical status of the state in order to find some solution to this problem (Campbell 1998). He argues that the state, as a political organization founded in a moment of contingency and violence, is never a stable entity. But this realization should not lead us to abandon hope, for it is the very deconstructability of the state that provides some possible avenues for alternative action. We can take Campbell's point about the state and reconsider the sources of state agency, which, as I have argued, are located firmly in the creation of a national history.

Thus we could interject new forms of agency into global politics, forms that do not necessarily depend on the presentation of the national history in a glorified way, but draw out moments from that history that may lead to empathy or a sense of responsibility. Note that this argument still assumes that states will be the ones that will act in world politics; even as new actors join in humanitarian projects, it seems that states will still be the dominant actors. But the state, for all our concerns about it, can still help to alleviate global problems. What we may need to do is sever the nation from the state in its capacity to act in the global sphere.[17] Thus it is still possible to envision intervention as a form of state agency. What we must do is provide ways in which humanitarian interventions derive not from sources that celebrate a past of exclusion and dominance, but which instead seek to find empathy and provide relief to those in need.

I have also suggested how the UN can be a possible global political agent, one with a history that provides a normative purpose to its actions. I do not, however, argue that the UN is an agent any less susceptible to the problems of states; indeed, I argue that in its interventions it falls victim to the same types of problems that states do. In other words, a solution to these problems will not necessarily be found in new agents; rather, solutions must be sought in new conceptions of agency.

We need an alternative vision of politics. The nation-state is necessary as a space for individual human political engagement but also detrimental to political practice in that it engages in a competitive contest with other states. Arendt's theory of narrative agency points us toward the national history of a state as a possible alternative source. And I have suggested, in outline form only, what an alternative history might be and do. In the conclusion, I develop this possibility more fully. But in the next three chapters, I explore interventions that demonstrate how the competition between agents who do not leave space for contestation will lead to the failure of intervention.

CHAPTER TWO

Intervention in Russia

INTRODUCTION

C hapter 1 laid out a framework for analyzing intervention based on state agents pursuing normative goals in a political context of competition with others. Using this framework, this chapter explores the American and British interventions in revolutionary Russia from 1918 through 1920.[1] The first section explores the American intervention in Russia, beginning with the *aide-mémoire* issued in July of 1918 by the Wilson administration and ending with the decision to withdraw American troops from Siberia and Archangel in December of 1919. The American intervention revolved around a normative discourse of saving the Czechoslovak forces and creating order out of chaos.[2] But these goals had to be accomplished through a state agent. And, as explained in chapter 1, this state agent, as a political actor, was concerned with presenting an image of itself. Furthermore, the political agency of the state led to the undermining of each of the normative goals being sought, as the contest of agents led to clashes among them. The political image that undermined the normative goals were: the American image of itself (ironically) as a noninterventionary power, the American image of itself as more liberal than its allies, and the American image of itself as the leader of the New World Order in contrast to the only challenger to that role, Leninist Bolshevism. The goal of creating a liberal polity in Russia and a liberal world order was undermined, ironically, by the American attempt to construct itself as a representative of those liberal values.

The next section addresses the British intervention in Russia, beginning with the British and French attempts to convince the Wilson administration to intervene in December of 1917, through their intervention in Archangel and Southern Russia, up until the withdrawal of troops from Northern Russia in September of 1919 and from the rest of Russia in October 1919. The

British intervention was initially prompted by a desire to open a second front in the war against Germany, but that reason was quickly overtaken by events as the war ended soon after the intervention began. As the original strategic reason became less tenable, two normative elements developed as justifications for the intervention: saving the Russian people from the anarchy of Bolshevism, and protecting the weak states of Eastern Europe from Bolshevism. As in the American actions, however, these normative elements were undermined by three political elements: the duty of Britain to protect other states based on its tradition of imperial rule; the duty of Britain to educate "uncivilized" populations, a category in which the Russians were placed in the course of the war and their revolution; and the duty of Britain to protect Europe from "Asian barbarism," the most recent manifestation of which was Bolshevism. As in the American intervention, the British intervention was substantially undermined by conflicts between their allies and conflicts within the government based on competing interpretations of its national purpose.

AMERICAN INTERVENTION IN RUSSIA

The American intervention in Russia can be divided into two separate actions: an intervention in Northern Russia, focused on the ports of Archangel and Murmansk; and an intervention in Siberia, focused on the port of Vladivostock and the railroad lines stretching from Vladivostock to Central and Western Russia. The idea was first broached by British war planners who suggested in December 1917 a joint action in which troops from the North and East would link up in the center of Russia. The British and French convinced the Japanese that they should intervene in Vladivostock and that the British and other Allies would intervene in the north.

This plan, however, floundered on the resistance of Woodrow Wilson and the American government. Wilson and his advisors argued that the Allied and Associate forces were incapable of creating an eastern front, and, even if they did, the war would be won on the western and not eastern front. After six months of continuous discussions, however, Wilson finally agreed to the intervention. In July 1918, Wilson sent an *aide-memoire* to the allies informing them that the United States and Japan would undertake "military action" in Vladivostock to rescue the Czechoslovak troops stranded in Russia, and to provide whatever aid they could to the Russian people. Wilson proposed that the United States and Japan both send 7,000 troops, which were sent to Vladivostock in August 1918. Meanwhile, in June 1918, prompted by British claims that the Germans were setting up a submarine base in the North Sea, Wilson agreed to send a contingent of American troops to Archangel. For various reasons, however, Wilson and Secretary of State Robert Lansing decided to pull all American troops out of Russia in December of 1919.

Intervention in the New World Order

The decision to intervene found its central justification in the need to "rescue" the Czechoslovak troops stranded in Siberia. A number of historians have argued that the rescue of the Czechs was simply an excuse used by American policy makers to justify their actions (Foglesong 1995; Unterberger 1956; White 1950). But in fact, the decision to aid the Czechs derived from two sources essential to the normative understandings of those engaged in American policy making in Russia. First, there was a desire to aid a group that was believed to be unjustifiably attacked by the Bolsheviks, a national purpose that coincided with the conception of America as an altruistic, nonimperialist nation. Second, the Czechs represented a nascent political community that especially appealed to Woodrow Wilson's belief in self-determination, a belief that drew on and helped constitute an image of America as an agent of change for developing countries (Steigerwald 1999, 97).

The rescue of the Czech troops is the stated aim of the intervention in both the *aide-memoire* delivered to the allies on July 18, 1918, and the announcement of the American intervention given to the American public. These troops were composed of Czech and Slovak soldiers who had either been part of the Czarist special unit, the *Druzhina*, or were soldiers from the Austrian-Hungarian army who had been captured or had deserted to the Russian side (Kennan 1956 II, 136–65; Unterberger 1989). After the revolution, the Allies recognized this combined force and put them under the command of French military leadership. This decision was made possible by Thomas Masaryk's role as representative of the nascent Czechoslovak nation. Masaryk went to Russia soon after the revolution to convince the Bolshevik authorities to allow the Czechoslovak soldiers to leave for France. Finding the Bolsheviks uncooperative, Masaryk turned to the Allied leaders. British leaders, however, saw in Masaryk's appeal a chance to recreate the Eastern front with a well-organized group of soldiers.

From January to May, the Czechoslovak legion had been moving slowly eastward through Russia while negotiating with the Bolsheviks over their departure. Meanwhile, at an Allied military council in Abbeville, France, it was decided that the corps should be split into two, with half going through to Vladivostock and the other half going north to Archangel. This coincided nicely with the British strategy of linking up forces from these two directions to recreate Russia as a wartime ally. But, due to a minor conflict that occurred between the Czechoslovak legion and a group of Hungarian prisoners at Chelyabinsk, the Soviet government denied the Czech legion its arms and refused to allow it to continue its escape. This decision by the Soviet government coincided with what later became the Chelyabinsk Congress, where the Czech leaders gathered and decided to fight their way to Vladivostock.

George Kennan, the American statesman and diplomatic historian, stresses that the American reaction to the Czech corps was the fundamental factor in the decision to intervene. On June 17, 1918 Wilson noted in a memo to Robert Lansing that the Czech situation provided a "shadow of a plan" for solving the problem of the Russian intervention (PWW 48, 335; Kennan 1956 II, 388). Others have read this as meaning that Wilson saw in the Czech forces an excuse for intervening, but Kennan takes seriously Wilson's attraction to the Czech cause. Even as the Allies continued to send the Administration various proposals and justifications for intervention, usually couched in terms of creating an eastern front, the State department and Wilson focused more acutely on the Czechs. "It was the reports concerning the Czechoslovaks, not the arguments of the Allied chanceries, that were determining Wilson's decision," (Kennan 1956 II, 391).

The final straw occurred in late June. On June 29 some of the Czech troops, after provocation by the Soviet authorities, seized control of Vladivostock. In response, British and Japanese forces landed,[3] thus effectively depriving the Soviets of control of the city. There was an American ship at this time located in the harbor of Vladivostock, *The Brooklyn*, commanded by Admiral A. N. Knight, who immediately requested instructions from Washington. The next few days in Washington saw a number of high-level State Department meetings and memos sent back and forth concerning a solution. On July 4, while on the presidential yacht, *The Mayflower*, Secretary of State Robert Lansing drew up a memorandum in which he argued that the Czech forces had provided a "sentimental element" concerning the question of intervention, and the United States had a responsibility to aid them (Kennan 1956 II, 395).[4] The next day Wilson gathered together his main military and diplomatic advisors and read them a copy of a memo that later became the *aide-memoire*. It was written entirely on Wilson's own and stressed the Czech troops as the main reason for the intervention. According to Kennan, this memo most accurately portrays the decision on the Siberian intervention. He notes that whether or not the aid for the Czechs was also intended to help overthrow the Bolsheviks is unclear; many in the State Department hoped this would be the case, but he argues Wilson was not so convinced.

Despite the claims of other historians, including later interpretations of Kennan, the war seemed to be the least important reason for the intervention from the American perspective.[5] Certainly concern with the war entered into the decision. But, there was a clear resistance to the intervention offered by members of the military community surrounding Wilson. General Peyton March, the Army Chief of Staff, was the most insistent in his disagreement with the intervention; when Wilson presented the *aide-memoire* to his advisors on July 5, 1918, March was the only one to openly voice his disagreement (March 1932, 126). March also points out that Wilson almost always followed the advice of his military advisors, with the intervention in Siberia and Archangel being the only times he did not (113). Thus the decision to intervene in Russia did not derive from the military needs of the Allies, as Kennan argues in his later interpretations. It appears that for Wilson the intervention must have had a different set of reasons than can be found in a military interpretation.

Undoubtedly, the diplomatic documents can be read in diverse ways. This book, however, seeks to demonstrate that one can find in those documents support for an interpretation more attuned to the normative concerns of the American policy making community. Wilson's struggle with the Russian problem and his personal involvement in the military aspects of it reflect a strong commitment to helping the Czech army and the developing Czech nation (Baker 8, 266). The Russian decision was important to Wilson, and the Czech forces played an important part in his decision. Moreover, in his later justifications of the intervention to other Allied ministers, Wilson reminded them that the intervention was not for political reasons, but mainly to help the Czechs (FRUS Paris Peace Conference 6, 644; FRUS Russia 1919, 346).

Wilson's concern with this issue prompted him to pen the *aide-memoire* himself. This policy paper is central to the intervention for two reasons: First, it remained the central justification for the intervention until approximately January 1919, when an agreement between the United States and Japan turned the Siberian intervention into an attempt to protect the Trans-Siberian Railroad. The paper was typed by Wilson himself on his own typewriter, about a week after he had informed his main military and foreign affairs advisors of his decision.[6] Second, it served as the only real formal instructions given to General William Graves, the commander of forces in Siberia (Graves 1931, 1–33).

It begins by reaffirming the United States' commitment to the overall war effort and stressing the importance of the Western front for winning the war. The document then moves to one of its central claims:

> It is the clear and fixed judgment of the Government of the United States, arrived at after repeated and very searching reconsiderations of the whole situation in Russia, that military intervention there would add to the present sad confusion in Russia rather than

cure it, injure her rather than help her, and that it would be of no advantage in the prosecution of our main design, to win the war against Germany. It cannot therefore, take part in such intervention or sanction it in principle. Military intervention would, . . . be merely a method of making use of Russia, not a method of serving her. . . . Military action is admissible in Russia, as the Government of the United States sees the circumstances, only to help the Czecho-Slovaks consolidate their forces and get into successful cooperation with their Slavic kinsmen and to steady any efforts at self-government or self-defense in which the Russians themselves may be willing to accept assistance. (FRUS Russia 1918 II, 288–9)

As is indicated by this quote, the decision to intervene is framed solely in terms of aiding the Czechs and the Russians, while the previous sentences deny that the creation of an Eastern front has anything to do with the decision. Furthermore, it is framed largely as a "rescue" mission, and not an intervention.

Two other documents from the same period support a normative interpretation of the decision. The first is a report from William Wiseman, the British head of intelligence operations in the United States, to Arthur Cecil Murray, a British foreign policy official, reporting on Wiseman's conversations with Wilson. Wiseman reports that Wilson would not be swayed by arguments concerning the creation of an Eastern front. Instead,

Anyone who has studied his Mexican policy will understand the remarkable parallel which the Russian situation presents, and realize that this is to him more than a passing political question, but a matter of principle. . . . I think we should realize that we are up against a new conception of foreign policy. . . . The Czech-Slovak position has, in my opinion, materially altered the situation, and will be, I think, the determining factor. The President recognizes that both the Allies and the United States are responsible for the Czechs, and if possible must render them assistance. (PWW 48, 523–4)

Wilson was at this stage not interested in the military advantages of intervention but believed that the United States had a responsibility to aid the Czechs. Reports from American consular offices along the Trans-Siberian railroad must have further supported this sense of responsibility. They revealed that American officials had in fact helped settle a number of conflicts between the Czechs and the Russians throughout June, creating strong feelings of concern in the American diplomatic community (FRUS Russia 1918 II, 184–7).

The second document is a memo from Robert Lansing written on July 4 and delivered to the President that day. In that memo, Lansing argues that the Czechs had introduced a "sentimental element into the question of our duty"; that is, had created a moral issue requiring United States intervention. Unterberger describes the memo in the following:

> He declared that if the United States failed to aid the Czechs and if they were destroyed, "we would be held culpable or at least generally blamed, especially by their compatriots in this country and western Europe." . . . he now emphasized that American responsibility was made almost imperative because the Czechs were being attacked by released Germans and Austrians. . . . There was, he added, "a moral obligation to save these men from our common enemies, if we are able to do so." (Unterberger 1989, 236)

Evidently, Wilson felt that saving the Czechs was the moral responsibility of the United States. That moral responsibility took on further significance for Wilson and his advisors in that the Czechs were a "young" nation worthy of American support. "Saving the Czechs" expressed the desire to help a nation newly forming, especially on the heels of World War I, a war fought to make the world "safe for democracy" and self-determination. The influence of Thomas Masaryk on Wilson provides important evidence of this. During the last two years of the war, various nationalities of the Austrio-Hungarian empire had been meeting and issuing declarations addressed to the Allied powers demanding that the dissolution of Austrio-Hungary be one of their war aims. The Fourteen Points speech that Wilson delivered in January of 1918 gave some hope to these groups, although it was not followed by anything more concrete. The Allied governments offered half-hearted support, providing some means to publicize the cause. In April 1918, the Congress of Oppressed Nationalities met in Rome, composed of the various national groups that made up the Austrio-Hungarian empire (Unterberger 1989, 120–32). This group, given tacit support by the British and other Allied powers, publicized the Czechoslovak cause. They demanded that the United States and the Allied powers give their full support to a policy of self-determination for all national groups.

At the same time that these proclamations were emanating from Europe, Masaryk arrived in America to convince Wilson to support his cause. He was received in Chicago on May 5 with a "spectacular reception," (Unterberger 1989, 126). For the next two months, aided by sympathetic State department officials, Masaryk sought an audience with Wilson. While he was not immediately successful, Masaryk was able to meet with a number of State department officials, including Lansing. It was probably more than a coincidence that on May 29 Lansing issued a public statement of support for the Congress of Oppressed nationalities (PWW 48, 438n3). Wilson had also received a memo from Masaryk in which he argued that the United States ought to recognize the Bolshevik government, *de facto*, and that in so supporting a strengthened Russia the nationalities of Eastern Europe would be protected from Germans and Austria-Hungarians (PWW 47, 549–552).

On June 19 Masaryk and Wilson finally met. In a discussion that lasted a little under an hour, Masaryk agreed with Wilson that intervention must not be undertaken to alter the Russian political situation. Masaryk further argued that the Czech forces were neutral in the conflict (an assertion that contradicts much of what we know about the conflicts between the Czechs and Bolsheviks along the Trans-Siberian railroad (Unterberger 1989, 170–200). He also asked Wilson to "help our men to be brought from Russia to France" (Unterberger 1989, 223). A few days later, having met with Masaryk, Lansing sent Wilson a memo on the nationalities question, in which he argued that the United States ought to support the demands of the Czechs unequivocally (PWW 48: 435–437). Wilson agreed, and on June 27 Lansing publicly announced the United States support for the oppressed nationalities (Unterberger 1989, 228–31). Only one and half weeks later, Wilson decided to intervene in Russia, largely in support of the Czech legion.

The parallel announcements of support for the oppressed nationalities and the intervention in Russia, along with Masaryk's meetings with Wilson, Lansing and others during this same period, provide strong evidence that Wilson and Lansing were motivated by a concern with helping the Czechs form a new nation in their decision to intervene in Russia. Lansing's memo of June 26 explicitly cites the principle of self-determination as one of the central reasons for supporting the oppressed peoples of Eastern Europe, an appeal that undoubtedly resonated with Wilson. Further, the fact that Masaryk supported Wilson's own beliefs on the question of intervention in Russia must have made the president all the more sympathetic to Masaryk's arguments. The ethic of saving the Czechs conformed to the United States national purpose, as understood by Wilson and Lansing. In fact, Lansing encouraged Wilson to announce his support for the oppressed nationalities in his July 4th address at Mount Vernon. While he did not explicitly mention any one group, Wilson did remind his audience that George Washington acted "not for a class, but for a people," a direct challenge to Bolshevik class ideology (PWW 48, 515). His address, in the midst of two weeks devoted to the intervention in Russia and support for the oppressed nationalities, further locates the intervention in a national ethic of support for self-determination and freedom.

Rescuing the Czechs, then, was not simply a fig leaf to cover over the more "realistic" reason of prosecuting the war. In fact, the decision to intervene was strongly influenced by the existence of the Czech legion in Russia. There existed in the minds of a number of American officials both in Washington and in Russia a moral obligation to save this group, as is evidenced by Robert Lansing's memo on the subject, and Wilson's agreement with it. Further, the role played by Thomas Masaryk in convincing Lansing and Wilson to support the Czech cause, at the same time that they were contemplating intervention in Russia, enabled Wilson and Lansing to place the intervention in terms of support for a policy of self-determination. Saving the Czechs provided an important normative explanation for the intervention in Russia, one that resonated with the decidedly liberal and American purpose of supporting self-determination.

Returning to the concept of norms developed in chapter 1, the norm of saving the Czechs not only regulated the behavior of the United States, it also contributed to shaping its identity. Just as America was a nation founded on a fundamental act of self-determination, so the Wilson administration saw the Czechs as attempting to determine their own future and constitute themselves. This important element of the norm of liberalism both guided policy toward the Russian revolution and also reinforced the image of the United States.

So it appears that a normative vision played a role in the decision to intervene. But while a normative vision may have prompted the intervention, a concern with politics—politics as I have defined it in chapter 1—effectively undermined that normative purpose. How?

The image of the United States as an agent for change in world politics constituted one of the central elements of Wilsonian foreign policy. Wilson and his advisors believed that America had to present itself as different from the other powers waging the war; entering the war as an "associated" rather than as an "allied" power was a good example of this. Wilson and those around him sought to present the United States as a state that does not intervene, but only undertakes forms of "military action" for noble goals such as restoring order or rescuing oppressed peoples. Two moments in the history of the intervention demonstrate how this concern with being a noninterventionary power undermined the success of the intervention: the March 1918 decision not to support the Japanese in the their intervention, and the *aide-memoire's* distinction between intervention and military action.

Before turning to these two moments, however, it is instructive to briefly examine the other major intervention undertaken by the Wilson administration. For it is in Mexico that Wilson learned how putting troops across an international border can damage the image of the United States.

After siding with a number of different leaders in Mexico, Wilson eventually sent troops into Mexican territory in March 1914 in pursuit of Pancho Villa. From the time when American troops met with the Mexican army to the time of their withdrawal from Mexico, the Mexican government sent a series of official communications to the United States demanding an end to the intervention. In response, Wilson argued, both in public and in private, that the action undertaken by the United States was not an intervention. In a speech before Congress asking for funds to continue the "action" in Mexico, Wilson declared:

> I am not willing to be a party to intervention in the internal affairs of Mexico. By this I mean an attempt to determine for the Mexican people what the form, the circumstances, and the personnel of their government shall be, or upon what terms and in what manner a settlement of their disturbed affairs should be effected. To such intervention I am, and shall remain, unalterably opposed . . . I have been bred in an old school of American principle and practice: I know what American history means . . . I know that [the American people] desire no one who professes to speak for them to interfere with the liberties of any people and that I am speaking their deepest principle of action when I say that we wish not a single foot of Mexican territory, not a single hour of political control in Mexico. (PWW 37, 301)[7]

Clearly Wilson had an understanding of what intervention entailed, and it was something he believed that the United States would never undertake again. Even more importantly, the desire to abstain from intervention derived not just from Wilson, but from the history of the American republic and the desires of the American people. Robert Lansing also argued that the Administration ought to avoid the term intervention in its presentation of its action in Mexico, because "Intervention . . . suggests a definite purpose to "clean up" the country (PWW 37, 276).

Wilson's insistence on the noninterventionary character of the American national purpose in the Mexican action developed out of a dialogue with various parts of the political system: Republicans (PWW 37, 180–1), Congress (PWW 37, 298–304), and the American public (*The Ladies Home Journal* on Mexico, August 1, 1916; PWW 37, 508–12). During the summer months of 1916, the United States had to deal with both the Mexican situation and the war in Europe. This meant presenting itself as both uninterested in acting like one of the "old powers" as they were in Europe, but simultaneously engaging in an action in Mexico that looked strikingly like what European powers had been doing throughout the nineteenth century in their imperialist policies. One way to differentiate the two actions was to make clear that the action in Mexico was mainly an attempt to protect the United States, especially after the Villa raid on Columbus, New Mexico; this is the line of argument suggested by Lansing. But this line of argument became less tenable as United States forces confronted a hostile Carranza government and were forced to engage in military action against the Mexican army. Thus the need for protection was adroitly combined with the need to change the Mexican government so that it would be more in accord with the wishes of the "Mexican people." Wilson concluded his address to Congress on the following note:

> The present situation, if fortunate in no other respect, is at least fortunate in this, that it affords us an opportunity to prove ourselves as great as our professions. We shall seek in the very act of protection our southern frontier to succor the people whose territory we enter, and to set them free to look to their own affairs, bring order out of their confusion. (PWW 37, 304)

Americans do not intervene, but they do act to protect themselves and to provide aid to those who need it.

Chastened by the hostile reaction of the Mexicans to American military forces in Mexico, Wilson was adamant that the United States would not be mistaken for an intervening force in Russia. In March of 1918 Wilson and Lansing agreed, tentatively, to a Japanese intervention in Russia. Although the force would not include Americans, the Administration agreed that perhaps Japan acting on its own could bring some order to the Siberian situation. On March 1, 1918, Wilson handed to Lansing a memo that agreed not to object to Japanese intervention in Siberia "as an ally of Russia, with no purpose but to save Siberia from the invasion of armies and intrigues of Germany" (PWW 46, 498). But the next day Colonel E. M. House, Wilson's personal advisor, concerned with the "moral position" of the United States in acquiescing to such an action, urged Wilson to recant his memo. It appears that House's appeal to the moral "position" or image of the United States convinced Wilson, for on March 5 he sent another note to the State Department withdrawing American approval of the action (Foglesong 1995, 147–9).

The appeal to the "moral position" of the United States, it seems, was not a question of "mere" image. Rather, the change from approval to rejection of the Japanese action resulted from a serious concern with the political image of the United States in Russia and around the world. House explained to British foreign secretary Arthur Balfour on March 4 that intervention would "mean a serious lowering, if not actual loss, of our moral position in the eyes of our own peoples and of the whole word, and a dulling of the high enthusiasm of the American people for a righteous cause. Unless we maintain our moral position we must expect a very formidable anti-war party here, a general weakening of the war effort, and a breaking-up of that practically unanimous support upon which the Administration can now count" (Foglesong 1995, 148). House believed, and it seems so did Wilson, that the American ability to act internationally depended on sustaining a vision of itself as a proponent of certain moral and political positions. One of those positions was nonintervention, in this case differentiating itself from the Japanese, and also German, desire for territory or political control.

In what way did this failure to support the Japanese undermine the success of the intervention? Of course, history does not lend itself to counterfactual arguments. Nevertheless, it does seem that an early Japanese action in March 1918 would have been more effective than the vacillating American intervention of late fall. The Japanese were prepared to move a large number of troops into Siberia and would have certainly defeated the Bolsheviks if given the chance.

The second moment of the intervention in which the American position as nonintervenor played an important role was in the *aide-memoire* itself. Recall that the *aide-memoire* specifically claimed that the United States was not intervening but was engaging in military action (FRUS 1918 II, 288–9). This seemingly semantic point derived from Wilson's, and Lansing's and House's, conceptions of the United States as a noninterventionary power. Instead, the United States could take action to solve a specific problem, especially one that involved saving Russia and saving the Czechs. The *aide-memoire* presents the United States as an altruistic power, not like the other powers that were interested in the intervention for their "selfish" reasons. Much to the chagrin of the Allied powers, Wilson made a point of saying that American military action should in no way "set limits" on the actions of the other powers. Instead, it sought to make clear the purposes of the United States in this action. This disavowal of joint action, in a memo intended to create a multilateral intervention, indicates the importance the American policy makers placed in their political image.

This desire to present itself as a noninterventionary power resulted in the United States sending a force that would have little impact on the course of the intervention. The decision to deploy only 7,000 troops in Siberia indicated that this force was not intended to have a real impact on the course of the Russian military situation. Indeed, the small size of the force resulted from Wilson and Lansing's desire not to be seen as interventionary, but instead as a force seeking to aid in very particular, and circumscribed, ways. Soon after the intervention began, the French and Japanese both sought to increase the number of troops and to allow them to travel farther westward along the Trans-Siberian railway. This request brought a swift reaction from Wilson and Lansing, reminding the allies that the agreement had been to "rescue the Czechs" and not much else (Unterberger 1969, 43). When Roland Morris, United States Ambassador to Japan, asked the State Department about possibly sending troops to Omsk to protect the White government there, Lansing responded with a note stressing the difference between the Americans and the allies:

> The ideas and purposes of the Allies with respect to military operations in Siberia and on the Volga front are ideas and purposes with which we have no sympathy. We do not believe them to be practical or based upon sound reason or good military judgment. (FRUS Russia 1918 II, 393)

Along with the refusal to agree to advancing troops farther west, the American policy makers refused to participate in any political coordination of military action. When asked by the French whether or not the United States would be willing to participate in a joint Allied council on operations in Russia, Wilson replied in the following:

> Please make it plain to the French Ambassador that we do not think cooperation in political action necessary or desirable in eastern Siberia because we contemplate no political action of any kind there, but only the action of friends who can stand at hand and wait to see how they can help. (Unterberger 1969, 43–44)

The American political leaders sought to differentiate themselves from all others in Siberia and represent a particular form of American political action. But that attempt to differentiate itself left the American forces hindered in their ability to accomplish any practical military objectives. The inability to aid the Czechs and provide the needed political order and physical supplies resulted from the combination of wanting to help yet also wanting to present a particular image of oneself.

It might appear that this desire to present itself as noninterventionary as it intervened in both Mexico and Russia is a clear example of the hypocrisy of international relations, or of the inability to rely on an interpretive approach in understanding foreign policy or world politics. But the presentation of America as a noninterventionary power in the midst of an intervention is central to understanding why the intervention followed the course it did, and why it failed as it did. The evidence indicates that Wilson, Lansing, House, and others sincerely believed that American action was not interventionary; that they were acting in Russia, as in Mexico, in support of aims that differed from those of intervening and imperial powers. But the need to differentiate itself from these other powers, who were in fact the allies of the United States in this action, prevented any concerted action throughout the intervention.

The political aspect of the intervention, the desire to present oneself in this action as representative of certain forms of political order and certain values, reveals why the United States could not cooperate with the other powers. And it is precisely this political element of intervention that this book is seeking to uncover. The politics of state agency, the performative element of foreign policy that not only influences others but presents the self, can be seen here as a key element in the failure of the intervention.

The Order of Liberalism

A second normative component of the intervention concerned order. Viewing the events of Russia from the United States (and Britain as the next section will demonstrate), many feared Russia's descent into chaos. This was especially the case for the diplomatic and consular officers of the United States. Accused by some as being conservative capitalists, motivations which certainly played a part in their thinking, Americans like Robert Lansing, David Francis, Basil Miles, and Frank Polk seemed to have been greatly disturbed by what they saw as a lack of political order. But order can be constructed in a wide variety of ways. The clash between imposing order of any sort and the actions of those on the ground responsible for American troops, specifically David Francis and William Graves, undermined the effectiveness of the American intervention.

One key figure who was especially concerned with the dangers of anarchy and the need for order was Robert Lansing. Lansing's states papers, dated December 4 and December 10, 1917, reveal that he supported a military dictatorship.[8] Some historians, such as the Marxist William A. Williams argue that the intervention derived, in large part, from Lansing's focus on the economic bases of American foreign policy. Williams adds that Basil Miles and Frank Polk, two advisors in Washington, Paul Reinsch, Ambassador to China, and Roland Morris, Ambassador to Japan, all of whom had conservative backgrounds, used their influence to convince Woodrow Wilson that the United States needed to adopt an anti-Bolshevik policy (Williams 1963, 25–8), based on their belief in an ideology focused on the expansion of American power. Williams argues that the decision to intervene was made at the end of January 1918. He bases this argument mainly on the policy papers of Miles and Polk and on an overview of the situation written by Robert Lansing on December 3, 1917. In that paper, Lansing argued that the leaders of the Bolshevik Revolution, Trotsky and Lenin, were not German spies but true revolutionaries who needed to be dealt with as such. Lansing claimed that the American system of government was the one on which the Russians needed to base the course of their revolution, for "The United States was dedicated to the 'the principle of democracy and to a special order based on liberty.' The Bolsheviks openly challenged that unique system and should be dealt with accordingly" (Williams, quoting Lansing, 1963, 37).

Williams overstates the economic basis of this state paper. The anti-Bolshevism found in Lansing's paper and others like it derived not only from simple economic motives, but also from the numerous reports emanating from Russia concerning the general chaos of the revolution and the terrorist activities of the Bolsheviks (cf. FRUS Russia 1918 II, 15, 102, 220–3). The source of American intervention was certainly anti-Bolshevism, but not only because Bolshevism hindered American economic expansion; rather, it also resulted from the belief that Bolshevism was a threat to the physical well-being of the Russian people.

Lansing's interpretation of Russia provides a revealing example of how the history of the intervening state plays a key role in the construction of its normative, national purpose. In the December 4 paper, he argued that the Bolsheviks, in taking over power from the democratically elected Kerensky government, had created a "class despotism." In this particular paper, Lansing argued that the dangers of class despotism manifest themselves most clearly in the Bolshevik appeal *vis-à-vis* their foreign policy:

> This arbitrary and irregular method of conducting foreign intercourse is a further evidence of the despotic spirit of the Bolshevik faction and of their utter disregard of constitutional and representative government, which is the very foundation of national independence and the safeguard of individual rights. Without submission to government resting upon the rule of majorities democracy is an empty word, and personal liberty becomes prey to tyranny and lawlessness. (PWW 45, 206)

Ironically, Woodrow Wilson's foreign policy was accused of exactly the same thing in his emphasis on national self-determination. And although Lansing followed the President in this question, he did express his doubts about basing foreign policy on self-determination. In a memo on a Bolshevik propaganda piece addressed to the "peoples and governments of the Allied countries," Lansing argued that such appeals are to classes and not to the proper authorities. Such a means of conducting foreign policy subverts not only domestic order, but international order as well:

> The address from beginning to end is to a class and not to all classes of society, a class which does not have property but hopes

to obtain a share by process of government rather than by individual enterprise. This is of course a direct threat to existing social order in all countries. . . . If the Bolsheviks intend to suggest that every community (though they state no unity as the basis for independent action) can determine its allegiance to this or that political state or to become independent, the present political organization of the world would be shattered and the same disorder would generally prevail as now exists in Russia. It would be international anarchy. . . . Such a theory seems to me utterly destructive of the political fabric of society and would result in constant turmoil and change. It simply cannot be done if social order and governmental stability are to be maintained. (PWW 45, 428)

For Lansing, the practices of the Bolsheviks, seen perhaps most clearly in their conduct of foreign policy, will be destructive of social order and stability. It is based on these views that Lansing advocated support for a "military dictatorship" in a December 10, 1917 memo, the same memo that Williams claims as proof of Lansing's concern with economic factors. Finally, in a memo of February 15, 1918, Lansing argued that the class despotism of the Bolsheviks is more dangerous than the autocratic despotism of the Germans, because the latter "has the virtue of order, while the other is productive of disorder and anarchy" (FRUS RLP II, 353).

Thus Lansing's suggestion of support for a military dictator derived from the same concern with political order that motivated much of the intervention in general. The concern with order can in fact be broken down into two categories: a concern with the lives and social order of the Russians themselves and a concern with the lives of the diplomats of the Allied countries. Each of these played an important role in the justification of the intervention. Indeed, Lansing's comments that the Bolsheviks are a danger to both domestic and international order demonstrate this twofold concern. Each justification is equally important for an ethic based on the United States national purpose: a concern with the domestic tranquillity of Russia reflects the image of the United States as embodying a foreign policy concerned with human rights; and a concern with danger to the diplomatic community reflects the American belief in an ordered international world, an order perhaps best exemplified by practices like diplomatic immunity and extra territoriality.

Lansing was not the only one to voice such concerns. Soon after the Bolshevik revolution, reports began arriving of the terrorist methods of government being employed by the Bolsheviks. It is important to note that this anarchy and terror was not interpreted as a product of revolution in general; rather, it resulted from the specific policies of the Bolsheviks. From Moscow, reports from David Francis (United States Ambassador to Russia), DeWitt C. Poole (Consul at Moscow), and Maddin Summers (Consul at Moscow) all stress the terrorist policies of the Bolsheviks. Francis eventually recommended intervention in a telegram of May 2, 1918 (FRUS Russia 1918 I, 519–21). His concerns with the Bolsheviks at this point, however, largely revolve around his interpretation of them as being controlled by the Germans (FRUS Russia 1918 I, 296; 505–7)). Francis' later interpretations of the intervention, however, stress more the threat of Bolshevism itself to the functioning of an orderly society (see Francis 1922, 330, 335, 349). Admittedly, the cables that Francis sent to the State Department throughout the winter of 1917 and the spring of 1918 sought an intervention in Russia because of the threat of the Germans. However, as these later interpretations demonstrate, he also believed that Bolshevism was a threat to "civilization"— that is, a threat to orderly society.

Two other foreign service officers in Russia argued that the Bolsheviks used terrorism. Maddin Summers claimed on November 27, 1917, that because the Bolsheviks seized power violently, they would need to employ violence to keep their hold on power (FRUS Russia 1918 I, 270–1). Poole pointed out, on August 26, 1918, that the Bolsheviks were getting worse over time:

> So-called [Commission against] Counter-Revolution again supporting a veritable reign of terror with many summary and baseless shootings each day. Among the Bolsheviks, saner elements giving way to the violent and completely irresponsible. (FRUS Russia 1918 I, 581)

Clearly, most of those in the American diplomatic community believed that the Bolsheviks were not representative of the Russian people, and that they were holding on to power by means of sheer terror.

The period that perhaps proved this to many in the diplomatic community, and policy making community, was The Terror which lasted from September to October of 1918, during which, after an attempt on the life of Lenin, the Bolsheviks wantonly killed random Russian citizens (FRUS Russia 1918 I, 680–721). These events took place after the initial decision to intervene, during July 1918. The intervention required a new set of justifications with the end of the war, and the events of late 1918 gave the American, and all Allied forces, a further justification for their presence in Russia. A telegram from Poole at the onset of The Terror perhaps best exemplifies how these events provided an important support for the continuation of the intervention:

> Since May the so-called Extraordinary Commission against Counter-Revolution has conducted an openly avowed campaign of terror. Thousands of persons have been summarily shot without even the form of a trial. Many have no doubt been innocent of even the political views which were supposed to supply the motive of their execution. . . . In sum, vengeful and irresponsible gangs are venting the desperation of their declining power in the daily massacre of untold innocents. The situation cries aloud to all who will act for the sake of humanity. . . . The . . . truly efficacious course is a rapid military advance from the north. Our present halfway position is cruel in the extreme. Our landing has set up the Bolshevik death agony. It is now our moral duty to shield the numberless innocents who are exposed to its hateful reprisals. (FRUS Russia 1918 I, 682)

In this report, Poole moves smoothly from a recounting of the terrors of Bolshevik rule (which he traces back to May, not just to the start of the current massacres) to a policy of further intervention, chastising the half-hearted efforts undertaken so far. The reports of the massacres clearly had an effect in Washington, as evidenced by a circular from Lansing to all diplomatic missions a few days later, on September 20, in which he condemns the actions of the Soviets and encourages all other governments to do so (FRUS Russia 1918 I, 687–8). On October 10, 1918, Francis, asking for a drastic increase in American troop presence, one that will enable them to take over Moscow and Petrograd, wrote,

> Major arrived [and gave] a horrible account of Bolshevik cruelties saying that 43,000 innocent men and women are imprisoned, hundreds being killed daily. My conclusion is for the Allies immediately to take Petrograd and Moscow by sending sufficient troops therefore to Murman and Archangel without delay; 50,000 would serve but 100,000 would be ample . . . Bolsheviks gain strength by terrorizing. (FRUS Russia 1918 II, 555)

The chaos and terror existed not only in Moscow, but in Petrograd and the surrounding areas, according to American diplomats. Reports from Siberia also detailed the horrors of Bolshevik rule, even though the Bolshevik presence was not particularly strong in these areas. J. Butler Wright, a consular officer in Vladivostock, reported on March 26, 1918, that the Bolshevik rule was bringing about "[t]he most arbitrary confiscation of property, execution of individuals, levying of loans and searches of trains . . . " (FRUS Russia 1918 II, 89). He goes on to recommend intervention so as to provide "law and order" (II, 104). A year after the intervention had been underway, the concern with chaos continued to justify military action. The American ambassador to Japan, Roland S. Morris, argued that:

> The population is exhausted, local administration is corrupt and inefficient, pestilence threatens. I think that we should make every effort to revive economic life and render it possible for the population to go to work. Otherwise I fear that the country will fall into political chaos and become a field of international intrigue if not conflict.[9]

There is a further dimension to the terrorism of the Bolsheviks that may have had an even more decisive effect on the course of the intervention. The threats to the Russian people were bad enough, but soon the Bolshevik rule began to threaten diplomatic representatives in Russia. On January 14, 1918, Francis and much of the diplomatic corps held an audience with Lenin concerning the arrest of the Rumanian minister in Russia, Constantine Diamandi. As reported by Francis, the diplomats protested vigorously to Lenin, in that the principle of diplomatic immunity should never be violated (FRUS Russia 1918 I, 477–82; Kennan 1956 I, 330–42). On August 31, 1918, a mob stormed what was left of the British Embassy and killed the senior British officer, Captain N. A. Cromie (Kennan 1956 II, 462–3). This death eventually played a role in the justifications for the British intervention, a point explored in more detail as follows. According to Charles Crane, one of Wilson's unofficial advisors on Russia, Francis held off a group of Bolsheviks who had threatened the American embassy soon after the November revolution (Cronon 1963, 249). Even the German Ambassador, Count Wilhelm von Mirbach, was assassinated on July 6, 1918 (Kennan 1956 II, 434). Undoubtedly, each of these events alone would not have alarmed the diplomatic and policy making communities. But occurring throughout 1918, soon upon the heels of the Bolshevik takeover, they would serve to further reinforce the Allied interpretation of the Bolsheviks as ruling through terror.

Both the threats to the Russian people and to the Allied diplomats made a vivid impression on American policy makers. While each event did not contribute to the decision to intervene, they all helped justify the action, thus giving it a moral purpose. The danger of anarchy and the terrorism practiced by the Bolsheviks were important normative components of the intervention. The American response to this anarchy indicates a concern with creating order out of chaos. Once again, we see how norms played a key role in the intervention. Here the legal norms of in the international system played a particularly important role. Recalling the distinction between positivist and legal constructivists, we see here the importance of the international legal norm of the diplomat. While diplomats are not any more important as human beings than nondiplomats, the attack on the diplomatic corps by the revolutionaries played a decisive role in generating support for a military intervention. The norm of diplomatic immunity not only helped construct the space within which diplomats can operate, it also, in this case, influenced the decision to prompt an intervention.

But what kind of order should be created? Political order comes in various guises, from a totalitarian order to a democratic one. The United States represented a new form of political order according to those engaged in the formulation and implementation of its foreign policy at the time of the intervention. Three important moments in the course of the intervention demonstrate how disagreements over what that American order should represent had a decisive influence on the outcome: the role of the Russian ambassador to the United States; the actions of General Graves in Siberia in support of American conceptions of justice and order; and the actions of Ambassador Francis in the governing of the Northern Russia provinces, especially in his overturning of a *coup d'état* supported by the British authorities there. Moreover, these actions were undertaken not by the decision makers, but those who had to put in place the orders from Washington—the soldiers and diplomats who enable state agency.

Liberalism is an essential part of the American national purpose, but what liberalism means has shifted throughout the course of American history. N. Gordon Levin presents Wilson as an advocate of a world order based on liberal principles. Some, like Arthur Link, have presented Wilson as an advocate of a Christian world order in which Wilson played the role of prophet (Link 1979). But Levin convincingly demonstrates that Wilson was in fact a supporter of liberal principles before he was a supporter of Christian ones. According to Levin, Wilson felt that America could be an "agent of the world's transformation from chaos to orderly liberal rationality" (Levin 1968: 5). The American nation had never experienced a preliberal past, thus making it well-suited to teach the world how a truly liberal political community could flourish. America differed from the autocracy of Germany and Czarist Russia, but also from the aristocratic imperialism of France and Great Britain. The unique history of the American nation made it best suited to play the role of redeemer of the world:

> For Wilson, the ultimate mission of a liberal exceptionalist America was to lead the rest of the world, without socialist revolution, to a universal liberal triumph over all elements of pre-bourgeois reaction and atavistic imperialism. (Levin 1968, 181)

Levin explains how Wilson's belief in liberalism and his reading of American history enabled him to see himself as both protecting the American national interest while simultaneously changing the world for the better.

> In the President's view, it was fitting for an American nation-state, whose own national tradition was based on an original triumph of progressive liberal values over European reaction to be the disinterested and trusted leader of mankind at the moment of liberal internationalism's final victory over the atavistic restraints of traditional reaction. (Levin 1968, 255)

Liberalism manifested itself in the intervention in a number of different ways. One was the relationship of the American political community to Ambassador Boris A. Bakhmeteff, the Provisional Government's representative to the United States. Bakhmeteff presented his credentials on July 5, 1917, after which Wilson and he "sang a rhetorical duet" on the promise of liberal democracy (Foglesong 1995, 52). Bakhmeteff was also welcomed by the United States Congress, where he addressed a joint session on June 23. He was introduced by Champ Clark, the Speaker of the House, who linked the Russian revolution to the example of America. Speaking of republics around the world, Clark said:

> In a large sense, we made them [republics], every one (applause)— not by conquering armies . . . but by the wholesomeness of our example; by teaching all creation the glorious fact that men can govern themselves. (*Congressional Record* 65, 4136–37)

Bakhmeteff answered in kind, praising the example of the American revolution as a guide for the newly invigorated Duma. Clark's introduction, along with the Wilson administration's welcome of Bakhmeteff, reveals how the American political community genuinely believed that the Russian political future was tied to the success of republican democracies worldwide, all of which owed their genesis in part to the very existence of the United States. The liberal example of the United States, that is, the political presence of a successful liberal democratic republic, thus played an important part in United States foreign policy toward Russia.

But after the Bolshevik revolution in November, Bakhmeteff's position became tenuous. Soon after the revolution, however, both Lansing and Frank Polk assured Bakhmeteff that he would continue as the official Russian representative in the United States. Furthermore, during the fall and winter of 1917 to 1918, Bakhmeteff cultivated friendships with both Lansing and House, thus giving him almost direct access to the president. This access played an important role in convincing the administration to intervene in favor of the White forces. On December 14,

Joseph Tumulty, Wilson's Press Secretary, delivered to Wilson a memo written by Bakhmeteff that outlined the importance of humanitarian aid and intervention for the success of orderly, democratic forces in Russia (PWW 45: 288–95). Perhaps even more importantly, the Russian embassy became a channel for funds delivered from the United States to the White forces in Russia throughout 1918 and 1919 (Foglesong 1995, 63–72; Maddox 1977, 80–3).

Most importantly for the intervention, however, was the assurance that Bakhmeteff gave to the American political community about the existence of "liberal" Russia. Many of the other Russian activists in the United States and in Europe, especially those advocating intervention, were far too monarchical for the likes of Wilson and other American policy makers. Bakhmeteff assured the American political community that there existed a Russian "people" who truly desired liberal American-style government. Bakhmeteff's tireless efforts contributed to the Wilsonian belief that intervention was in the interests of the Russian people (Foglesong 1995, 68). Thus the recognition of Bakhmeteff as the ambassador to the "true" Russia, the Russia of liberalism and democracy, played an important role in the decision to, and continued justifications of, the American intervention (Foglesong 1995, 51–75). The belief in a liberal Russia was ensured by the recognition of a liberal ambassador, even when that ambassador no longer represented any real country.

The actions of General William S. Graves, the commanding officer of the American troops in Siberia, provide yet another instance of the liberal character of the American intervention in Russia. Graves, a military man, did not think that his actions, especially in light of the *aide-memoire*, could be political in any way. Instead he believed that he would be helping to guide the Czech forces out of Russia and help guard the Trans-Siberian railroad. Neither of these courses of action would appear to have any connection with the political issues driving the civil war in Russia. But Graves soon learned otherwise:

> When I left the United States for Siberia, I did not anticipate that I would be involved in the political squabbles of the Far East, but very soon after my arrival in Vladivostock, I learned that every act of an American, civil or military representative, was represented as designed for political effect in the Far East. This was true of all Russians and practically all Allies. (Graves 1931, 65)

In other words, Graves soon learned the fact that this essay has been arguing all along; that is, the actions of state representatives in a public arena, even if they are intended to accomplish seemingly nonpolitical ends, will inevitably be interpreted as political.

Over the course of his tenure in Siberia, Graves came to the realization that the White forces had very few of the characteristics of American democracy or liberalism. He singled out four White Russian leaders, Generals Kalmikoff, Semenov, Ivanoff-Rinoff, and Admiral Kolchak as particularly autocratic and violent. He believed that General Kalmikoff's men were so outraged by his barbarity that 300 of them mutinied in early 1919 (Graves 1931, 129–31). The troops under the command of the White leaders in Siberia "were roaming the country like wild animals, killing and robbing the people" (108).

One incident in particular demonstrates the way Grave's belief in American liberalism shaped the course of the intervention. In the spring of 1919, a group of deserters were taken captive by Ivanoff-Rinoff, who wished to send them to Semenov for execution. Graves objected to this vehemently, believing that Semenov represented the worst type of Russian White leader and that the deserters would be killed without a trial. He thus called together the Allied representatives and proposed to send a note to Ivanoff-Rinoff, stating that:

> as the Allies were responsible for order in Vladivostock it was incumbent upon them to see that justice was shown to all, therefore, we would not permit Russians to be arrested and taken out of Vladivostock where their guilt or innocence should be determined, and, if tried, we claimed the right to send a representative to the trial with a view to determining if it was a bona fide trial for an offense. (Graves 1931, 172)

Here we see one of the major tenets of a liberal political system being imposed on a political community, the right to a fair trial. While such a right seems undisputed to an American, especially an American raised in a military culture of rules and regulations, it was clearly not the norm at the time in Siberian Russia. Thus Graves' ability to impose on the Siberian White leadership his visions of a liberal America, even if in a small instance such as this, indicates that the political presence of a liberal American played a role in shaping the intervention.

The conflicts between Graves and others, however, reveals how such divergent interpretations led to the conflicts of the intervention. A memo written by W. G. Haan of the United States General Staff explains the conflicts between the United States and the Japanese forces:

> Notwithstanding the fact that the announced object of sending troops to Siberia of the United States and Japan were the same, it soon became apparent that our ideas as to carrying out these policies were diametrically opposed. Acts which appeared to me

as being the most flagrant violations of the policy of non-inter-
ference in internal affairs were claimed by the Japanese military
representatives as being necessary in order to maintain order
in Siberia.[10]

Such conflicts undermined Graves authority, who came to be considered a
communist by not only some British and Japanese officials but also United
States diplomatic officials. When the commanding United States military
officer refuses to cooperate with the other allied forces, one can imagine
how this would undermine the effectiveness of military action.

The final manifestation of American liberalism in the intervention
occurred in the Northern Russian theater. In February 1918, the American
diplomatic mission, along with a number of the other diplomatic missions,
moved to Vologda in order to escape the terror of the Bolshevik anarchy
and to avoid having to recognize or deal with the new Bolshevik government. During July of that same year, when the American political community had finally decided on intervention, Ambassador Francis began a
telegraph conversation with Gregori Checherin, the Bolshevik Minister for
Foreign Affairs. Checherin sought to convince the diplomatic community
(Francis was the dean of the diplomatic community at this point) to move
to Moscow where they would be "safer." Francis and the others realized
that the Bolsheviks were not going to let them remain in Vologda but also
did not wish to move to Moscow. Francis told Checherin that the diplomatic community was going to move from Vologda, but he did not tell
him that they had decided to move to Archangel.

On August 2, Allied forces, led by a British officer, General F. C. Poole,
had begun to land in Northern Russia. The Allied forces had been invited
to land by the Sovereign Government of Northern Russia, led by a Russian
socialist, N. V. Chaikovksy. Soon after the Allied troops had arrived, on
September 4, a *coup d'état* occurred, in which Captain G. E. Chaplin, a
Russian naval officer, overthrew the Chaikovsky government and sent
them into exile on Solovetski Island in the White Sea. In explaining his
actions to Francis and the Allied diplomats, Chaplin claimed that the
Northern Government was "socialistic" and poorly organized. Francis and
the other Allied diplomats immediately objected to this action and sent a
warship to the island to bring back the deposed government. Over the
next month, Francis worked closely with Chaikovsky to create a government (Francis 1921, 272–84; Strakhovsky 1944).

The actions of Francis and the other Allied diplomats in overturning
the *coup* by Chaplin provide further evidence of the political elements of
the intervention. Two aspects of that action in particular are worth noting.
First, the very act of bringing about a change in government is clearly

political. "Francis felt that he had to back Chaikovskii and his naive, impractical colleagues in order to preserve popular support for the Allies in the north" (Foglesong 1995, 212). Again, we see an American belief in itself as representative of the virtues of self-determination, even if those in power could not rule themselves. The fact that this decision was taken largely by Francis, without consultation with the White House, and that Francis was a quintessentially Mid-Western politician, hint at the fact that these beliefs did not just exist in Washington. They made up the larger skein of American beliefs about itself and its place in the world.

The fact that the *coup d'état* may have received tacit support from the British commanding officer provided another opportunity for the United States to differentiate itself from the other allied powers. A few days before the intervention, Francis had cabled the following to the State Department:

> British who are colonizers by instinct and practice, and in control of Archangel port since war began are disposed to treat the government contemptuously, but I remonstrated, arguing that must avoid repetition of German expansion in Ukraine. (FRUS Russia 1918 II, 518)

Note that in this quote, Francis seeks to differentiate the American intervention from both the Germans in the Ukraine and the British, the allies of the Americans. Francis also sought to ensure that Colonel George Stewart, the commanding American officer, reported directly to him and not to General Poole (Francis 1921, 271). The belief that Poole may have supported Chaplin comes out in Francis' memoirs:

> As to the position of General Poole, I am satisfied he did not want to establish a government of his own, but British soldiers have been colonizers for so long that they do not know how to respect the feelings of socialists. I do not mean to say that is the policy of the British Government, but British officers have had to do so much with uncivilized people, and Great Britain has done so much colonizing that its officers do not feel as American officers do. (Francis 1921, 272–3)

Again, the British are seen as colonizers while the Americans represent the virtue of self-determination. The actions of Francis in overturning the Chaplin coup, and his claims that the British may have contributed to this action, demonstrate an important political element of the intervention.

Once again, the American interpretation of itself and desire to present itself in a particular way played a key role in the lack of cooperation between the British and Americans. While this lack of cooperation did not cause the failure of the intervention on its own, it certainly contributed to it. Once again, Arendtian politics of agency, manifested in state agents rather than individual persons, can be seen as playing a key role in the politics of intervention.

Conflicts of Purpose

While conflicts between allies certainly played a role in undermining the intervention, some of the most important disagreements over what the United States represented came from within the American political establishment. When United States intervention became a public question, debates over what the United States was doing became debates over what it represented. And those debates played a key role in the decision to end the intervention.

United States intervention began as covert military aid to the Southern Russian forces. After discussions between Wilson and Lansing in early December of 1917, undoubtedly prompted by the memos from Lansing on the need for an orderly government, Lansing sent Wilson a memo in which he requested the Secretary of the Treasury to send funds to the British and French in support of General A. M. Kaledin, whose forces were located in Southern Russia. Wilson approved of the memo and, despite resistance from House and certain State Department members, funds were provided for three months, up until Kaledin's suicide on February 11, 1918 (PWW 45, 274–5; Foglesong 1996, 76–105).

Was the Siberian and Northern intervention simply a continuation of previous attempts to finance White forces throughout Russia? As the previous section demonstrates, the decision to send in American troops had a great deal to do with the "rescue" of the Czech forces, a factor that does not seem to be simply an excuse to cover over a more insidious intervention. In fact, it seems unclear why the American policy-making community would not have simply continued to finance various groups secretly rather subject the administration to the Congressional and media scrutiny to which it was eventually exposed. Unclear, that is, until we realize that it is this public character of sending troops that makes an overt military intervention a very different action than a policy of covert aid. The decision to send troops to Russia can be seen as the presentation of the United States as a nation representing certain values and traditions.

That need to present the United States in a particular way took on so much importance because of the challenge to those liberal values from communist Russia. On November 11, 1917, only a few days after the Revolution, the new Bolshevik government issued a peace proposal to both the Germans and the Allied powers. In that decree, Leon Trotsky and

Lenin requested the cessation of hostilities and the creation of a new international order, one based on open diplomacy and an end to war. In January 1918, both Wilson and David Lloyd George, the British Prime Minister, presented their visions of the war aims and the future of world politics. Arno Mayer explains how both Wilson's and Lloyd George's speeches may well have been direct reactions to Lenin's proposals (Mayer 1959, 368–93). Not only was Lenin attempting, in the eyes of American and British policy makers, to disrupt the domestic life of Russia, he was also trying to overturn their visions of the world order.

This kind of direct challenge could not be answered by means of secret diplomacy and covert intervention. Instead, one might assume, Wilson and Lloyd George both saw a need to eliminate Lenin and the Bolsheviks because of the challenge they posed to a liberal world order based on the newly forming idea of a League of Nations. The decision to overtly send military troops to Russia, then, appears to be part of the broader attempt by Western states to alter the political image of the United States and Great Britain. It is the type of political action that Arendt discusses in her understandings of politics, action that allows the agent to appear in a public space in a way that it chooses. The United States would appear to the world as the representative of liberalism and, ironically, a state in support of self-determination, something that implied a noninterventionary foreign policy. The intervention as it took place in Siberia and Northern Russia was an attempt to present the United States as representative of the new values that would constitute the world order.

But that public action, and the need to support it in a democratic context, contributed to the failure of the intervention. In the United States itself, it resulted in a public, Congressional debate over the purposes of the intervention, especially after the war had ended. The American force sent to Northern Russia was the 339th Infantry Regiment, most of whom came from Michigan (Rhodes 1988, 33). As the intervention advanced, Senators and Representatives from Michigan began to demand explanations as to where their constituents' sons and husbands were and the reasons for which they were fighting. This Congressional activity soon brought testimony from State department officials and an official reply from President Wilson. The difficulties that the Administration had with Congress over this issue contributed to Wilson's decision to withdraw the troops.

An important point to note in this debate is that the Congressional resistance to the intervention resulted from the fact that the action had to be justified publicly, not just to the world community, but to the domestic American community as well. This public justification resulted in a debate over the overall purpose of American foreign policy, with different actors interpreting the history and moral purpose of the American community in radically different ways. While the Michigan senators objected to the intervention mainly on the grounds of their constituents' demands for the return of their "boys," other senators, especially the Progressives, sought to debate the wisdom of the intervention on the grounds of the American purpose. Hiram Johnson of California introduced Senate Resolution 384 on December 12, 1918, demanding all information on the intervention, and then Senate Resolution 411 on January 14, 1919, demanding an end to the intervention. In support of the bill, William Borah declared "The Russian people have the same right to establish a socialistic state as we had to establish a republic," (Lasch 1962, 164). Only a vote by Vice President Thomas Marshall prevented Johnson's resolution from being passed. Christopher Lasch's book on the liberal reaction to the Russian revolution demonstrates how American foreign policy toward Russia led to a split within liberal political groups, with those in support of ending the intervention basing their claims on anti-imperialism, a tenet that differentiated America from France and Britain (Lasch 1962). The Congressional agitation had a direct effect on the course of the intervention. In Paris, House "cited such congressional resistance and public distrust in America when he opposed a proposal by Winston Churchill to enlarge and intensify the military campaigns against Bolshevism," (Foglesong 1995, 229).

In other words, in an attempt to create a liberal world order, especially important in relation to the challenge of communism, the Wilson administration prompted a series of public debates over what constituted the liberal national purpose of the United States. The Progressives argued that international liberalism must be founded on nonintervention, while Wilson and others believed that a more muscular international liberalism required the use of American power to enforce its ideals. The political action of sending troops to Russia to accomplish a moral goal both sides agreed on led to a debate that resulted in the pullout of American troops. Once again, an attempt to accomplish a moral goal was undermined because that goal required the construction of a particular type of state agent, a state agent that clearly did not have the full support of the community it supposedly represented.

While resistance from within the American political community certainly played an important role in the failure of the intervention, perhaps the most important reason for its failure was the active resistance of the Bolshevik government. Even more importantly, the ability of the Bolsheviks to resist the intervention and consolidate their power derived in large part from the intervention itself. Bruce Lockhart recounts how the Bolsheviks were on the verge of losing power in the spring of 1918. But just at the point when they were failing, the intervention of foreign troops on Russian soil allowed them to become the representatives of a free Russia; free, that is, from the forces of outside interference. Moreover, the particularly weak force that was landed, a weakness due to American combination of ethical desire with political concerns, led to the hope that encouraged the Bolsheviks and their supporters to rally the population:

> In Lockhart's view, the "direct effect" of landing without sufficient force to reach the capital "was to provide the Bolsheviks with a cheap victory, to give them a new confidence, and to galvanize them into a strong and ruthless organism." At the same time, the weak intervention diminished Allied "prestige among every class of the Russian population." (Foglesong 1995, 221)

Thus the intervention, combining political and ethical elements in a unique way, tended to give support to a community that the Allied and Associated forces refused to address, the Bolsheviks. This further emphasizes the fact that when state agents attempt to provide aid they fail because political communities that they wish to "help" refuse to be denied a political presence. Even though many may not have believed that the Bolsheviks would be a better government than the Whites, the fact that the Bolsheviks did not give into foreign demands and foreign control played an important part in their ability to stabilize their power. Interventions, while begun and understood as attempts to help communities, fail because the process of politically presenting a state will inevitably deny the political presence of the community into which the intervention is being made. Put differently, the very nature of intervention in the twentieth century, an action that denies the political presence of the state against which the intervention is taking place, will lead it to failure as those political communities denied a political presence vigorously resist the intervening forces. The battles fought in Archangel and Siberia give testament to this resistance in the case of the Russian intervention.

The actions of American military and diplomatic representatives in Russia were part of the American attempt to present itself as conforming to the ideals of liberalism. Unfortunately, these attempts to teach the Russians the values of liberalism did not contribute to the task of securing order. United States actions in both Northern Russia and Siberia undermined the capacity of White Russian leaders to assert any authority in situations that may have called for strong political control rather than participatory democracy and protection of civil rights. This is not to justify the policies of the White Russian leaders, but only to point out that the attempt to alleviate anarchy and terrorism in Russia may have required the support of authoritarian personalities. And the public debates over what the United States represented led to a lack of Congressional support that eventually ended the intervention. These debates, by raising the political question of what the United States represented, both weakened the United States' resolve and strengthened the Bolsheviks. In other words, one of the central normative goals of the intervention was undermined by debates over what the United States represented—a political image that overwhelmed a normative impulse.

The combination of the ethical and political elements of the intervention contributed significantly to the failure of the overall mission. That the intervention was a failure is a generally agreed upon conclusion by historians. As one says "The small United States expedition and the many shipments of supplies to anti-Bolshevik forces were enough to provoke dissent at home and resentment in Soviet Russia, but not sufficient to secure the goal of a reunited democratic Russia" (Foglesong 1995, 187). The American troops pulled out of Northern Russia in September 1919 and out of Siberia in January 1920. Neither force accomplished its goal of supporting the forces of order over those of anarchy, nor of providing food aid to the starving Russians.

BRITISH INTERVENTION IN RUSSIA

The United States was not the only country to intervene during the Russian revolution and civil war. Great Britain, France, and Japan also played important roles. While both the American and British conceived of their interventions as attempts to "save" certain groups, the specific character of the British action came from a much different source than did the American. While Americans saw themselves as representatives of liberalism, the British agents saw themselves as protectors of Europe, Central Asia, and the Russian people. Thus their attempt to reform Russia derived not from a messianic liberalism, but from a colonial paternalism. Interestingly, this colonial paternalism lent itself to many of the same humanitarian concerns as the American desire to liberalize Russia, while its manifestation led to a much different set of actions.

The British began planning an intervention soon after the Bolshevik Revolution. At a series of British War Cabinet meetings in November and December of 1917 the prospect of intervening in Russia was seriously considered at the cabinet level; in early December, they began sending aid to General A. M. Kaledin in Southern Russia. In April of 1918, as the existence of the Czech forces in Russia became known to Allied war leaders, the British proposed using these troops to recreate the Eastern front. But disagreements with the French, who wanted the Czech force to go to the Western front, prevented any clear decision from being made. Meanwhile, in the Northern theater, the British sent General Poole to aid the Murmansk Soviet in its attempt to defeat the White Finnish forces who were supported by the Germans. At the same time, Bruce Lockhart, the British quasi-official representative to the Bolsheviks, was pursuing talks with Trotsky on the possibility of an invitation from the Bolshevik government to the British and other Allied troops. These talks soon collapsed, however, as British and American troops began to arrive in full force in Archangel, Siberia, and the Transcaucasus. On August 31, 1918, the British embassy in Petrograd was attacked by Anarchists who killed a British military attaché. Soon thereafter, Lockhart was taken prisoner by the Bolsheviks, who did not release him until late October 1918.

The initial British intervention, occurring in Northern Russia, Siberia, and Southern Russia, was motivated and justified by the need to recreate a Russia that could draw the Germans off the Western Front. But when the Armistice was signed in November 1918, the British had to decide whether or not to continue their intervention. The debates and state papers of the period from November 1918 through April 1919 are thus the most interesting sources for understanding the British intervention. In fact, their troops were pulled out by the summer of 1919, due largely to the will of David Lloyd George. But the debates of this six-month period provide an important insight into the ways in which such events are formulated, undertaken, and interpreted.

Finally, it is also important to remember that the British intervention occurred in different theaters, each of which took on an importance for different reasons. The forces sent to Northern Russia were devoted mainly to defeating the Bolshevik forces of Moscow and to recreating a Russian government in European Russia—the colonial image motivating this action relied on a British perception of themselves as protectors of Europe, specifically in the Baltics and Poland. The forces sent to Siberia and Transcaucasus were devoted to reestablishing political order in the Central Asian republics, motivated by traditions of imperialism in India and the Middle East.

The British ethic of intervention revolved around two main themes: a humanitarian desire to quell the anarchy of Bolshevik Russia, anarchy that touched directly on British diplomatic representatives, and a colonial belief in the need to protect Eastern Europe, especially the Baltic and Central Asian countries from the anarchy of Bolshevism. It is important to stress that these ethical aspects of the intervention only really came into play after the November 1918 armistice; the intervention originally took place to recreate the Eastern front. This section also emphasizes how different normative impulses can be part of the same intervention.

The attempt to order the chaos in Russia reflected a humanitarian norm, while the desire to protect the peoples of the south and east reflected a colonial norm.

Order, Intervention, and Coup d'état

The normative impulse of creating order out of chaos prompted the British action in the same way that it prompted the American action. But because of the divergent political histories of the two countries, the response to that normative impulse led to different interpretations and policies. For the British, intervention would help recreate a functioning Russian political and social system. In order to do so, however, the British turned to the autocratic White forces and supported *coups d'état* in the different theaters. This support for the Whites and attempts to meddle in the internal governance of Russia contributed to the failure of the Allied intervention.

While the March Revolution was welcomed by both the government and the opposition in Great Britain, the growing strength of the Bolsheviks throughout the summer and fall of 1917 caused great consternation in British policy-making circles. One set of reports that was widely circulated in the British policy making community came from F. N. A. Cromie, the British Naval Attaché stationed in St. Petersburg.[11] Cromie, whose death at the hands of a mob in the summer of 1918 further increased support for the intervention, sent a series of reports to various naval officers describing the chaos the Bolsheviks were creating in St. Petersburg. He described various scenes in which British naval officers provided protection from Bolshevik masses: "Ladies were seven deep around each Englishman, clamoring for protection," (Jones 1973, 357). When some Russian sailors claimed they were modeling their revolution on the British political system, Cromie retorted indignantly:

> . . . after dinner the red flag crowds came down the pier, preaching rank anarchy and demanding a Republic. . . . I again explained that we were used to order and justice and expected it from those who sought to imitate our Government. (Jones 1973, 358–9)

Moreover, perhaps because Bolshevik strength was strongest in the shipyards of St. Petersburg, Cromie was also witness to the way Bolshevik ideology affected military discipline.

> Discipline does not exist, smoke everywhere, never salute off duty or on, dress as they please, start cleaning ships at 8:00 A.M., knock off all work at 3, and then go ashore until 8 the next day. (Jones 1973, 364)

Undoubtedly the comments about the breakdown of the Russian military were of the most concern to the British policy makers. Yet one cannot ignore the fact that Cromie's letters do not just describe a breakdown in military discipline, but a collapse of the social order as a whole. Such descriptions of Russian society began to appear more often as Bolshevik power increased.

Other British diplomatic agents in Russia also reported this same breakdown of the social order. Interestingly, as with Cromie, their comments focus on the status of women in Russian society. By highlighting the precarious status of women in Russian society as a result of the Bolshevik takeover, these reports drew the attention of British policy makers to what they saw as the particularly abhorrent elements of Bolshevik power. General Alfred Knox was the British military representative to the Russian military staff during the war. In his memoirs Knox describes an incident in which the Bolsheviks captured 137 women and had them beaten. Only upon the demands of Knox were these women allowed to leave (Knox 1921, 712). George Buchanan, the British Ambassador to Russia, describes a state of general drunkenness, with soldiers invading private wine cellars (Buchanan 1923, 240). And Buchanan's daughter, Merial, who wrote a number of works on her father's diplomatic career, described Russia "with the rising tide of Bolshevism and anarchy" as full of "long-haired men and short-haired women," (Buchanan 1928, 220–1).

This breakdown of order derived not just from Bolshevism, but from the very nature of the Russian people themselves. This ethnic essentialist argument justified the colonial mentality so common among the British at that time. It assumed that the Russians were not only incapable of governing themselves, but that they were children who needed education in the most basic of concepts. The British vice consul in Irkutsk, C. Mash, reported the following on August 31, 1918:

> In my first report, I mentioned that politics were the curse of the country and I have no reason to change my mind. Political strifes [sic] are sapping the country of its real strength and the Allies will have to take the law in their hands, and save the Russians from themselves, if they are wanted back in the fighting line. What is wanted is a MILITARY DICTATORSHIP as the people are not fit to govern themselves. . . . The people do not understand the meaning of the word 'freedom'. . . . What they require is the whip to be laid on harder to bring them to their sense and, instead of building new universities, it would be much more to the point to start with kindergarten schools, and educate them that life does not consist of insincere speeches only.[12]

Some of the most interesting comments on the Russians from a British perspective come from the War Diaries of the Elope Force sent to Archangel. These troops, initially sent to guard war supplies in the midst of the war, eventually ended up fighting the Bolshevik forces alongside of the White forces. At the level of the private, British soldiers tended to see the Russians as dirty and unkempt, leading to a directive that "British personnel have to control hygiene and care of all prisoners".[13] At the level of the officers, British staff were encouraged to set the proper example for the Russians, while also being sensitive to the perceptions they would create among their fellow officers:

> The Liaison officer's first duty is therefore to encourage the Russian officer to take command of his men in the sense that we understand it. . . . All this must be done by influence and example, without the slightest tinge of patronage, for the Russian officer is easily offended, but equally easily guided . . . [14]

Attitudes like these justified military intervention as diplomats and soldiers convinced themselves and their superiors that Russians needed the positive influence of a military intervention.

Reports of social anarchy, however, did not just exist in letters and despatches from Russia. The British Foreign Office also recorded a breakdown of order and prevalence of chaos in Russia. On March 14, 1918, the British War Cabinet, composed of those members of the Cabinet who were directly concerned with the conduct of the war, approved a history of Russia from March 1917 through January 1918. October 4, 1917 notes "anarchy is spreading," and November 22, 1917 claims "Chaos continues," (Jones 1973, 233). It concludes with the following:

> When it is remembered that perhaps 80 million very poor people are in a state of complete anarchy, that arms and explosives are plentiful, it is a matter of some wonder that more terrible happenings have not yet been recorded. (Jones 1973, 236)

Such descriptions of chaos and anarchy, however, were not converted directly into intervention. As noted in the introduction to this section, the British intervention was motivated initially by the demands of the war. In the North, British soldiers were to protect the supplies that had been clogging up the harbor and prevent the Germans from creating a submarine base in the North Sea. In Siberia the purpose was to use the Czechs to recreate an Eastern front. And, in the south, the troops of Major General L. C. Dunsterville were to prevent the Turks from capturing the oil fields of Baku. But all these reasons became irrelevant with the signing of the armistice on November 11, 1918. On what basis could the British forces remain in Russia with no threat from Germany or her allies? In the House of Commons, such questions were raised only two days after the armistice, in debates on November 13 (110 H. C. Deb. 2798). Clearly a new rationale for the intervention was needed.

Such a rationale came from the pen of Bruce Lockhart, who had returned to London in mid-October 1918. In fact, Lockhart's imprisonment in Russia throughout 1918 gave an important impetus to the intervention. As noted above, Lockhart negotiated with Bolshevik leaders, especially Trotsky, about the possibility of having the British intervene by invitation of the Bolsheviks. They had appeared close to an agreement when the April landings of British and Japanese forces in Vladivostock scuttled the agreement. Up until this point, Lockhart had been adamant in his resistance to uninvited intervention in Russia by the Allies. As he learned more about the Czech forces in Siberia, and when he believed that the Soviet government had unjustly attacked them, Lockhart changed his views and argued for intervention in support of the Czech forces, but only on a large scale (Lockhart 1933, 285–7).

Events in the month of July further convinced Lockhart, and British officials, of the dangers of Bolshevik rule. On July 4, the German Ambassador in Russia, Count Wilhelm von Mirbach, was assassinated, and on July 17 the Czar and his family were executed in Ekaterinodar. These events were interpreted by Lockhart and others as evidence of the barbarity of the Bolsheviks. These concerns were further reinforced by the death of Lt. Cromie on August 31. Soon thereafter, based on a Bolshevik belief in a "Lockhart conspiracy," Lockhart himself was thrown into jail. During the months of September and October, Lockhart remained imprisoned, while the British authorities in London worked for his release. He was eventually exchanged for Maxim Litvinov, a Russian Bolshevik held in a British prison, who would later become an important foreign affairs minister in the Soviet Union.

When Lockhart arrived in London, he set out to write a policy paper on the subject of continued intervention. His arrival in London was concurrent with the armistice, a time when British officials were looking for new justifications for the intervention. Lockhart had previously supported intervention in a memo he had sent to the Foreign Office on May 5 (Ulman 1961, 165). That memo had argued in support of intervention mainly on the grounds of aiding the Czechs, whom he saw as being unjustly terrorized by the Bolsheviks (Lockhart 1933, 285–7). But the memo he wrote while in London is based on a much different set of reasons. He sets out three options for British policy: (1) leave after securing the Czechs and establish relations with the Bolsheviks; (2) support anti-Bolshevik forces clandestinely to prevent Bolshevism from spreading to other parts of the former Russian empire; and (3) full-scale military intervention. He concludes that the third option is the most viable, both to destroy the Bolshevik forces and "to restore peace and order in Russia" (Young 1973 I, 49–50). He further developed the importance of providing order and food to the population, which became the main justification for the intervention as a whole. No longer was he concerned with the Czech forces, protecting the Baltics, protecting the Transcaucasus, or any of the other British concerns in operation at the time. He argued:

> that our intervention is justified on humanitarian grounds, and that we should do better by proceeding openly against the Bolsheviks, than by trying to suppress them surreptitiously. . . . No intervention in Russia can be really successful unless it is accompanied by large surpluses of food stuffs and manufactured goods for the starving populations and no economic relief can be given without a military occupation. (Young 1973 I, 50)

Lockhart's reasons for the continuation of the intervention, based on his experiences of a year in Russia, and the last two months in a Russian prison, had moved away from the British imperialist concerns and more toward the need to create an orderly and well-fed Russian polity—that is, toward a more humanitarian basis. Moreover, because of his widely publicized prison experience, Lockhart had become something of a cause célèbre in Great Britain on his return and was invited to lecture on his experiences and relay them privately to many officials (Lockhart 1934). Thus it seems evident that his arguments would have been disseminated throughout the British policy-making community. While those arguments may not have had a profound effect on the course of the intervention, it is important to realize that the mere fact that Lockhart would voice them, and that his voice was heard and respected in London, indicates that such arguments played a role in the debates over the continuation of the intervention after the armistice.[15]

But the dangers to Russian citizens were not the only concern of the British. As with the Americans, the British became especially concerned when the nationals and diplomats of foreign countries, especially British nationals and diplomats, were threatened by the Bolsheviks. Such threats not only jeopardized the lives of those individuals, they also threatened international order as a whole by challenging notions of diplomatic immunity around which the nation-state system is organized. Moreover, as one of the Great Powers of the era, Great Britain had a particular concern that such aspects of world order were not violated.

On April 4, 1918, British forces landed in Vladivostock in response to the death of some Japanese merchants and concern for the safety of British subjects; as Foreign Secretary Arthur J. Balfour wrote, "Our present action has been entirely local, simply to protect British subjects in Vladivostock" (Kettle 1988, 36). This action was thus undertaken less for the strategic reasons of holding Vladivostock or of controlling the Siberian Railway, the reasons eventually given for sending forces to Siberia, but instead for the protection of innocent civilians.

Even though the British tried to play down this incident, it seriously hampered the efforts of Lockhart to induce the Bolsheviks to acquiesce to an intervention. The Bolsheviks immediately issued a statement saying that the landings were a pretext for a full-scale military intervention, and Leon Trotsky, the Bolshevik Foreign Minister, informed Lockhart that the attempts to reconcile the Allied and Russian positions on invited intervention had been dashed by the incident (Ulman 1961, 147–8). The evidence seems to indicate that this landing of a few British marines, who were soon withdrawn, was not at all a pretext for a full-scale intervention, but was in fact exactly what Balfour described it as: an attempt to secure the safety of British subjects in Vladivostock. This action, encouraged by the reports of anarchy and social breakdown that had been arriving in London ever since the Bolshevik takeover, could be called humanitarian. It was an attempt to save the lives of British subjects. But the Bolshevik reaction to it demonstrates once again how ethical concerns, when translated into state, especially military, action, lead to vigorous political resistance. The Bolshevik reaction was undoubtedly encouraged by Balfour's further arguments that the Soviet leaders were to blame for the deaths of the Japanese merchants (Ulman 1961, 149). By denying the Bolsheviks the ability to control their own territory, especially in relation to foreign nationals, Balfour and the British only exacerbated the Soviet resistance to any form of intervention.

A further incident concerning a diplomatic representative is the death of Lieutenant Cromie. Cromie and a skeletal diplomatic staff had been stationed in St. Petersburg during the spring and summer of 1918. As Michael Kettle details, Cromie was at this time engaged in efforts to destroy the Russian Baltic fleet to prevent it from falling into the hands of the Germans (Kettle 1992), efforts of which the Bolsheviks were fully aware. On August 30, M. S. Uritsky, the head of the Cheka (the secret police of the Bolsheviks) was assassinated and on August 31 an assassin attempted to take the life of Lenin. Kettle argues that while the British had no role in the attempt on Lenin, they undoubtedly were aware of and supported the assassination of Uritsky (Kettle 1988, 327). In response to these acts, The Terror began in Moscow and St. Petersburg, leading to the deaths of thousands of Russians, a series of events that supported the decision of the Americans and British in their incipient intervention. Perhaps even more relevant for the

British, on August 31 a mob attacked the British Embassy and killed Cromie. As Kettle points out:

> Cromie's murder had a great moral effect in both Russia and England. It aptly signified the end of any British presence whatsoever in the old Russian capital—a presence that had once been so strong. In London, it was taken by some to justify British intervention on its own; no further excuse was needed. (Kettle 1988, 324)

Note here the importance of the international legal norm of protecting diplomats. While the British intervention found justification in the domestic abuses of the Bolsheviks, it also found support in the violations of the international legal norms that governed the global political context. Norms that structure the domestic and international systems played a key role in the British intervention.

Nor was the British parliament hesitant to condemn the Bolsheviks. On November 14, 1918, the War Cabinet authorized the collection of "as much material as possible regarding the behavior of the Bolsheviks for 'full and speedy publication' " (Ulman 1968, 142). Importantly, this authorization took place three days *after* the official end of the war that had previously justified the intervention. This decision, the result of promptings by Sir Basil Thomson, a British propaganda official, led to the publication of a British bluebook, *A Collection of Reports on Bolshevism in Russia*. Released in April, this collection of reports detailed numerous abuses of the social, economic, and political order flourishing under the Bolsheviks. The report describes the horrors of Bolshevism in graphic detail. In a section on public health, it reports, "Corpses of horses, dogs, and human beings lie about the streets, everything in a state of unutterable filth, no attempts being made to clean buildings, streets, railway stations, market places, etc., the sanitary conditions were terrible" (Issaiev 1919, 24). Reports were also circulating concerning the "nationalization of women," a claim the report does not substantiate but clearly implies. And, returning to the terrorism that played such an important role in the American intervention, the report details numerous instances of wanton and brutal murders. It even included pictures of the dead, giving the report a strange macabre element.

Ulman points out that the report "can only be described as a wildly hysterical piece of propaganda" (Ulman 1968, 141). It appears that this judgment is accurate; even Lockhart argued that the Bolsheviks had been creating an orderly political system in Moscow before the assassination of Uritsky (Lockhart 1933, 256). But even if the report was exaggerated, it clearly had an effect on the public debate over intervention. Released in April, just as David Lloyd George, the Prime Minister, was arguing that full-scale intervention was not the answer, the report was cited numerous times in Parliament on April 9 (Ulman 1968, 143–4). When one member tried to point out that the report was propaganda, he was shouted down with cries of "Shame, shame!" Furthermore, the newspapers were provided with copies of the report at lower than cost prices, and the report was thus widely circulated throughout the country.

The effect of the report, along with the earlier reports of anarchy in Russia from diplomats like Bruce Lockhart, provided supporters of continued intervention with valuable ammunition. We must be careful, however, not to simply regard such reports as propaganda. If we accept the argument that the reasons given publicly for action have some legitimacy, then the reports of Bolshevik atrocity certainly played a role in the decisions to leave British troops in Russia after the armistice. As we can see from the reports of Lockhart and the British bluebooks, the concerns of the British military and foreign policy staffs had a strong humanitarian component. The next section emphasizes that the intervenors relied not just on these humanitarian beliefs but on colonial ones as well.

How did these concerns with order translate into the policies of the intervention itself? In both Archangel and Omsk, the British were suspected of supporting coups, and in both cases the forces that come to power were more concerned with creating order than with supporting democracy. While the American diplomats and military leaders interpreted these events as evidence of a British penchant for authoritarian government (thus emphasizing the American national purpose), the British officials involved in the events saw them more as policies in accord with the proper administration of a colonial territory. This British view of itself as a power that knows how to control colonial territories further reinforced British perceptions of itself as an old hand at the game of power politics and as a power with responsibilities for international order.

As detailed by Kettle, the British seemed to have played an important role in the *coup d'état* in Omsk. Prior to the coup, which occurred on November 18, 1918, Siberia had been run by a group of moderate White political figures, known collectively as the Directorate. Due to a disgruntled military community, however, combined with the vacillation of the Directorate on various issues, a group of military leaders overthrew the civilian leaders and put into power Admiral Alexander Kolchak, who is presented in many of the Allied reports as a sort of Cincinnatus figure who reluctantly takes over for the sake of his country. At this time the British had in Omsk two figures who came to play a key role in the *coup*: Lt. Col. J. F. Neilson and Lt. Col. John Ward. Neilson was the officer in charge of the British military mission in Siberia, left in charge after General Alfred Knox had returned to London for consultations. Ward, a Labour MP, was in charge of the Middlesex Regiment, a company of troops that came to play an important role during the *coup*.

Neilson had been made aware of the imminent *coup* through his connections with Russian military leaders in Omsk. In his notes on the *coup*, Neilson claims that he informed them "Neither I personally, nor as British Military Representative, nor the Government I represent, can take any part, direct or indirect, in the formation of new Governments, or the destruction of old" (Kettle 1992, 12). On the day before the *coup*, the conspirators asked Neilson his opinion of their action, wishing to ensure the approval of the Allied forces before acting. Neilson wrote in his notes:

> I think perhaps I lay myself open to the accusation of having moved slightly in advance of the very halting policy, or rather lack of policy, of our Government. I had a most difficult task with no one to help me, and with no precedent to guide me. In full charge of British interests during by far the most difficult period up to date, I picked my men, backed them, and consider that I chose the right men. What they can give to history now remains with them. I personally am certain that I adopted the right course. (Kettle 1992, 14)

With Neilson's seeming acquiescence, one might even say support, of the *coup* the officers acted and placed Kolchak in power. The morning of the *coup* the streets remained calm, due largely to the actions of Lt. Col. Ward, who turned out his Middlesex Regiment as soon as he heard of the arrests of the Directorate. Ward's actions, which he took independently of Neilson, undoubtedly gave the impression that the British were supporters of the *coup*. Ward in fact accused Neilson of deceiving him in helping him to put a "reactionary" into power (Kettle 1992, 17), although it does not seem that Neilson intended Ward to provide troops. Nevertheless, the impression of British support was further strengthened when Neilson arrived with Kolchak at the French High Commissioner's train; the French, in fact, were most critical of the British role. Neilson had decided by this time that with Kolchak in power it was the responsibility of the British government to support him "in the restoration of order" (Kettle 1992, 17). While officials in London were at first concerned that Neilson had acted beyond his mandate, they soon came to support his actions, with approval coming from Curzon himself (Kettle 1992, 29).

Kettle attributes these actions to Neilson alone and implies that Neilson's official report misrepresented his actions. Kettle also implies that Ward's actions during the *coup* were much more innocent. But I would argue that both Ward and Neilson were simply acting in accord with the British political image of itself as guarantor of order and stability in Russia.

While Neilson supported the *coup* plotters because he felt that a strong military government was necessary to bring about peace, Ward's placing of troops on the streets in the midst of a *coup* demonstrates the same belief that order and stability are more important than democratically elected government. This is not to judge either of their actions as a mistake; rather, it is to point out that their support for forces of order, especially military order, coincide with a British vision of itself as the force of order and stability in Russia.

Yet another *coup d'état* took place in Russia during the intervention, this one in Archangel. British forces had first landed at Murmansk on June 28, 1918, although in small numbers. British control over the situation in Northern Russia vastly increased, however, in August when a Russian voluntary force was organized with British funds, supplies, and command. The British conducted the training of officers and soldiers alike, giving them great control over the political actions in the area (Strakhovsky 1944, 43–44). The British commander in charge of these Russian and Allied forces, General Poole, also dictated to the civilian government, headed by Nicholas Chaikovsky, various administrative issues, including the creation of military courts to try convicted political prisoners. More interestingly, Poole explicitly discouraged freedom of speech for the inhabitants of Archangel.[16] Such interference was adamantly resisted by Chaikovsky and the other civilian leaders, although they usually acquiesced.

In the midst of this British control of the military and, by extension, political situation in Northern Russia, the Russian head of the Russian forces, Commander George Chaplin, overthrew the civilian government of Chaikovsky and sent them to an island monastery in the midst of the Dvina River. According to Strakhovsky, while General Poole warned Chaplin not to overthrow the government, the British and Allies clearly had some role in the *coup*:

> Although there is not direct proof of Poole's actual complicity in Chaplain's coup d'état, little doubt exists about the participation of certain high-placed Allied officers, particularly Colonel Thornhill, chief of the British Intelligence, and Count de Lubersa, of the French Second Bureau. The fact that Thornhill's office was across the street from the government's residence, and that the Allied military patrols were conspicuously absent from the streets that night, later led to a belief both among foreigners and Russians "that some of the General's subordinates were not only aware of the plot, but had a hand in getting it up." As a further proof, Chaplin received "warm" congratulations from Allied Offices,

"from generals all the way down to subalterns," in the days after the coup d'état. (Strakhovsky 1944, 51)

Such evidence indicates that the British had a role to play in the *coup*, a role that fit only too well with General Poole's previous interference in the administration of the government.

As discussed earlier in the chapter, the American response to this *coup* led to its being overturned soon thereafter. Poole, moreover, was eventually replaced by General Ironside, and British troops were withdrawn in August 1919. But the actions of the British military authorities in Northern Russia provides further evidence of the fact of the British political image of itself as able to handle colonial outposts by means of military governors. This political image of itself as orderer not just of the international realm, but as internal order of many of the communities of the world, significantly contributed to the failure of the intervention. In Omsk and Archangel, the White Russians were treated just as badly as the Bolsheviks, leading to a lack of cooperation between the Allies and the forces they were supposedly supporting. And, as discussed in the section on the American intervention, the friction created by the British support for the coup in Archangel severely undermined the cooperation between the Allies in this important theater of war.

Order, Intervention, and the Balance of Power

Internal order prompted the British intervention in part. But a further important normative element was the British view that it was responsible for ordering the world. As world power, the British believed that their civilizing mission in the East and their protection of Europe from Russia were essential elements of their national purpose. While the first of these two is usually seen as clear evidence of colonialism, the second is usually conceived of differently in the diplomatic literature, by attributing to Britain the role of "balancer" in the European system.[17] The impulse to protect these smaller European states from the power of Russia and Germany, however, appears to have a similar set of ethical underpinnings as does the British role as "civilizer" of the rest of the world. What is behind both conceptions is a belief that the world needs an orderer and that Britain, with its traditions of self-government and democracy, is best suited to provide that order. In other words, the history and governmental institutions of a political community, that is, its national purpose, contribute to its foreign policy, especially in its interventionary behavior. Moreover, this belief that the British were better at ordering the world than others led to their refusal

to allow the other allied governments to play any real role in the governance of Russian territories. This refusal led in a number of important
ways to the ineffectiveness of the intervention.

A key decision maker in the War Cabinet was George Curzon, who
was appointed Foreign Secretary in January 1919. In a biography focusing
on Curzon's tenure at the Foreign Office, Harold Nicolson describes his
colonialism as drawing on traditions of the Roman empire and Christian-
ity. For Curzon, according to Nicolson, the British empire had to follow the
example of the Roman empire in imparting to its colonies not only a political order but the benefits of a technologically advanced society. But more
importantly than these benefits was the sense of responsibility that the
Romans taught in their administration of empire. Because of their duty to
order the world, both the Romans and the British were obligated to intervene and correct situations of disorder.

> England was Rome's inheritor, tempering dominion with sanita-
> tion, dominance by public works. Among the qualities which he
> most consistently admired and practiced was the old Roman
> quality of *gravitas*, that seriousness which comes from a profound
> consciousness or world responsibility . . . This sense of responsi-
> bility, with its associated virtues of duty, sacrifice and justice
> dominated his conscience. (Nicolson 1939, 12, 14)

This conception of empire manifested itself in a number of ways in
Curzon's views on international affairs. One of the most important was
his belief that the British needed to focus more on Asia than on Europe in
its foreign relations. This was undoubtedly linked to Curzon's travels as
a young man throughout Central Asia and the Middle East, and his
tenure in India. When some advocated pulling out of its colonial position
around the world after the war, Curzon believed that to question the idea
of responsibility that supported these colonial adventures was to "harm
the soul of the British empire," (Nicolson 1939, 21). He was insistent on
remaining in Egypt and Persia after the war, despite the growing nationalist sentiments in both countries, and his views generally prevailed,
keeping the British firmly in place throughout the world for the next
forty years.

Arthur Balfour, the Foreign Secretary during the war, also believed
that the British had to strengthen their empire. But Balfour's conceptions
of that empire differed from Curzon's in some important ways. In his collected writings Balfour addresses the question of the British empire as it
relates to idealist conceptions of international order. One might think that
an idealist, very much in agreement with the beliefs in self-determination
and democracy of Wilson and Lloyd George, would necessarily conflict

with an imperialist. But Balfour, and many others, believed that the British empire played an important role in civilizing the world. The following quote demonstrates this and how it differs from Curzon:

> But my hope for the future is largely founded on the fact that the British Empire, whatever else it is, is not a selfish Empire. If we have acquired sovereignty over huge tracts of the earth's surface, at all events we rule those tracts in no selfish or narrow spirit. We do not desire to exclude other nations from the full benefits that may be derived from British freedom, from British traditions of government. On the contrary, though our colonies are ours indeed legally and by affection, they are not limited to the enterprise of citizens of this country. They are open to the world; and the world, if it pleases, may take advantage of this. . . . (G)reat empires make for peace. (Balfour 1912, 200, 204)

While both Balfour and Curzon advocated the continuation of the British Empire, they clearly did so for different reasons. Curzon believed more strongly in the conception of empire as a tool to "civilize" parts of the world and undertook that mission with all the *gravitas* that such a project demanded. Balfour, however, was able to reconcile his beliefs in democracy and self-determination with a conception of empire by seeing it as a link between different cultures and governments in order to bring peace. Indeed, one can hear a faint echo of Kantian Theory and the European Union in these ideas of closer contact bringing about peace.

Thus we have these two conceptions of empire operating within the policy-making circles of Great Britain at the time of the intervention. Both variations played a role in the British intervention in South Russia. On November 14, 1918, the War Cabinet had approved a policy of support for General Denikin in finances and weapons, occupation of Krasnovodsk and the Batoum-Baku rail line, and the extension of British control over various other areas in the South (Kettle 1992, 32). During this time, the French were undertaking actions in the Ukraine, occupying Odessa and some of the surrounding areas.

The debates that occurred during December 1918 over this British action provide some important clues to the purposes and ideas underlying the intervention. On December 2, Curzon argued before the Eastern Committee that "it was essential to the interests of the British Empire, and of India in particular, that Britain should exercise some measure of political control over Transcaucasia" (Ulman 1968, 67). He presents this argument largely in terms of the need to protect access to India and the importance of the oil fields in Batoum, arguments that could fall into a traditional realist appraisal of British foreign policy. Curzon, however, was soon challenged by others on the committee, who pointed out that the defense of the lines to India and the oil fields did not necessarily require the complete political control that Curzon advocated. On the suggestion that the French should be in control of more of these areas, Curzon responded that "[The French] national character was different— they had a certain way with Eastern peoples—and their political interests conflicted with Britain's in many cases," (Ulman 1968, 70). A week later, on December 9, Curzon continued this line of argument, claiming that the French should not be allowed to challenge the British empire, an argument he once again puts in terms of India and oil. Yet, once again, he was challenged by those in the Cabinet, especially Balfour and Robert Cecil (one of the most important voices in the establishment of the League of Nations) on the grounds that Britain should not be seen as an imperialist power.

> Curzon replied to Balfour and Cecil with some moralism of his own: if the British government did not take responsibility for the Caucasus, he asked, how could it prevent "these little peoples" from being crushed by the Russians? Balfour answered: "If Russia is in a position to crush them, why not? We should not go there to protect them from the Russians. It would be folly, from a purely military point of view, for us to try and keep a military force there." [sic] Curzon's reply begged the issue: "I do not want to protect them against anybody; I want to give them a chance of standing on their own feet." (Ulman 1968, 72)

Curzon went on to argue, after more challenges, that "We are talking only of staying in the Caucasus to see the people on their legs there" (Ulman 1968, 73). These conversations continued, and on December 16, Curzon succeeded in having the Cabinet agree to a set of thirteen propositions concerning the continuation of the British occupation forces, despite the objections of figures like Balfour, Lloyd George, Cecil, and Edwin Montague, the Secretary of State for India.

These sentiments were not confined only to Curzon; a memo by a General Bridges on August 12, 1919, concerning the political situation in the Caucasus, claims:

> The outstanding feature of the present conditions in the Caucasus is the racial conflict between Christian and Mussulman. This has been held in abeyance by British occupation. (BDFA I, 266)

Thus not only were the British the only ones who could help these people gain the advantages of Western culture, they were even able to disarm ethnic and religious tensions in their calming influence in the area.

Ulman interprets these discussions, and Curzon in particular, as being an example of the importance of oil in world politics (Ulman 1968, 81). His reading, however, is flawed because it fails to take into account Curzon's general views on empire and the role of the British in bringing order to the world. Two points are important to stress here. First, Curzon and others believed that the French were incapable of providing the sort of order that Britain could provide. The French, it was argued by Curzon, have a peculiar "national character" when it comes to colonies, one that is far worse than the British. Second, when he was pressed over his arguments concerning India and oil, Curzon reverted to what was undoubtedly the more important reason for him and others. The British had a responsibility to control and organize these areas of the world, not for their own self-interests, but for purposes of "putting these people on their own two feet." Such sentiments, brought out in the heat of Cabinet discussions, and clearly ones that informed much of Curzon's ideas of British foreign policy, played an important role in the development of that policy. Moreover, the decision, or nondecision, to continue the operations in South Russia based on Curzon's thirteen points, provide further evidence that, despite some objections, the moral purpose of ordering the "uncivilized" areas of the world undoubtedly played a role in the intervention.

The second aspect of the British norm of intervention focuses on the protection of Europe from the power of Russia and Germany. This British foreign policy objective has often been interpreted by historians and political scientists as part of a balance of power system. Hans Morgenthau claimed that Great Britain has been "the outstanding balancer in modern times" (Morgenthau 1986, 214). The idea that it is the "balancer" results from the British conception of itself as the savior of Europe from those who wish to dominate it. Winston Churchill argued that:

> For four hundred years the foreign policy of England has been to oppose the strongest, most aggressive, most dominating power on the Continent. . . . Thus we preserved the liberties of Europe, protected the growth of its ever-growing fame and widening Empire, and with the Low Countries safely protected in their independence. Here is the wonderful unconscious tradition of British foreign policy. (Churchill 1948, 207–8)

Unlike the neorealist interpretation of the balance of power (cf. Waltz 1979), British actions in Russia and elsewhere indicate that the balancer must in fact make a political decision to continue playing the role of protector of a certain system. The British conception of itself as balancer of power in Europe clearly draws on a moral foundation. In other words, the ethic of the balancer was the ethic of Great Britain in its relations with Europe.

This ethic becomes all the more important during the Bolshevik revolution and concurrent Allied intervention. With the Bolsheviks, the British saw an ugly combination of traditional Russian expansion westward into the Baltics and Poland combined with the fervent ideological expansion of Bolshevik ideology. A number of different participants in the British community make arguments revolving around the protection of Europe from Bolshevism. Lockhart's memo of November 1918, justifying the continuation and increase of the intervention on humanitarian grounds, refers to the importance of protecting Europe from the dangers of Bolshevism: "It is perhaps no exaggeration to say that Bolshevism is now a far greater danger to Europe than German militarism" (BDFA I, 36). Henry Wilson, the Chief of the Imperial General Staff, recorded in his diary on December 24, 1918 the following:

> Boyle firmly believes that if we don't attack and crush Bolshevism in Russia it will spread all over Europe and lead to an almost frightful state of affairs. He was really very terrifying. (Callwell 1927, 157)

While Wilson argued for pulling out of Russia (as did many military professionals in both the United States and Great Britain), he vacillated at times, concerned with the dangers of Bolshevism, and believed that the British had a responsibility to stop the spread of it.

These concerns were especially prevalent during the Paris Peace Conference. The Hungarian Revolution of early March, which brought to power the communist leader Bella Khun, led many in the Allied political councils to fear the worst from the Bolsheviks in their relationship to Europe. Curzon wrote a memo to Balfour on March 28 in which he asked for a policy decision on the role of the Allies in the Baltics. In that memo he warned:

> These states [Estonia, Lithuania, and Latvia] are now exposed to the menace of extinction, either immediately from the forces of Bolshevism, or, in the event of the collapse of the latter, from a revived Czarism, whatever be the actual form that it may assume. . . . There is reason, then, to anticipate that, unless the Allied Governments take some more active steps than are at present in contemplation to render assistance, the Baltic States may be confronted at no very distant date with entire extinction. (BDFA I, 67)

A memo written on April 15 by the British Delegation in Paris makes a similar point:

> The establishment of the border States on a stable basis will not only be a fulfillment of the obligations of the Allies towards some

of these States, but will protect Western Europe from the spread
of Bolshevik ideas by direct contact. (BDFA I, 91)

This quote reveals the subtle shift in justification that occurred during
the Peace Conference concerning the protection of Europe. While the role
of balancer continued to play an important role, the argument for a continuation of the intervention focused more on a sort of contagion argument; that is, it was necessary to prevent the spread of Bolshevik ideas to
Europe, much like controlling the spread of disease. This argument was
also employed by Marshall Foch, the French general who had led the
Allied forces in the war, and it was one that convinced many in the British
delegation (cf. Kettle 1992, 100–192).

A final manifestation of the need to save Europe came from the discussions over the League of Nations along with the general idealist sentiments in Great Britain. Because they were the most ardent supporters of
the League of Nations, after the Americans, the British believed that they
had a certain responsibility to ensure that these forms of conflict resolution
should succeed. In fact, this sentiment persisted throughout the interwar
period, as has been argued by participants and historians alike (see Carr
1964 and Eden 1962). One figure who was not, in fact, a strong supporter
of the League concept, unless it supported British foreign policy interests,
was Churchill. Nevertheless, Churchill argued in Parliament on March 3,
1919, that the British had an obligation to remain in Russia because:

> We are simply discharging a duty to the League of Nations or to
> the League of Allied Nations, and endeavoring to prevent new
> areas of the world from degenerating into the welter of Bolshevik
> anarchy. (113 H. C. Deb. 81)

Thus the British normative concern with protecting and ordering the
world manifested itself in two ways: protecting the "uncivilized" areas of
the Middle East and Central Asia, and protecting the weak European
states from the spread of Bolshevik ideology or general Russian aggression. These concerns reveal the overall British national purpose of protecting international order, a norm that played a fundamental role in their
decision to continue the intervention. But how did these concerns translate
themselves into political actions?

As argued above, one of the most important aspects of the politics of
intervention, specifically multilateral interventions, is the belief on behalf
of each state agent that its national traditions and ethic are far superior to
those of its fellow intervenors. Just as the United States interpreted the
British, French, and Japanese actions as motivated by selfish, usually colonial, beliefs, so the British viewed the policies of Japan, United States,

France, and Italy as lacking the means to accomplish the ends of the intervention. Three aspects of the British intervention in particular demonstrate this sentiment: first, British beliefs that the Americans and Japanese failure to act in Siberia displayed an "immaturity" in terms of international political action; second, the British interpretation of the French pullout of Odessa in the Ukraine in April 1919, which they saw as an example of the inability of the French to successfully govern; and third, a resistance to the suggestion that the Italians take over the mandate of the British in the summer of 1919 based on the belief that the Italian national character could not inspire the type of liberal democracy necessary for the developing Central Asian Republics.

As has been detailed in the first part of this chapter, the British and French sought throughout the winter and spring of 1918 to convince the Americans and Japanese of the importance of intervening in Russia to recreate the Eastern Front. It was only the appearance of the Czech forces that convinced the Wilson administration to intervene. This action then convinced the Japanese to join the Americans and British, although their forces soon outnumbered the other Allies. The British interpretations of this American and Japanese resistance to action demonstrates their view of their own political presence, and how that presence was the only one suited to successfully solve the problems of Russia.

The period of negotiations between the British and Americans resulted in a certain amount of friction between the two countries. One point of friction between the Americans and the British was the appointment of General Alfred Knox to head the British military mission in Siberia. Based on the reports of the British ambassador in Washington, the cabinet learned that Knox was considered too close to the reactionary forces in Russia for the purposes of the intervention. This interference in what the British leaders considered to be a strictly internal British appointment resulted in a number of telegrams and discussions in the cabinet highly critical of the Americans. Both Lloyd George and Henry Wilson expressed their anger at the Americans, leading to a high level of friction between the two leading forces in the intervention right from the outset (Ulman 1961, 220–3).

This attitude is perhaps best expressed in an official history of the negotiations written by a British civil servant. Ian Malcolm wrote on June 21, 1918, approximately three weeks before the American government decided to intervene, a report summarizing the communications concerning the Russian situation. In his conclusion to that report Malcolm claims, first, that Woodrow Wilson's refusal to agree to the intervention arises from his wish to appear as "the prince of peace" and his concern with the upcoming American Congressional elections. But he also argues that

Wilson and the American community refused to cooperate with the Japanese because of racism:

> The American hatred of all yellow races is thinly, if at all, disguised; the very thought of the yellows being brought in to redress the balance of the whites is repugnant to them, especially when it may involve the consequent of loss of commercial advantages in the new and lucrative market of East Russia. It is for these reasons that our cogent arguments to President Wilson . . . have fallen upon intentionally deaf ears. (BDFA I, 32)

Implicit in this comment is the belief that the British are not racist and would certainly welcome the Japanese participation in the intervention. But the Japanese do not escape from Malcolm's pen unscathed.

> [Japan] makes no secret of her power and readiness and intentions to swoop down upon Siberia if and when it may suit her to do so. Like other "young" nations (including America), she prefers playing a "lone hand." . . . her working knowledge of alliances is small and not altogether satisfactory. (BDFA I, 33)

Within this brief passage we see the British conception of itself as decidedly not a young nation, but rather an old hand at the game of international politics, one that has the satisfactory knowledge of international order necessary for a successful foreign policy. This differentiation from the Americans and Japanese contributed significantly to the failure of the intervention, especially in Siberia.

A second area in which the British saw themselves as very unlike their fellow Allies occurred in Southern Russia, specifically in the Ukraine. On December 23, 1917, the British and French had signed a "Convention between France and England on the subject of activity in southern Russia," which created separate "spheres of influence" for the two nations. That agreement became the basis for the intervention of the French in the Ukraine and the British in the Caucasus region. But after the war ended and the stress of keeping a force in a hostile territory began to wear down the French, they decided to pull out all of their troops from the Ukraine, including the city of Odessa. After rumors of the evacuation of French troops began to spread, panic spread throughout the White Russian community, leading to demands that the French evacuate all White sympathizers along with their own troops.

The British reaction to this unorganized and panic-stricken evacuation reveals their belief that the French could not handle such situations. The British Consul in Odessa, John P. Bagge, reported on the conditions on the French ships that shipped many Russians to Constantinople: ". . . the

French went out of their way to ill-treat and insult [the Russians], and the ill-feeling which had been growing during the French occupation of Odessa has now become one of intense hatred" (Kettle 1992, 256). As a consequence of this treatment, J. D. Gregory, the head of the Russian Desk in the British Foreign ministry, reported that:

The French have certainly let us down horribly over all this. The result of it all is that all the Allies, including ourselves, are cordially detested by all classes of Russians, Bolshevist and non-Bolshevist alike. (Kettle 1992, 257)

Finally, the British also saw their image improved by the French debacle, despite Gregory's warning to the contrary. Captain George A. Hill, a political agent in Constantinople who reported on the Southern Russian situation, wrote the following appraisal on May 19, 1919:

To the British popularity is not due so much to the failure of the French, but more the conduct and sympathy of all hands of our services during the panic, as well as to the voluntary aid we gave in a zone outside our own, and likewise to the faith we have in Denekin and the material and technical aid we have given him. Our popularity locally continues to grow, owing to the comparisons, favorable to us, which are continually being drawn [between] our treatment of the Russian refugees at Prinkipo and Malta as compared to that of the refugees at Kalki and Salonica, under the French. (BDFA I, 195)

Such sentiments are certainly not ones conducive to the successful operation of a multilateral intervention. The politics of an intervention, however, in which the intervening state(s) attempt to present themselves as representative of specific sets of values, played a key role in the official British interpretations.

The final point of differentiation also comes in the context of Southern Russia. Faced with a lack of political will to remain engaged in Russia, up to the level of Prime Minister, British diplomats in Paris during the Peace Negotiations sought for some way to continue the process of keeping order in the Caucasus region. They decided to bring the Italians in as a replacement for the British, believing that the more involved they were in various parts of the world, the more responsible they would feel toward keeping the peace. In March 1919, Wilson and Balfour arranged for Italian troops to take over for the British. Characteristically, however, Curzon immediately objected. He wrote a private note to Balfour against the plan, claiming that giving the Italians control over this region would result in "disorder, bloodshed, and anarchy of a most shocking description"

(Ulman 1968, 228). When the Italian government was defeated in elections in June the new administration resisted taking up this mandate. Curzon and others saw this as further evidence that such a policy of colonial control should not have been left to such an untrustworthy force. Curzon was undoubtedly encouraged in this belief by the reports he was receiving from Batoum. On May 14, 1919, Consul Stevens reported on the proposed substitution of British troops with Italian ones:

> [The news of the replacement] has been received with bitter disappointment by all classes of the population in this country. . . . Furthermore, since our occupation of the Caucasus this end [of creating order] was being pursued with considerable success, and although probably the desired standard of order and tranquillity has not yet been attained, the progress made in the desired direction has been great, and the population, under the just and equitable guidance of our military authorities, was gradually settling down to peaceful conditions. . . . The few men that have been allowed to land from the Italian ship in the roads in order to march through the streets of Batoum have created anything but a favorable impression on the inhabitants of the town. Their slouchy gait is in striking contrast to the portly demeanor of our troops, both British and Indian; dirty brass musical instruments and other indications of the lack of all those qualities which play such an important part in inspiring Eastern peoples with the required sense of authority is being greatly criticized, and it is generally admitted that the effect of the wholesome influence of our men on the local population, in the course of a short time, will be completely effaced. (BDFA I, 193)

Such a report almost requires no commentary; the belief that the public presence of troops, not even fighting but marching in the streets, will influence the course of the intervention further supports the theme that politics is about the public presentation of the state agent in the target state. Italians, with their sloppy marching and dirty instruments, as well as their susceptibility to socialist ideas, would severely undermine the British civilizing mission.

Each of these aspects of the intervention demonstrate the importance of differentiating the British presence from the other forces. For that public presence is the political element of the intervention, the cultivation of which severely undermines any possibility for successful multilateral intervention. As each state focuses on its image, images that differ drastically from the other Allied powers in Russia, they failed to coordinate their policies and thus failed in their mission. Again, the Arendtian politics of agency combined with Morgenthau's understanding of national purpose gives us insight into reasons for and failures of intervention. British officials not only wanted to accomplish certain normative aims, they also wanted to present the purpose of their state in relation to others as the provider of order in the international system. This focus on a particularly British form of order gives an important explanation for the failure of the British intervention.

Churchill versus Lloyd George

This section deals with the conflict between David Lloyd George, the British Prime Minister during the intervention, and Winston Churchill, the head of the War Department during the later half of the intervention. For the conflict between these two figures captures better than any of the preceding discussions the way in which an intervention is really about a national purpose and not a national interest. In the case of Churchill and Lloyd George the conflict between them became a conflict over different versions of the British national purpose that manifested itself as a direct conflicts over military and foreign policy in Russia. These two figures believed in two different images of the British national purpose and the differences between them had a fundamental effect on the course of the intervention, and, more importantly, its failure.

While the differences between Churchill and Lloyd George manifested themselves in a number of different contexts, this section will focus on two in particular: one, the trip Churchill made to Paris on February 14 in which he pursued a more aggressive Russian policy than Lloyd George had suggested; and, two, Lloyd George's failure to make a definitive decision after Churchill repeatedly demanded guidance throughout the month of March. Both of these incidents reveal how disagreements over policy in Russia severely undercut the effectiveness of the British intervention, and they also reveal that these differences were not just about the British "national interest" but were differences over the historical role Britain was to play in post-war Europe.

Churchill became a member of the War Cabinet after the November armistice and after some of the more important debates concerning intervention had already taken place. He had previously been Minister for Munitions, and was thus "only an interested bystander" in the matters of the intervention (Ulman 1968, 90). But with his appointment to the post of Secretary of State for War, Churchill was moved to the all important War Cabinet, where he became a vociferous proponent for increased intervention in Russia. In fact, he more often demanded from the Cabinet simply a decision, deploring the vacillation that had marked the debates throughout November and December. He first entered debate on the issue on December 23, during which he and Lloyd George argued vigorously over the merits of increasing the intervention. Churchill wanted all five powers to engage in collective intervention to remove any vestige of Bolshevism from Russia. In a paper of January 27, 1919, Churchill wrote his first statement on the Russian intervention for the Cabinet. In it he again placed his arguments in terms of the need to make a decision; as minister in charge of the soldiers in the field he did not feel it right to continue there with little or no policy direction. But he again implied that the British must increase its force, although mainly in the South (he advocated pulling out of the Northern theater) (Kettle 1992, 92–3). And in Cabinet meetings of February 12 and 13, Churchill again argued for the continuation of the intervention. But, due largely to the resistance from Lloyd George, Churchill pursued the theme of collective intervention. He went so far as to argue that Germany ought to be convinced to join the action, warning that a Bolshevik Russia would not be a "friendly" Russia (Ulman 1968, 118–19).

The evening of February 13, Churchill, Henry Wilson and Lloyd George met in the Prime Minister's room in the House of Commons. That day, Lloyd George had been defending the British policy of slowly pulling out to the Conservatives who wished a more active campaign against Bolshevism. As leader of a coalition government that relied heavily on Conservative support (Lloyd George himself was a Liberal), the prime minister sought to convince the MPs that Britain could not afford to act alone. But he also raised the issue that became a central part of his argument against the continuation of the intervention when "[h]e asked the House to turn occasionally from the newspapers to read about the French Revolution. 'Is experience to teach individuals, and never to teach nations?' " (Kettle 1992, 116). This request to read about the French Revolution referred to Lloyd George's belief that the British were about to repeat the mistakes they made during the French Revolution, which was to try to squash the birth of freedom in a new nation. The prime minister had in fact raised this point in the same December 23 meeting in which Churchill had pursued a policy of joint intervention.

> [In the French Revolution] (t)here had been "horrors as bad as, or worse than, any of the Bolsheviks, perpetrated by a small fraction." But the very fact of British intervention had enabled Danton "to rally French patriotism and make the terror a military instrument." France had thus become organized "as a great military machine imbued with a passionate hatred" of Great Britain.

To the Prime Minister the parallels were clear: the one sure way to perpetuate the power of Bolshevism in Russia was to attempt to suppress it with foreign troops. (Ulman 1968, 97)

Lloyd George used this reason to resist further intervention both in the Cabinet and in the Parliament. It became an important means by which to resist Conservative demands for aggressive military action.

During the meeting in the Prime Minister's room, Churchill and Lloyd George agreed that Britain must pull its troops out and that they would only supply the White forces with munitions and food. It was further decided that Churchill was to go to Paris the next day to force the Peace Conference to make a decision on this issue. Thus on February 15, Churchill arrived in a meeting in which President Wilson was presenting his proposals for the League of Nations. As the meeting was breaking up, Churchill interjected that he wished to ascertain the Council's views on the situation in Russia. On his way out the door (and on his way out of France; he was returning to America that day to face the Senate), Wilson agreed that he would "cast his lot with the rest" whatever decision they made. Churchill took this as acquiescence to any policy he could push forward, believing that the Council was "entitled to count on American participation in any joint measures which we may have to undertake" (Kettle 1992, 124).

The following day, the French proposed an aggressive military campaign against the Bolsheviks. That afternoon, Churchill, attracted by the French plan, but knowing it needed further diplomatic justification before being approved by Lloyd George, suggested a two part policy: one, demand an answer to the Prinkipo Proposals[18] and, two, set up an Allied military and political council to deal with Russia. The American delegation, composed now of Lansing and House, agreed to the letter but refused to set up a council. Philip Kerr, the official British secretary for the conference, telegramed that night to Lloyd George, the following warning about Churchill's proposal:

But I cannot conceal from you that in my opinion Mr. Churchill is bent on forcing a campaign against Bolshevik Russia by using Allied volunteers. . . . He is perfectly logical in his policy, because he declares that the Bolsheviks are the enemies of the human race and must be put down at any cost. (Kettle 1992, 127)

Thus it appears that Churchill had gone beyond the mandate Lloyd George had issued to him and was pursuing a policy of collective intervention in Russia. Churchill in his memoirs of the event claims that he was only following the instructions he had received from Lloyd George at their meeting in the Prime Minister's room (Churchill 1929, 172–86), but most everyone at the conference agreed that Churchill had pursued a much more aggressive policy than that of Lloyd George.

This point of disagreement between two of the leading members of the British delegation to the Peace Conference, Lloyd George and Churchill, hurt the ability of the Conference to come to any clear policy, a detriment to the success of the intervention in that the Peace Conference had become the place where Allied countries were making many of their foreign policy decisions of the time. This disagreement between the two of them continued into the month of March as Churchill continuously sent messages to Lloyd George requesting a clear policy statement on Russia. In the first six days of March, Churchill requested a clear policy from Lloyd George at least four times (Kettle 1992, 158–91), none of which Lloyd George answered. This refusal to come to a decision on Russia resulted in a foreign policy based on, in historian Michael Kettle's words, an unanswered letter. Churchill, after numerous failed attempts, wrote a letter to Lloyd George on March 8 in which he laid out the policy to be pursued, but described it in a way that would allow him to try various other schemes for involving Allied forces in Russia throughout the spring and summer of 1919. On March 21, still having heard nothing from Lloyd George, Churchill simply informed the War Office that policy would be based on the unanswered letter. As Kettle writes, however, this decision both epitomized and finalized the complete failure of the British intervention in Russia:

> It was in fact, in this farcical way—on the basis of an unanswered letter—that British policy for Russia was fixed for the next five months. Thus, while French "major intervention" in the Ukraine galloped on to a rapid and humiliating defeat, the British were committed to a course of action which the entire War Cabinet recognized could lead to no result, and would only prolong bloodshed in Russia. . . . Thus, as the War Cabinet refused to face the Russian dilemma, and Churchill tried to extricate them by unending military adventure, Russia was to be ruined, the Bolshevik regime consolidated, and the seeds of the Cold War sown. (Kettle 1992, 191)

Thus the disagreement between these two principle figures clearly undermined the intervention and may have contributed to later problems between the West and Russia. What constituted the difference between the two? More importantly, what did it have to do with their political image of Great Britain? For Churchill, the British represented both the honorable leaders of world order and the protectors of Europe. He differed from

Curzon's attempts to focus more on Asia, believing that the British needed to recreate Russia for the good of Europe. At one point, Curzon argued for the protection of the Central Asian republics from any form of Russian aggression, while Churchill sought to recreate a unified Russian empire under the command of Denekin or Kolchak (Kettle 1992, 61–3). Perhaps the most revealing comment from Churchill came on February 21, after his failure in Paris, in an attempt to convince members of the cabinet that the British had an "obligation" to continue its intervention:

a) An obligation of interest to the seceding States on the Western front of Russia which have claimed the protection of the League of Nations. b) An obligation of honor to Russian leaders, like Denekin and Kolchak, whose armies were called into the field by our appeal and with our support in order to take the pressure off the Western front during the German war. (Kettle 1992, 143)

Note that these obligations are not to the Asian republics trying to break free, a focus of Curzon's, but specifically to Europe. Churchill's vision of Great Britain as the defender or Europe prevented him from accomplishing any of the moral goods initially outlined in the intervention.

While Churchill's vision of Great Britain emphasized its relationship to Europe, Lloyd George's vision, living up to the name of his political party, the Liberals, believed the Great Britain was a country that, above all, did not intervene in the internal affairs of other states. In his speech before the House of Commons on April 16,1919, in presenting the case for an end to intervention in Russia, Lloyd George argued:

there is the fundamental principle of all foreign policy in this country—a very sound principle—that you should never interfere in the internal affairs of another country, however badly they are governed. . . . We cannot interfere, according to any cannon of good government, to impose any form of government on another people. (114 H. C. Deb. 2940)

In that same speech Lloyd George raised an alternative vision of responsibility, the responsibility of a government to its own people, and claimed that an intervention in Russia would be "the greatest act of stupidity ever undertaken by a government" (114 H. C. Deb. 2942). This conception of Great Britain as a country that never interferes in the affairs of others, the image of a nonintervening great power that respects the sovereignty of other states, coincides with a form of world order that the British wanted to represent. It also coincided with the American understanding of itself as a liberal orderer of the world, and it was not an accident that of all the Allied leaders, Lloyd George and President Wilson were most in accord in their views.

Thus the differences over the intervention were really differences over the political image of Great Britain; that is, differences over the definition of the national purpose. And this clash of visions of what the British national purpose was led to the downfall of a policy that had been begun for reasons of defeating the Germans, but had turned into a battle over what the state agent of Great Britain represented.

CONCLUSION

This chapter has presented a detailed historical account of how an intervention can be motivated by an ethic of wanting to help quell anarchy and provide tangible aid, yet can also fail because of the need to present a state agent as representative of certain values and purposes. Certainly, the strategic and material reasons for the intervention were important. This chapter, however, has explored a number of alternative interpretations of intervention. As noted in the introduction, these interpretations will also help to resolve some of the dilemmas raised by the practice of humanitarian intervention, dilemmas that I address more directly in the final chapter.

As noted in Chapter 1, interventions rely on different norms, what I have called liberal, colonial, and humanitarian. The intervention in Russia reveals the liberal and colonial most clearly. United States intervention sought to create a liberal political system in Russia, one that focused on the rule of law, civilian government, and due process. The pursuit of these aspects of liberalism exist in the decision-making debates and papers of Woodrow Wilson and his advisors. They also exist in the actions of Ambassador David Francis and General William Graves, United States representatives in Russia. Interventions should not be seen simply as decisions, but must be assessed as analytical wholes; hence, the liberalism of the United States intervention can be found in Washington, Archangel, and Siberia.

Furthermore, this norm of liberalism was expressed by a political agent, the United States. This agent, in seeking to reveal its purpose on a public stage, generated a series of conflicts both internally and with other agents. Internally, the conflicts of interpretation between the executive and legislative branches concerning what constituted liberalism undermined the ability of the Wilson administration to continue with the intervention. Certainly, not every political system allows such conflicts to have an effect on an outcome. The specifics of how divergent normative visions of United States purpose caused the failure of the intervention are less important than the fact that those conflicts caused a failure at all. The conflicts between the allied states also resulted from the politics of agency. The

United States' failure to support the Japanese proposal to intervene in much stronger terms in March 1918 arose from a United States belief that only their specific form of military intervention could benefit the Russians.

The British intervention in Russia represents the colonial norm. The norm of colonialism, as noted in chapter 1, derives from a feeling of responsibility, part of the *gravitas* that Curzon believed so essential to the running of an empire. It manifested itself not only in the view that Britain would have to protect its colonies, but in the broader view that Britain could best aid the Russians in copying their forms of governance. This meant supporting military governments in Siberia and Archangel. It also meant that Great Britain continued to see itself as the key to protecting Europe. Since the time of Napolean's conquests, British officials had seen themselves as the protectors of Europe—a form of colonialism or responsibility. This led, in part, to the view that only Britain could protect Europe from the scourge of communism.

But, as in the case of the United States intervention, the politics of agency led to conflicts within Britain and among its allies, conflicts which helped undermine the intervention. The most significant internal conflict was that between Lloyd George and Churchill on what Britain represented, a protector of Europe (Churchill) or a noninterventionary power (Lloyd George). The conflicts generated among Britain, France, and Italy further contributed to the failure of the intervention.

My argument that the conflicts generated by the intervention—between allies, within states, and by the target states—all derive from the clash of normative visions with the politics of state agency may seem simplistic. These conflicts could certainly be explained in other ways. Nevertheless, I believe that a focus on how normative visions generate political conflicts is useful for understanding the problems of intervention.

Before moving on to the next chapter, the following quote allows me to capture some of the sentiments that this narrative has explored. In a memo on the British evacuation from the Caucasus region, a Professor Simpson presents an argument that could just as well have been made in 1993 to justify action in Somalia, or 1995 to justify action in Rwanda, Haiti, or Bosnia-Hercegovina. It is a statement of why certain states believe themselves to be the standard bearers for certain images and values, coupled with a genuine moral urge to prevent revolutionary anarchy. And it captures the tensions that this chapter, and the following chapters, have revealed:

> The smaller the world becomes as a the result of increased speed in means of communication by land and sea and in the air, and the more the best feeling and culture of the different nations are

linked together in a league, the more will the doctrine of nonintervention retreat into the background and the more will the idea of rendering practical assistance and existing moral pressure have to be developed in the interests of the world civilization as a whole. If it is the case that no region of the world coming under review as the result of peace negotiations has asked for any country other than Great Britain or America to act in the role of mandatory, it seems to the writer no use to either shut our eyes to this fact and its implications, or refrain from letting it be known throughout the world and acting on it, full regard being always given to the reasonable expectations of other Powers. Anything less is really treachery to civilization. (BDFA I, 179)

CHAPTER THREE

Intervention in Egypt

INTRODUCTION

This chapter continues to explore the normative and political nature of military intervention by analyzing the British and French intervention in Egypt in 1956.[1] This intervention provides a good "test" of the argument for a number of reasons: One, this attack on Egypt is rarely considered to have originated from within any normative framework. It is usually explained as an attempt by France and Britain to hold on to the strategically important Suez Canal and to ensure the flow of oil through it, an argument more in line with an amoral realist account of intervention. Two, the public lies, or "collusion," that surrounded this intervention make it a difficult one to which one may ascribe any morally good purpose. Three, the reason for the failure of this intervention is generally thought to reside in the American resistance to the British and French actions and not to any "political response" from within Egypt or anywhere else.

Each one of these points has some important truths to it, and this chapter will not attempt to disprove any of them with the discovery of new documentary material. Instead, this chapter, as with much of this book, provides an alternative lens through which to view the events of the intervention. While concerns over the continued flow of oil certainly played a part in the decision to topple Nasser, other concerns, focused on a set of moral obligations felt by both the French and the British, played just as important a role. The British norm revolved around three central tenets: First, although their empire was now in the process of being turned into a commonwealth, the British still believed that they had a number of important "responsibilities" in Africa and the Middle East. Those colonial responsibilities were reinforced in the Middle East by an Orientalist discourse that surrounded British interpretations of the Arabs and Egyptians. Second, the British felt themselves to be the protectors of an international morality and law that they believed Nasser had violated in his duplicitous comments about his aims and in his nationalization of an "international" waterway. Third, many British leaders and members of the House of Commons saw Nasser as Hitler or Mussolini. Importantly, the aspect of Nasser that was analogous to the dictators in this view was not his internal policies but rather his international conduct, especially his failure to keep promises. Thus the British responded to the Hitler/Nasser who invaded Czechoslovakia and Poland and not the Hitler/Nasser who created Auschewitz and Buchenwald.

The French also had a set of normative concerns that motivated their participation in the intervention. First, the French believed that they also had a set of responsibilities emanating from their colonial past. These responsibilities took on two different manifestations. One, the French believed that Nasser was undermining their ability to promote French culture, which embodied the best of Western civilization, throughout the Middle East and Northern Africa. Two, the French sought to protect the most important of their colonial possessions, Algeria. The second ethic behind the intervention was the French "tacit alliance" with Israel. While that alliance certainly had elements of a traditional security relationship, it also involved a bond based on a particular reading of French and Jewish history, especially concerning the Holocaust. Third, the French also saw Nasser as Hitler, leading them to respond vigorously to his actions in seizing the canal. Because of their more direct experience of Hitler, many of the leaders of the French government, who had also been participants in the French resistance, refused to allow another dictator to act freely in the world. These elements of the French action reveal what can be best described as a combination of a colonial and a humanitarian norm.

Yet, while these ethical concerns motivated the French and British actions in the Middle East, they soon came into conflict with the politics of state agency, leading to the downfall of the intervention. The British insisted that they were not like other countries in this area, especially the United States. Thus while the Eisenhower administration sought to find a peaceful solution to the crisis, the British saw this as a typical American refusal to recognize danger, citing their failure to enter both world wars until after Britain and Europe had already born the brunt of the struggle. Second, the British image of itself as protector of the Arabs world prevented it from acting openly with Israel to defeat Nasser. The "collusion" that has become a subject of so much controversy in the literature resulted from Eden and Lloyd's refusal to treat Israel as an equal, instead viewing them as a distastefully necessary partner. This treatment of Israel contributed in a number of important ways to the failure of the intervention. Finally, the British conception of itself as guarantor of international morality, not necessarily international law, prevented it from acting through the United Nations. Taken over by forces of anti-colonialism and third world nationalism, the UN did not represent the type of international society in which the British believed.

The French political images of itself also conflicted with its normative concerns. Also believing itself to be the only power capable of acting to defeat dictators, the French refused to work with the Americans to bring about a peaceful resolution of the conflict. In fact, the French were further motivated by the wish not just to distance themselves from American inactivity, but, more importantly, to move themselves out from under American "tutelage" and return to their mission of being a leading world power. The French also believed that the British were too reliant on American influence to successfully take up the burdens of the Middle East. Eden's collapse in the face of American pressure was seen as a perfect example of the need to act alone in foreign affairs. Even outside of the British reliance on the Americans, the French believed that the British would fail to carry out the intervention with sufficient force; days before the intervention, French generals were astonished that Anthony Head, the British Defense Minister, came to Cyprus to remind the forces that they should try to avoid civilian casualties.

Finally, resistance in the Arab world played an important role in undermining the intervention. The usual explanation of the failure of the intervention focuses on American lack of support for the British. But American policy derived in some important ways from the public voice of the Arab world in the UN and elsewhere. President Dwight D. Eisenhower believed that by supporting the British and French action, the United States would be tarred with the brush of colonialism that would hamper its efforts to act worldwide. Such a conception of itself as a noncolonial power certainly arose in part from the American national purpose; but it is instructive to see how such a national purpose developed in a dialectal fashion with the nascent nationalism of the Third World. Second, the British were sensitive to their image as defenders of the Arab world. When Jordan, the state that owed its existence to the British, failed to support their policy, the British understood that their political image was being seriously damaged by the intervention. Thus, Arab resistance to the intervention played a key role in its collapse.

This chapter presents an alternative interpretation of the intervention in Egypt. It demonstrates that a focus on the ethics and politics of intervention reveals new and instructive aspects, ones that do not fit so easily within a realist explanatory framework. And, it reveals how a colonial mindset can produce normative reasons for action; the belief that those against which an intervention is undertaken would not be able to rule themselves if left unattended, and that only by forcing a government on them could they become productive and "civilized" members of international society.

BRITISH INTERVENTION IN EGYPT

On November 6, 1956, British and French forces intervened in Egypt ostensibly to separate the Israeli and Egyptian armies, prompted by an Israeli attack on the Sinai peninsula. As testimony and participants' memoirs later revealed, however, the intervention was really an attempt to overthrow the regime of Gamal Abd El Nasser, the Egyptian leader who had four months earlier nationalized the Suez Canal in direct defiance of the Western powers. When Nasser nationalized the canal on July 27, 1956, the British Conservative government, led by Anthony Eden, argued that this violation of international morality could not prevail. The French, led by the socialist government of Guy Mollet, also quickly announced their opposition to the Egyptian actions, in such harsh terms that the Egyptian ambassador in Paris refused to accept their formal response. By the beginning of October, the French and British were massing forces on Cyprus for a joint attack on Egypt, and Nasser was continuing to publicly assert Egypt's right to nationalize the canal.

During September, however, the French and Israelis had been meeting to determine the possibility of a tripartite action against Nasser. These secret negotiations continued while the British and French brought their case to the UN Security Council. At the UN, it appeared as if a peaceful resolution might have been possible, but on October 18, Selwyn Lloyd, the British Foreign Minister, was called to London where Eden informed him that he was to attend a secret meeting with the French and Israelis. At this meeting, held in a Paris suburb, it was decided that the Israelis would attack at the Sinai Peninsula, followed by a British and French ultimatum being delivered to both sides demanding the withdrawal of Egypt and Israel from the Canal Zone. The Western forces would then intervene with military forces, take control of the Canal Zone, occupy Cairo, and force the downfall of Nasser.

The Israelis attacked on October 29. British and French bombers attacked on October 31, and their combined ground forces were introduced on November 5. On the very next day, the British and French were forced to accept a cease-fire, and negotiations were begun in the UN concerning the establishment of a peacekeeping force in Sinai. Eden was forced to resign in January of 1957, and Mollet resigned some months later. The Atlantic Alliance was severely strained, with the British and French blaming the United States for refusing to aid them, and the United States claiming that the British and French had acted out of colonial motives. Israel and Egypt were the only states to seemingly gain from the intervention; the Israelis halted the *fedeyeen* attacks sponsored by Egypt, and Egypt became the star of the Arab world for standing up to the West.

The British role in these events reveals a normative concern with keeping order in the international system. This concern, manifested through notions of empire, colonialism, and good governance is a normative one. But the politics of putting into place such normative concerns generated the resistances that led to the failure of the intervention. Furthermore, the clash between the normative concerns of different state agents participating in an intervention, here the French and Israelis, led to conflicts that could not be resolved. The following section explains how the interactions between politics and ethics can lead to such failures.

The Responsibilities of Empire

By 1956, British colonial obligations were becoming a burden on the the economy. In 1952, as Secretary of State for Foreign Affairs, Anthony Eden wrote a memorandum examining ". . . where if anywhere our responsibilities can be reduced so as to bring them more into line with our available resources" (Porter 1989, 164). In that memo Eden argued that Britain had to scale back its commitments in a number of areas and turn certain obligations over to the United States. But even within that memo, Eden pointed out that the British still have a number of obligations deriving from their "Imperial Heritage" including "Defense of the British position in Egypt and responsibility for security in the Middle East generally" (167). And while that Middle East security obligation was one that Eden considered devolving onto the United States, he believed that defense of the area should become an "international responsibility," something that involved *both* Britain and the United States (170).

But even as British leaders were realizing their limited resources, many continued to believe that Britain had a number of important responsibilities in the world, especially those that derived from its "imperial heritage." That heritage now involved gradually leading the former colonies towards self-government, and "gradually" was certainly the key word to many in the British foreign affairs establishment. Importantly, however, that process of self-government was not one that these countries would be able to develop on their own. Instead, as memos over the situation in Cyprus demonstrate, the British insisted on retaining some measure of sovereignty over these areas (Porter 1989, 310–18). Former colonies simply were not prepared at this time to govern themselves without the guidance of the British model.

This colonial, or imperial, ideal manifested itself in many countries during the eighteenth and nineteenth centuries, and Great Britain was one of the leading exponents of it. In *The Imperial Idea and Its Enemies*, A. P. Thornton describes the idea of imperialism as a "faith and an emotion before it became a political programme" that gave it longevity in British politics despite the arguments marshaled against it.

> It became their faith, that it was the role of the British Empire to lead the world in the arts of civilization, to bring light to the dark places, to teach the true political method, to nourish and to protect the liberal tradition. It was to act as trustees for the weak, and bring arrogance low. It was to represent in itself the highest aims of human society. It was to command, and deserve, a status and prestige shared by no other. (Thornton 1966, ix–x)

While there were certainly other elements that helped to constitute the colonial idea, Thornton stresses the importance of the ethical, that sense of responsibility found throughout the official and nonofficial explanations of imperialism.

The leading British figure behind the intervention, Anthony Eden, explicitly expressed this sentiment in his memoirs. In describing his views on nationalism within the developing countries, Eden writes:

> Everywhere through our Commonwealth and our Empire nations are growing up. This places a heavy responsibility upon the parent. He has to be sure that patience is shown, that guidance is given, that experience is passed—as warning but not as command. (Eden 1960, 379).

> In terms of the happiness, welfare and security of the great mass of the population, a hurried end of colonial administration may yield bitter fruit . . . Colony after colony, inspired or infected by the universal bacillus of nationalism, has tried to run before it could walk. (427–8)

For Eden, the responsibilities of Great Britain may no longer involve placing High Commissioners in the former colonies, but there certainly remained the responsibility of guiding these new peoples toward forms of self-government that would provide them with "happiness, welfare, and security." The metaphor of the parent and the child resonates with the type of paternalism that played an important role in British policy.

Nor was Eden alone in taking this view of the relationship between Great Britain and its colonies. C. M. Woodhouse, a member of parliament at the time of the intervention, wrote a history of British foreign relations in 1961, in which he argued:

Britain has, in the first place, obligations towards people in many parts of the world arising simply from past history, even if the historical origin of those obligations may well have been self-interested. Some go far back in history; examples are the old dominions, India, and Egypt, and many of the colonies. In most cases a residual responsibility remains, however much attenuated it may be by the conferment of independence and subject to developments. (Woodhouse 1961, 168–9)

John Glubb, the British military officer who became the head of the Trans-Jordanian military during the 1940s and 1950s, and whose dismissal played an important role in the construction of Nasser as a fomenter of troubles throughout the Arab world, wrote that:

Americans have little or no appreciation of the immense amount of love and benevolence which thousands of Englishmen have devoted to many Eastern races. (Glubb 1957, 327)

Leon Epstein's study of British politics during the Suez crisis also places an emphasis on this colonial element in British foreign policy. He argues that these concerns were not simply motivated by self-interest, but came from a deeper sense of obligations: "The consciousness of responsibility for the welfare of subject peoples was no doubt genuine. Seeing British interests alone was not enough to justify the task" (Epstein 1964, 11).

These more general views of the obligations of Great Britain in its former colonies display two distinct aspects, paternalism and a link to history. They are paternalistic in that they present the British as "parents" who are "devoted" to their "children," or expressing "benevolence" and "love" for the "Eastern races," an attitude that appears to have been an important part of the views of many involved in the British intervention. But there is also a link with history, as Woodhouse explains. Even if those obligations were developed originally from economic concerns, they soon became moral obligations that had to be respected.

In the course of the intervention, this ethic manifested itself in terms of protection: protecting Africa, especially the Sudan, from Egyptian aspirations and protecting the Arab world from Egyptian aggressiveness. Both of these aspects reflected a British interpretation of Egyptian foreign policy and "national character." This protective impulse in the British colonial ethic previously included an attempt to protect the Egyptians from themselves. But such a conception did not have the same legitimacy in 1956 that it had when Great Britain occupied Egypt in 1882. Thus, while the idea of protecting the Egyptians from the tyranny of Nasser did play a role in the House of Commons debates during the intervention, it was more accept-able for British statesmen to argue that other areas needed to be protected from this aggressive dictator. This colonial attitude not only led to the intervention, it partly contributed to its failure. Not only did managing an empire mean stopping Nasser, it did not include siding with Israel. The collusion that played such an important part in the intervention can be seen as result of the British refusal to deal on equal terms with any non-Western government.

Under the liberal government of William Gladstone, Great Britain had intervened in Egypt in 1882 to suppress a revolt by an Egyptian army colonel, Ahmad Pasha Arabi (Vatikiotis 1991). That initial intervention, undertaken to prevent the Egyptians from misruling themselves, led to a British presence in Egypt for the next 80 years. But during those 80 years the Egyptians continued to agitate for a British withdrawal. That with-drawal only occurred when Nasser came to power in 1954, and it resulted in a British pullout from what was an important military base in the Middle East. Ironically, the last British soldiers left Egypt only months before Nasser nationalized the canal.

While the British could justify their presence in Egypt based on riots and civil unrest in the early twentieth century (*British Blue Books*, 1918–1956), this justification no longer held the same legitimacy as it once had. But the colonial norm persisted, now manifesting itself in a reaction to the aggressive, from the British perspective, attitudes of Nasser. He was first viewed as the type of leader with which the British could deal (Schuck-burgh 1986), but as his espousal of Arab nationalism began to undermine the British position in the Middle East, the British foreign policy establish-ment began to look at him less generously.

Perhaps the clearest expression of the British concern for Nasser's influence on Africa comes from Julian Amery, a Conservative member of parliament who led what was called the "Suez Group" in the House of Commons. This group had been formed in 1954 to protest the negotiations with the Egyptians over the British withdrawal from the Suez Canal Base. Composed mainly of conservative and former military members of parlia-ment, they argued that giving up the base in Egypt would be the final step in the breakup of the British empire. Interestingly, even though Winston Churchill was the prime minister at the time of the signing of the treaty, he himself was not fully convinced that Britain should withdraw; Amery reports that while Eden, as Foreign Secretary, was trying to convince par-liament of the wisdom of the pullout, Churchill was supporting the Suez Group's opposition by clandestine calls to Amery and others (Amery 1990, 114; Schuckburgh 1986, 75). They argued vigorously for military action against Nasser two years later when he nationalized the Canal. In a retrospective written in 1990, Amery claims that the consequences of the British pullout from Egypt were severe for Africa. He claims that the withdrawal from British "responsibilities" in Africa resulted in:

> catastrophic consequences which we have witnessed in the Sudan, Uganda, the Congo, Tanzania, right down to South Africa itself. . . . Idi Amin is one of the children of our defeat at Suez. (Amery 1990, 124–5)

This conception of the British role in Egypt and Africa as preventing chaos and anarchy played an important role in the intervention. Eden also believed that the effect of Nasser in Africa was dangerous. In a letter to Eisenhower during the early stages of the crisis, Eden wrote:

> We have many friends in the Middle East and Africa who are shrewd enough to know where the plans of a Nasser or a Mossadeq would lead them. But they will not be strong enough to stand against the power of the mobs if Nasser wins. The firmer front we show, the greater chance that Nasser will give way without the need to any resort to force. (Carlton 1989, 104)

Such concerns also found their way into the British cabinet debates over the proper response to Nasser's action. On August 28, Harold Macmillan, Chancellor of the Exchequer, and one of the strongest supporters of the use of force, argued that:

> The Governors of Aden, Somaliland, and Kenya have already given warnings that the Arabs in those colonies were waiting for the outcome of this contest between Colonel Nasser and the Western Powers and that, if it ended in triumph for Nasser, British influence among the Arabs in those countries would be destroyed. (Carlton 1988, 136)

But concerns over Nasser's influence in Africa may have had the most decisive effect on the British Foreign Secretary at the time of the intervention, Selwyn Lloyd. Lloyd's concerns focused on one country in particular, the Sudan. Before exploring Lloyd's reaction to Nasser in terms of his influence on the Sudan, it is instructive to briefly relate the British role in Sudanese-Egyptian relations, a role that many in Britain saw as key to preventing anarchy and intervention in the Sudan. The relationship between the Sudan and Egypt had become one of the points of contention in the final stages of negotiations over the British military withdrawal from Egypt in 1954.[2] Negotiated and advocated before the House of Commons by Eden himself as Foreign Minister (which included convincing his own

Prime Minister, Winston Churchill) the agreement signed in July 1954 stipulated that all British troops would be withdrawn from the Suez Canal
Zone, a withdrawal that was completed only months before Nasser
nationalized the Canal in July 1956. But negotiations over the withdrawal
had actually begun in late 1950. In December of 1950, Salah ad-Din Bey,
the Egyptian Minister for Foreign Affairs, in a conversation with Ernest
Bevin, the Labor Secretary of State for Foreign Affairs, argued that the
British "responsibility" for the Sudanese had been based on its presence in
Egypt. In that this presence was coming to an end, the Egyptian government believed that it was now responsible for the protection of the Sudan.
To this argument, Bevin responded that "His Majesty's Government, however, as one of the two Powers responsible for the Sudan, could not dis-
charge its responsibilities without taking steps to help Sudan's political
development." He continued by arguing that the British administration of
the Sudan was far preferable to the Egyptian:

> [Bevin] himself had been personally interested in the develop-
> ment of the Sudan and had repeatedly sought Egyptian coopera-
> tion, as the Egyptian Ambassador could testify. He considered,
> without wishing to make invidious comparisons, that the stan-
> dard of administration and the development of the country com-
> pared well with Egypt. (*British Blue Book* 1952, 17)

The next day, as the conversations continued, Bevin pointed out that
British policy in the Sudan was "based on one primary interest, the welfare of the Sudanese people and their progress towards self-government"
(21). The British Ambassador also compared the administration under the
two governments, arguing that "It seems to me that Egypt's idea of self-
government for the Sudanese means Egyptian control of many phases of
Sudanese life whereas the British idea is eventual full self-government and
self-determination" (37).

These negotiations eventually broke down and the Egyptian government of Nahas Pasha abrogated the Anglo-Egyptian Treaty of 1936, which
had included the Sudan Condominium. This agreement had stipulated
that both Great Britain and Egypt were responsible for the governance of
the Sudan. But Nahas's Wafd government declared that the Sudan would
be under the control of the Egyptian King, leading to strong opposition
from the British. In the meantime, however, the royalist government in
Egypt was overthrown in 1952 by the Free Officer's movement, placing
General Neguib in power. Neguib and the Free Officers believed it was
more important to keep the British out of Egypt than to covet the Sudan,
so they dropped the previous insistence on control of the Sudan. This led
to a renegotiation of the treaty as a whole, resulting in the 1954 agreement

that removed British forces from Egypt, including a treaty in February of 1953 that formally declared the Sudan to be independent.

What is important to note about these negotiations, especially from 1950 through 1952, is that the British government had agreed to withdraw its troops from Egypt, including the Canal Zone. What they objected to was the Egyptian attempt to intervene in the Sudan, an area for which they felt a special "responsibility" one they felt they could better fulfill than could the Egyptians (Beloff 1991, 323). The resistance to allowing the Egyptians full control over Sudanese affairs thus relied more on Britain's belief in its colonial role than on its strategic or material self-interests.

Lloyd's concerns echo this history of British and Egyptian competition over the Sudan. He argues in his memoirs that the abrogation of the 1936 treaty by Nahas, especially the provisions concerning the Sudan, gave rise to the crisis of 1956 (Lloyd 1978, 8). Citing attempts by Egyptians to take over the Sudan throughout the inter-war period, Lloyd claims that "We believed that we had preserved the Sudan from Egyptian imperialism and exploitation" (10). Moreover, Lloyd believed that Nasser held it against the British that they had frustrated Egyptian control of the Sudan (despite the fact that the Free Officer's had been instrumental in agreeing to British demands that this issue be dropped from the new Treaty!) (15). For Lloyd, the danger to the Sudan from Nasser demonstrated the type of dictator that he was and revealed that only by toppling him would the Sudanese be allowed to develop their political lives unmolested. Perhaps even more importantly, Lloyd believed that the "traditional" Egyptian interventionary attitude toward the Sudan needed to be quelled by the British.

It is important to note here that Lloyd was not one of the strongest supporters of the intervention, based on reports from French and American diplomats who worked with him (*Documents Diplomatiques 1989*, 483). He, along with many others, saw the degree to which Eden's personal antagonism toward Nasser was an important factor in the decision to intervene. Moreover, while he remained a loyal member of Eden's cabinet, it seems that he was appointed by Eden more because the Prime Minister believed himself to be an expert at foreign affairs and less because of Lloyd's own capabilities as foreign minister.[3] Thus he may not have been fully in support of a policy that was the brain child of his prime minister, but he did not wish to fail in his support of Eden. His emphasis on the protection of the Sudan allowed Lloyd to take the action away from Eden's seeming personal antagonism toward Nasser and into the realm of British control of the aggressive Egyptian national character. Through his emphasis on the Sudan, Lloyd and others were able to fit the intervention into a more traditional pattern of British foreign policy.

Concerns over the fate of African colonies played a role in the views of some important members of the British leadership, including Anthony Eden and Selwyn Lloyd. But perhaps more important was the concern with Nasser's influence in the Middle East. What followed from that concern, combined with British views of its responsibilities in the Middle East and British interpretations of the relations between Arabs and Egyptians, constituted one of the most important aspects of the British ethic of intervention in the Suez. In a speech at Guildhall in November of 1955, Eden stated: "Our country has a special responsibility in all this, for we have a long tradition of friendship in the Middle East" (*Documents on International Affairs* 1958, 384). And that special responsibility led to the ill-fated attempt to topple an Arab leader who insisted on disputing that history, and who threatened the position of Great Britain in the Arab world.

How did this "special responsibility" develop, and what sustained it throughout the period of the intervention? This responsibility, like many others in international relations, resulted from a particular reading of history. That reading painted the British imperial role in the Middle East as one that brought peace, prosperity, and civilization to the area. The British intervention in Egypt in 1882 brought them into direct military control of the area, a position they would hold for the next eighty years. But the British did not have a presence only in Egypt. They also took up protectorates in Palestine and Iraq during World War I. After the war, those protectorates became mandates from the League of Nations, specifically in Iraq, Palestine, and Transjordan, with the French controlling Syria and Lebanon. In Palestine during the inter-war period the British sought to find ways in which to please both the Zionist immigrants to the area and the Arab populations already living there; what resulted instead were terrorist activities directed against the British, riots, and continued conflict until World War II (Laqueur and Rubin 1984, 44–124; Fromkin 1988). With the creation of Israel in 1948, the Hashemite kings, under the protection of the British, took power in Iraq and Transjordan.

What was it about Iraq and Jordan that demanded the attention of the British? Part of the reason undoubtedly derives from the British role in the "Arab Revolt" during World War I. The Hashemite family, prior to the war, controlled the holy cities of Mecca and Medina. Those cities were lost to the Turks during the war, along with much else in the area. The British at first did little to battle the Turks, allies of the Germans, and the Arab tribes were left to fight on their own. The British did, nevertheless, retain a command center in Cairo, and were in constant contact with the Arabs fighting the Turks. In 1917 a young civil servant, T. E. Lawrence, was sent into the Arabian peninsula to report on the status of the Arab troops fighting the Turks. To the British, the rest of the story is part of a myth that combines British tenacity with Arab simplicity. Lawrence led the Hashemites, who gathered around them other Arab tribes, and led the defeat of the Turks not only on the peninsula, but in Palestine, Syria, and Iraq as well. This victory of the Arabs, indispensably aided by the British, led to the creation of the modern Middle East. For the Hashemites became the rulers of Transjordan and Iraq, and were able to hold their positions there thanks to British help.[4]

This history gave to many British statesmen of the 1950s a sense that they still had a special role to play in the Middle East. There developed two sets of connections with the Middle East, those with Jordan and Iraq, and those with Egypt. The connections with Jordan and Iraq were based on these links with the Hashemites and the legend of British aid to the Arabs during World War I. The fact that the thrones of both Transjordan and Iraq were still occupied by Hashemite kings further reinforced that connection. The connections with Egypt were much weaker, due to the stronger resistance to British rule during the interwar period. The connections with Egypt also tended to be more focused on military issues, due to the canal and the use of Cairo as a base of operations during World War II (Eden 1965).

The British also believed that they had a responsibility to defend this area of the world based on the fact that they "created" these states. As Julian Amery argued in Parliament in 1954:

> . . . 72 years in which Cromer, Milner, Allenby, Kitchner, Lloyd and Killearn built modern Egypt as we know it; 72 years in which we built the foundations of what became a British empire in the Middle East after the First World War and has remained so until the other day. It is an area to which the force of the Commonwealth came twice in a generation to defend freedom and civilization. (Epstein 1964, 24)

Eden himself claimed in his memoirs that "Jordan was a country for which we had a special responsibility; we had brought it into being" (Eden 1960, 381). Thus the British not only had a responsibility to defend this area of the world from outsiders based on their role as defenders of the empire, they also had a responsibility to defend it from those, even those within its borders, who would change the character of the area largely because they had helped to create it.

These responsibilities were reinforced by a second overarching theme in Anglo-Arab relations: knowledge. Because of their long-standing interest in Oriental languages and culture, an interest that often found its way into the foreign service, the British believed that they had a knowledge and understanding of this area of which few other states could boast. The best example of this is Anthony Eden himself. Eden studied classical Persian at Oxford, with a minor in Arabic. In a revealing passage from his memoirs, Eden describes his Arabic teacher in the following way:

> He is said to have addressed Baghdad University in Arabic so pure as to be almost unintelligible to his audience. They were impressed as we might be if we were harangued in the language of Wycliffe, and only a little more enlightened. (Eden 1960, 212)

Mohammed Heikel, a confidant of Nasser's and editor of the Egyptian newspaper *Al-Ahram*, notes that Eden tried to discuss Arabic poetry with Nasser and even spoke to him in classical Arabic at their first meeting (Heikel 1986, 72–3). What is important to note here is Eden's description of his English professor's Arabic, "so pure as to be almost unintelligible." The British, including Eden, had come to believe that their studies of classical Arabic and Persian placed them in the position of being the teachers of their subject peoples, even in those people's own culture and language.

Eden's education in Persian and Arabic is in fact part of the larger discourse of Orientalism. While the term Orientalist was once simply a professional term indicating scholarly research on the Middle East and Asia, since the publication of Edward Said's *Orientalism* in 1978, it has taken on a whole new meaning. Said argues that this discourse was a way in which knowledge enabled the West to view the East as a place of danger, mystery, sensuality, emotion, oppression, and cruelty. This creation of the East further reinforced the image of the West as a place of rationality, common sense, democracy, and good will. And this cultural characterization relied heavily on the type of linguistic and cultural education that Eden experienced at Oxford. Eden studied only classical Arabic and Persian, along with pre-Islamic poetry and some early Islamic theology, as was the norm for an Orientalist education. This education reinforced the image of the Middle East as an area mired in the past with no possibility for growth and change (unless that change came from the West). Said points out this connection between Western attitudes and the textual study of the Orient:

> When a learned Orientalist traveled in the country of his specialization, it was always with unshakable abstract maxims about the "civilization" he had studied; rarely were Orientalists interested in anything except proving the validity of these musty "truths" by applying them, without great success, to uncomprehending, hence degenerate, natives. (Said 1978, 52)

While Said is describing an Orientalist from the nineteenth century, his description applies well both to Eden's description of his Arabic teacher, and Heikel's description of Eden's first meeting with Nasser. To understand the British approach to the Middle East during the 1950s, especially the approach of Anthony Eden, the concept of Orientalism provides an important aid.

Furthermore, that knowledge of the Middle East did not only rely on language. It also included an important distinction, for the purposes of this particular intervention, between Arabs and Egyptians. In the parliamentary debate of September 12, 1956, Patrick Wall pointed out that "(i)n the Arab world in general, we must remember that Egyptians are not an Arab people. Many of the Arab nations dislike and are jealous of the Egyptians. . . . [Iraq] is the future leader of the Arab race" (558 H. C. 48–9). John Glubb, the British commander of the Arab Legion in Transjordan, claimed that:

> As a race, Egyptians are physically inclined to be lethargical, a quality doubtless to be attributed to their climate. . . . They prefer to settle their problems by intellectual means, rather than by physical action. They are extremely expert at intrigue, politics, demagogy and subtle argument, but rarely meet success in war. (Glubb 1957, 32)

Albert Hourani, an Arab historian, suggests that "Eden may have shared the belief of many British Arabists of his generation that somehow the Egyptians were not true Arabs, but a mongrel race who had no right to claim the leadership of the Arab world" (Hourani 1989, 397).

These arguments derive from a Western supported racial and cultural theory that posited that the Egyptians could not lead the Arabs because they were not as "pure" as the Bedouins who had rode with Lawrence in the desert. The theory had both racial and cultural overtones. First, there was a difference between Arabs of the city and Arabs of the desert. Those in the city, with Cairo being the largest and most important city in the Arab world, were not as "purely Arab" as the Bedouin of the desert. Describing this difference between the desert and the town in the Western imaginary, Childers writes:

> By the early 1900's, innumerable travel books had appeared about the Arab desert, and a genuine fixation for it was growing among Westerners of superior social and educational status . . . it was the sheer contrast of vast silent, clean expanses, peopled by a mere handful of proud and self-confident tribal sheiks and their followers: the contrast of this experience with the dirt, the 'Turkish' cunning, the corruption and seething violence which was all most Westerners could see in Middle Eastern towns. In a very real sense, it was in the Arab desert that a Westerner seemed to find the refu-

tation of his own inherited prejudices about Islam; and in the Arab city that those prejudices seemed so apt. To many a Briton picking his way through a Cairo slum, there was something downright degrading about the sight of a ragged man praying towards Mecca on a dirty mat surrounded by garbage. But the homage of the Bedu tribesman out in the desert was clean, intriguing, strangely disquieting and attractive. (Childers 1962, 46–7)

And because Egypt was largely a country of cities clustered along the Nile, while Jordan and Iraq and the Gulf states all had sparsely populated towns spread throughout the desert, this contrast between the clean desert and the dirty city became a contrast between the dirty Egyptian and the pure Jordanian or Iraqi. Such attitudes would certainly help reinforce British conceptions of themselves as defenders of "pure" Arab culture against attacks from Egyptian infiltration.

But the contrast between city and desert was not the only font of this distinction. Childers also points out that Egypt was seen as an "older" civilization that stood for the pharaohs and pyramids before Islam and Arab nationalism. This distinction was important for the administration of the Middle East for Great Britain, especially because the Egyptians were the ones that proved least amenable to British rule, from Arabi to Nasser. Childers notes:

An entire political and administrative tradition grew up around the thesis that "the Egyptians" were a race unto themselves—utterly different from the "Arab" world. The very departments and channels of British policy were different for the two parts of the Middle East: the character of the men also are different. In short, it is quite impossible to imagine a Lawrence organizing a revolt-force of Egyptian peasants. It is quite certain that a Glubb could never have come to love Egyptians. (Childers 1962, 56)

British military and political strategy continued to differentiate between Egyptians and Arabs, as the course of the intervention reveals.

Finally, these attitudes were reinforced during negotiations with the Egyptians in 1954 over withdrawal from the Suez Canal Zone. One British civil servant wrote memos describing the Egyptian political scene in disparaging terms, warning that they are not to be trusted (Louis 1991, 46). Schuckburgh says the same thing, asserting that you cannot make long-term agreements with the Egyptians because of this inability to trust them (43). These attitudes were surrounded by a discourse of the Egyptians as dangerous to the larger Arab world, and the need for the British to remain engaged there to prevent those Egyptian ambitions from being realized.

It is important to recall that these different attitudes concerning Arabs, Egyptians, and the British role in the Middle East region can be considered as norms. Because they have racist overtones, such norms can be difficult to see as normatively "good" in the sense that we think of morality and ethics. But, when considered in terms of the forms of normative analysis presented in chapter 1, such attitudes may be understood as norms. Using the "positivist constructivist" approach, the colonial norm previously described can be seen as a set of positive facts, things that played a role in the decision to intervene and latter justifications of this intervention. But to make such a claim, it is important to answer a key question: These attitudes about the differences between Arabs and Egyptians may well have been in the background of the Suez crisis, but were they actually aspects of the intervention, especially in terms of a colonial ethic of protection? They clearly played a role, in many different forms. The belief that Egyptians were skilled at demagogy and subtle argument was the root of British interpretations of Nasser's radio broadcasts throughout the Middle East. These broadcasts, Nasser's most influential means of transmitting Arab nationalism to the other countries of the area, were seen by the British as Nasser's attempt to overthrow the "safe" Arab leaderships. In parliament on August 2, only days after Nasser had nationalized the canal, Eden claimed that "We have been subject to a ceaseless barrage of propaganda. This has been accompanied by intrigues and by attempts at subversion in British territories" (557 H. C. Deb. 1606). Selwyn Lloyd claims that Nasser possessed a propaganda machine that even "Dr. Goebbels would have envied" (Lloyd 1978, 34). And Glubb holds that "Perhaps in the West lies are more liable to be exposure than in the Middle East, because people are more sophisticated and have more varied sources of information. But in the Middle East, the gullibility of the masses is unending. The Egyptian radio broadcasts told continuous lies . . ." (Glubb 1957, 385). Clearly, many of the key players in the intervention believed that the Egyptians were deceitful and, more importantly, were spreading those deceits by means of their radio broadcasts.

Even before the seizure of the Suez canal, the British believed that Nasser was fomenting unrest in Jordan. In 1955, the British joined an Iraqi-Turkish pact that had been signed in February 1955. Britain's participation in what became the Baghdad Pact, later joined by Pakistan and Iran, was meant to be the new means by which Great Britain retained its influence in the Middle East. For the British, the pact was a way to counter Arab nationalism. In December 1955, Sir Gerald Templar was sent to Amman to win the Jordanian government over to the cause of the Baghdad Pact. But while in Jordan, perhaps because of Israeli attacks on

Syria in which fifty-two Arabs were killed, the Jordanians turned against the pact, believing that it was inspired by Israeli and Western colonial interests. The Jordanian government fell and rioting broke out throughout Jordan. As one author notes "Radio Cairo deliberately exploited this popular confusion, calling the pact a Zionist-imperialist plot aimed at dividing the Arabs, strengthening Israel and betraying 750,000 Palestinian refugees made homeless in the 1948 war. If Jordan joined, Cairo Radio warned, Arab military secrets would be available to Israel through friends in England and elsewhere and eventually would be used against Arab states" (Neff 1981, 176).

Whether or not Radio Cairo did exacerbate the political divisions within Jordan, it is clear that British leaders believed this was the case. Harold Macmillan claimed that the rioting was provoked by Egypt (Macmillan 1971, 90). Eden, in reviewing the wisdom of the British withdrawal from the canal zone, claims that "It is probable that the absence of British forces from the canal zone, however circumscribed they had been, facilitated aggressive Egyptian activities, both covert and overt, against her neighbors" (Eden 1960, 290). One important clue as to the link between Eden's views about Nasser's infiltration of the Arab world and the "special responsibilities" of Great Britain comes in a revealing passage in his memoirs. When Eden was informed of Nasser's nationalization of the Suez Canal, he was at a dinner honoring King Feisal, the king of Iraq, along with Nuri El-Said, the Iraqi Prime Minister, and others from the British and Iraqi foreign services. In the passage describing this scene, he first connects this young Feisal to the Feisal who rode with Lawrence:

> As I listened to Feisal's speech given at the dinner given in his honor at Buckingham Palace, my mind went back to my first meeting with his grandfather, founder of Iraq and of his dynasty, who had ridden with Lawrence and been our ally in the first world war. Feisal I would have been proud of his grandson that evening. (Eden 1960, 471–2)

He then goes on to describe Nuri as a bulwark against Egyptian expansion, and laments the death of both Feisal and Nuri during the Iraqi revolution, describing their deaths and linking them to the emotional masses that Nasser had created with his propaganda:

> The naked bodies were dragged through the streets of Baghdad amid scenes of unmentionable beastliness. A British officer was shot within the embassy. Three Americans were torn to pieces by the mob, with faint protest by their government. (Eden 1960, 471–72)

The implicit criticism of the American government is addressed in the following, but consider how Eden links all these themes to the description of his initial reaction to Nasser's nationalization of the Canal. Not only does he recall Lawrence, who popularized the relationship between the British and the Arabs, but he also implies that Nasser is responsible for the brutal deaths of those Arab leaders who represented the positive aspect of the relationship. Clearly, Eden saw Nasser's nationalization of the canal as an attempt to disrupt the productive British influence in the area.

Further evidence, at least for the British, of Nasser's nefarious plans was provided in March 1956, when King Hussien of Jordan summarily dismissed General Glubb as commander of the Arab Legion. Even though Glubb did not believe that Nasser had anything to do with his dismissal, ascribing it rather to the young king's need to assert his authority, the British political leadership exploded. Anthony Nutting, a British foreign secretary who resigned in the midst of the intervention, claimed that the Suez drama began the day Glubb was dismissed. Nutting focuses in particular on Eden's visceral reaction to Nasser, who he had once believed could be a leader with whom the British could deal, and whom he believed was the force behind the firing of Glubb (Nutting 1967, 35). Schuckburgh, previously Eden's private secretary and later head of the Middle East section of the Foreign Office, wrote in his diary on March 3, the day after the firing: "[Eden] is now violently anti-Nasser, whom he compares with Mussolini, and he spoke darkly (to the Americans) of having a good mind to revise the evacuation of the Suez" (Schuckburgh 1986, 341).

Even Hugh Gaitskill, the leader of the Labor opposition at the time of Glubb's dismissal, argued that this action was both dangerous and due to Nasser. He claimed that Glubb had played an important role in keeping infiltraters out of Israel by means of the disciplined Arab Legion which he led (*Documents on International Affairs* 1958, 15–16).[5] Selwyn Lloyd explicitly connects the stereotype of the deceitful Egyptian with Glubb's firing. Lloyd was, in fact, in Egypt when news arrived that Glubb had been fired. In a dinner with Nasser, Lloyd was informed of the firing, and the next day confronted Nasser with the news. Nasser, having learned of the firing himself only that morning, congratulated Lloyd on the wisdom of the British move in eliminating a relic of colonialism. Lloyd, offended that Nasser would lie to him so baldly, later claimed that this was simply part of Nasser's conspiratorial nature. As he wrote in his memoirs "[Nasser's] life had been conspiracy after conspiracy and we must understand that fact" (Lloyd 1978, 45). The conspiratorial Egyptian had undermined the British position in the Arab world in the most direct way possible, by dismissing a man who professed his "love and benevolence" for the Arabs.

Finally, Eden indicates in his own memoirs how the firing of Glubb affected him. While he does agree with Glubb that the dismissal was due more to King Hussein's jealousy than Nasser, he hints that Egyptian influences played a part in the general chaos in Jordan that contributed to the act. He also blamed Radio Cairo for the outbreak of violence and refusal to join the Baghdad Pact. "Egypt was inciting the people of Jordan to civil war and to attacks on her British ally" (Eden 1960, 387). Furthermore, it is in this same passage that Eden reminds the reader of Britain's special responsibility for Jordan based on the fact that it had "created" it.

The last aspect of the British role in protecting the Arab world from the Egyptians can be seen in the secret Anglo-American plan to bring peace to the Arab-Israeli conflict, code named Project Alpha. A series of secret messages had been exchanged by Nasser and Israeli Prime Minister Moshe Sharret during 1954 and 1955. The British and Americans facilitated these talks in an effort to bring an end to the most contentious conflict in the region. In early 1955, Schuckburgh wrote up a formal plan for bringing about some resolution of the conflict. Importantly, the agreement called for unification of Jordan and Egypt, something that would appear to be anathema to a Britain concerned with the power of Egypt to take over the Arab world. But, by having Jordan and Egypt come together under British auspices, the British would be able to retain their position in the Arab world (Shamir 1991, 84). Even as it became evident that Nasser would not be part of any plan with the British in control, they still believed that Nasser was "an erratic or even opportunistic leader who, with some skill and patience, could be manipulated to a reasonably Western posture" (90). The plan collapsed in early 1956, and the nationalization of the canal that year further diminished any chances of Great Britain playing any constructive role in bringing peace to the Middle East.

These colonial sentiments provided the normative justification for stopping Nasser. They also played an important role in the modality of the intervention. One of the most hotly debated issues of the Suez crisis was the "collusion" with Israel and the denial of it by the British and French. The decision to act with the Israelis arose from the shared interests of all three states in removing Nasser. A more interesting point to explore, however, is how the refusal to admit that they were acting in concert, especially the British refusal to admit that they had cooperated with Israel, arose from similar colonial sentiments. Unlike the French, whose bond with Israel had a more normative basis (see the following), the British saw the Israelis as confounding their protectorate over Palestine. The attacks by the Israelis on the British prior to 1948 derived from an anti-colonial liberation type movement. More importantly, this refusal to act openly with the Israelis significantly contributed to the failure of the intervention.

France played the decisive role in bringing the three states together, a point explored in the next section of this chapter. For the British were not at all enthusiastic about collaboration with the Israelis on any action in the Middle East. Despite the fact that they had helped launch Project Alpha with the Americans, the approach was directed more at the Arabs than at the Israelis. For it was the Arabs whom the British believed themselves to be protecting, creating a political presence that in some important ways depended on how those Arab states interpreted British actions. The British thus refused to openly collaborate with the Israelis, leading to the secret negotiations at Sèvres and the false pretext of "separating the combatants" as the reason for the intervention. This secrecy contributed to the failure of the intervention by making one of the participants, Israel, openly hostile to the British and the other, France, dismissive of the lack of British will.

Certainly there existed in Great Britain support for Israel. Arthur Balfour authored the famous document that bears his name, promising Zionists British support. And Winston Churchill was a committed Zionist, especially after World War II. Nevertheless, in the British foreign policy establishment, the support for Arab states was much stronger than was support for Israel. Describing the British position at the time of Project Alpha, Simon Shamir writes:

> It seems that at that stage Whitehall still had difficulty in viewing Israel as a fully established sovereign state. British officials who had for many years been accustomed to seeing the Jews as a controversial community in a country under their mandate were somehow impeded from coming to grips with the realities of Israeli statehood. (Shamir 1991, 91)

Kyle also reports on British animosity towards Israel; indeed, only weeks before the beginning of the intervention, British military officials were considering a joint attack against Israel and Egypt (Kyle 1991, 124).

This sense that Israel was not exactly an ally of the British stemmed from a number of historical circumstances. The most important was the British mandatory period, during which the British were attacked by Zionists agitating for their own homeland in Palestine; the attack on the King David hotel that housed a number of British officials during the Mandate period certainly did not contribute to feelings of goodwill between the two sides. Moreover, with a British officer in charge of the Jordanian army and bases in Egypt and the Gulf states, the British military community had a much stronger link with the Arabs than with the Israelis. Finally, the British traditions of Lawrence and the establishment of the Hashemite kingdoms led to a strong orientation toward the Arab states. Nor was there any love lost by the Israelis in relation to the

British. David Ben-Gurion, the Prime Minister of Israel during the intervention, states in his memoirs that the two enemies of the Zionists as they were establishing their state were the Arabs and the British (Ben-Gurion 1963, 24). As one of the chief architects of the Israeli-French war plans, Moshe Dayan, the Israeli Army Chief of Staff, was jailed by the British Mandatory authorities in 1939 (Dayan 1976, 31–42). These experiences of the leading Israeli authorities at the time of the intervention only contributed to the distrust between the two sides during the course of the negotiations.

The events leading up to the French and Israeli cooperation are examined in more detail in the following section. The French had been providing the Israelis with weapons since early 1955, and when Nasser nationalized the canal, the French and Israelis saw their opportunity to eliminate a joint enemy. On September 28, 1956, an Israeli delegation arrived in Paris for talks. These talks resulted in plans for a joint intervention, perhaps even without the British (Dayan 1976, 158). But Christian Pineau pointed out that any decision would have to await the outcome of the talks at the Security Council. Dayan describes how this continual delay contributed to the "military headache" of planning the intervention, delays that were largely the result of British indecision and refusal to work with the Israelis. As discussions with the British continued, but only through the French intermediaries, Dayan and Ben-Gurion become more and more annoyed.

On October 14 French officials arrived in London and held secret meetings with Eden and Anthony Nutting, then Under Secretary for Foreign Affairs. At those meetings, the French proposed a plan in which the Israelis would attack and the British and French would intervene to separate the parties, but then take over Egypt and replace Nasser. This led to the infamous meetings at Sèvres, a Paris suburb, from October 22 through October 24, during which the French and Israelis discussed plans for the attack, but then had to await British approval. The British, represented on October 23 by Lloyd, demanded that the Israelis not attack Jordan and that the attack on Egypt be serious enough to warrant an intervention by the British and French (Dayan 1976, 174–94). Ben-Gurion, wanting assurances that Israeli cities would be protected in case of Egyptian air attacks, was incensed when Lloyd would not promise protection. Dayan had to convince Ben-Gurion that the opportunity of having the British and French act with Israel to defeat Nasser was too great an opportunity to pass up, and they would simply have to accept the British conditions. The agreement was eventually signed, although Eden sought to have all the copies of it destroyed; luckily for historians, Ben-Gurion insisted on keeping his own copy.

The British refusal to treat Israel as a legitimate partner in the enterprise derived from their political presence in the Arab world. Even as they were disparaging Nasser and his seizure of the canal, the British continued to seek out the advice of other Arab states and political leaders. To act with the Israelis would jeopardize this presence, one to which most British leaders were strongly attached. And this refusal to cooperate with the Israelis led to a number of difficulties that contributed to the overall failure of the intervention. First, by not dealing directly with the Israelis, the British destroyed the goodwill among allies that is necessary for a successful joint military operation, especially one formed in secret. As Dayan writes about the British attitude:

> Britain wished us to fulfill this exalted function of villain, or scapegoat, without her having to meet us and discuss it face to face. (Dayan 1976, 161)

This attitude on the side of the British led to the Israelis making only a weak feint into the Sinai, sending a small contingent near the Suez Canal, thus making the British and French ultimatum appear as a sham. Without the appearance of a real threat to the canal from the Israelis, the need for peacekeepers was simply nonexistent. Moreover, the entire concept of the need to separate the combatants and take over the canal zone required a stretch of the imagination, in that the Egyptians could not really be seen as a threat to the canal unless they were using it to stop the Israelis, a tactic they certainly would not have employed.

The second consequence of the secret negotiations was the secrecy within the British cabinet and administration that prevented key players from knowing what was transpiring. As noted above, Lloyd was near to an agreement with the Egyptians on a peaceful resolution of the crisis when Eden recalled him from New York on October 18. The danger that Lloyd would resolve the conflict before the British could throw Nasser out was exacerbated by the secrecy surrounding the British and French machinations (Kyle 1991, 125–27). This type of secrecy on the eve of a major military action could only confuse the participants and lead to a lack of military precision and planning necessary for a successful action. The French diplomatic liaison on Cyprus, where the British and French troops were preparing to attack, reported that up until the day of the attack, many in the British military command structure had no idea that they would have to act as peacekeepers between the Arabs and Israelis (Baeyens 1976). One British general thought he would be able to count on a division from Libya up until just weeks before the intervention, a lack of communication that only aggravated the problems experienced by the British military staff.

Thus the lack of equality between the British and Israeli forces contributed to the overall secrecy that hampered the intervention. This refusal
to treat the Israelis as equal partners derived in large part from the British
need to continue their presence on the world stage as a colonial protector
of the Arabs. Again, recalling the theoretical framework of state agency
presented in chapter 1, we can see how the conflicting normative visions
of the three states generated a set of conflicts between them that could not
be resolved and that contributed to the failure of the intervention. As
noted previously, this intervention failed, in part, not because of a lack of
norms but because of an excess of them.

Defending International Norms

Defending international norms played an important role in the decision
to intervene in Egypt. Both the historical background that the British had
in creating these norms and their experience in resisting dictators in
World War II engendered the view that it was their responsibility to
respond to any violation of those norms. Moreover, their political conflict
with the United States resulted in part from their belief that the Americans were only interested in making money and not ensuring order. This
normative vision and political action both sprang from the same source,
and the combination led in a number of important ways to the failure of
the intervention.

It is significant that the British realized soon after Nasser's public declaration and the publication of the Egyptian law that nationalized the
canal, that they were on slim legal grounds to challenge his action (see
Documents on International Affairs 1959, 77–115 for both the speech and the
law). The only legal ground upon which they could possibly challenge
Nasser was the Constantinople Declaration of 1888 in which the major
users of the canal, including the Ottoman Empire which at that time had
sovereignty over Egypt, signed a treaty guaranteeing free passage (*A Selection of Documents Relating to the International Status of the Suez Canal* 1956).
The only country Egypt would not allow through the canal was Israel—a
clear violation of the treaty. But, because the British and French had
allowed Egypt to prevent Israel from using the canal prior to Nasser's
nationalization, they were unable to use this as a legal pretext for objecting
to the nationalization.

Thus the public pronouncements from the British quarter took on a
different character. They stressed not a violation of international law, but a
violation of something else, a vaguely undefined sense of international
morality and respect for international norms. These protests began in Par-

liament. On July 30, the government announced to Parliament that "No arrangements for the future use of this great international waterway could be acceptable to Her Majesty's Government which would leave it in the unfettered control of a single power which could, as recent events have shown, exploit it purely for purposes of national policy" (557 H. C. Deb. 919). On August 2 in the House of Commons, Eden claimed that Nasser had implicitly endorsed the agreements keeping the Canal outside of the control of any one power. He went on to say that "These understandings are now torn up, and one can have no confidence in the word of a man who does that" (1603). One of the leaders of the Suez Group pointed out on that same day that there were two sides to the issue, a legal side and that of "decency between nations" (1618). And on September 12, in one of the debates on the Suez issue, Eden claimed that Nasser had "taken away the international character of the canal" and had "de-internationalized" it (558 H. C. Deb. 5).

These protests continued in the ensuing months. In a public speech on October 13, Eden argued that:

> The responsibility which rests upon us and our allies is to ensure that justice is done and that international obligations are fulfilled. After all, the UN Charter was set up to discourage breaches of international engagements and not to allow them to pass with impunity. (Eayrs 1964, 117)

And even Lloyd, a lawyer by profession and one who appeared to want a legal pretext for attacking Nasser, seemed to move away from the international law argument. In a broadcast on November 3, after the British ultimatum had been issued, he argued that "Law and order cannot be maintained in any country without a policeman. The burglar is not deterred because a society of property owners passes a resolution condemning house-breaking. Unlawful wrongdoing is not stopped because the victims may all condemn violence. So it is in international society . . ." (Eayrs 1964, 220).

Were these concerns simply a matter of public consumption? In examining some of the internal debates, it appears that the British had a very strong sense of themselves as defenders of something far more important than the UN or formal international law. In a British cabinet meeting on July 27, Eden argued:

> From a narrow legal point of view, [Nasser's] action amounted to no more than a decision to buy out shareholders. Our case must be presented on wider international grounds. Our argument must be that the Canal was an important international asset and

facility, and that Egypt could not be allowed to exploit it for a purely internal purpose. (Carlton 1988, 133)

The belief that the nationalization of the canal violated international norms also played a role in the first tripartite talks between the United States, Great Britain, and France. The three parties were first concerned with a statement condemning Nasser's actions. Before the arrival of the United States delegation, British and French diplomats had prepared a draft statement which read in part:

> The three Governments note with grave concern that the Egypt-
> ian Government in proclaiming that they were acting in a spirit
> of retaliation, have given a political character to their action of
> July 26, 1956. . . . They deplore the fact that the Egyptian Govern-
> ment have had recourse to what amounts to a denial of funda-
> mental human rights by compelling foreign employees of the
> Suez Canal Company to continue work under threat of impris-
> onment. (*FRUS The Suez Crisis* 1990, 58)

This statement was rejected by the American delegation, and the final statement issued on July 31 was more focused on the violation of law that Nasser's actions entailed. But the initial statement by the British and French, at least the sections quoted here, indicates a much different conception of Nasser's actions. First, by pointing out that the seizure was "political" the Western powers could claim that their response was not an enforcement of a legal violation, but a much more important issue of protecting international norms. Further, their reference to "fundamental human rights" was an attempt to place the action in direct violation of one of the most important of those international norms. In this way, the British and French tried to construct the action as a violation of the norms that they believed they were destined to protect.

Eden's memoirs give further evidence of the importance of these international norms. Eden and many others in the British foreign policy establishment of the 1950s had been schooled in the interwar period on the dangers of dictators and the need for collective action. The British especially were on the forefront as defenders of the League of Nations, even when it failed to stop the aggressive behavior of Japan and Italy (Carr 1964). Eden recalls in his memoirs the importance of collective security and the international norms that it protects. In a speech given in April 1935, having returned from a mission to convince Hitler to not rearm Germany, he states:

> We [the British] shall always be arrayed on the side of the collec-
> tive system against any government or people who seek by a

return to power politics to break up the peace which by that system we are trying to create. (Eden 1962, 211)

Later, upon describing Hitler's violations of various treaties, he writes:

Once obligation to uphold international engagements is evaded, pretext will follow pretext, until the structure of confidence is destroyed and respect for treaties hangs like a rusty nail in monumental mockery. Asia and Africa have already furnished their examples in flouting engagements with impunity. (ibid., 413)

Note that he implicitly connects "Asia and Africa" with this abrogation of international "obligation," thus connecting Nasser with those same dictators. British foreign policy is designed to uphold the "structure" of confidence by enforcing the moral norms that constitute that structure.

Finally, Eden's letters to Eisenhower during the crisis further reveal this sense that the violation is one of international morality and not international law. Because the two had developed a friendship during World War II, both sought throughout the crisis to convince the other of his position. Eden, knowing the American predilection to interpret international affairs through the prism of international law, sought to dissuade Eisenhower of these notions throughout the crisis. On July 27, Eden wrote:

We should not allow ourselves to become involved in legal quibbles about the rights of the Egyptian Government to nationalize what is technically an Egyptian company, or in financial arguments about their capacity to pay the compensation which they have offered. I feel sure that we should take issue with Nasser on . . . broader international grounds . . . (*FRUS The Suez Crisis* 1990, 10)

In two further letters to Eisenhower, Eden links this violation of international norms to Britain's specific responsibility to respond to such actions. On September 9 he wrote:

it seems to us that our duty is plain. We have many times led Europe in the fight for freedom. It would be an ignoble end to our long history if we tamely accepted to perish by degrees. (Carlton 1988, 120)

And on November 5:

History alone can judge whether we have made the right decision, but I do want to assure you that we have made it from a genuine sense of responsibility, not only to our own country, but to all the world. (ibid., 131)

In seeking to convince Eisenhower that this was not a matter of "legal quibbles" Eden revealed the connections between the structure of an international system grounded in moral norms and the British responsibility to uphold that system.

The norms of international responsibility and moral diplomacy that lie behind these British attitudes fall somewhere in between legal and ethical norms. They are not truly legal because of the way in which the British wished to differentiate their notion of norms from that of actual international law. International law set in stone certain rules that the British, and other great powers, felt the need to violate to uphold a higher moral norm. These norms were not to be disrupted by "legal quibbles" as Eden claims.

A final point in understanding Eden's views on Nasser and international morality concern the analogy with Hitler and Mussolini. Eden titled the first volume of his memoirs *Facing the Dictators*, a title that described both his interactions with Hitler and Mussolini as part of the Foreign Office, and also his sensational resignation in response to Neville Chamberlain's policy of appeasement. Indeed, it was Eden's resignation in February 1938 that made him such a popular figure in both Great Britain and the world, and Eden saw himself as vindicated when the Chamberlain government fell and he became part of Winston Churchill's government in September 1939. His time spent with both Hitler and Mussolini, and his later reactions to their breaking of international agreements, led to a very strong set of views on what constituted proper international behavior. And Eden believed that Nasser was repeating many of the same strategies that Hitler and Mussolini used in his attempt to take over the Arab world. The belief that Nasser was Hitler gave a strong moral impetus to the British reactions to the Suez seizure, and these reactions helped constitute an ethic of "facing the dictators."

Some of the initial reactions to Nasser's seizure of the canal drew a parallel with Hitler. In Parliament on July 26, only one day after the seizure, one member drew a rather mundane comparison with Hitler, pointing out that both used the same timing in their actions: "Is [Eden] further aware that this 'weekend technique' is precisely the technique which we got used to in Hitler's day? Is he also aware of the consequences of not answering force with force until it is too late?" (557 H. C. Deb. 779–80). And it was Gaitskill, the leader of the opposition, who made a further parallel with Hitler in his official response to Eden's opening statement on August 2 (1612). Lloyd also drew on this similarity, claiming that Nasser's actions in taking the canal were like Hitler's actions in taking the Rhineland (Lloyd 1978, 192).

But the most important analogy came from Eden. Schuckburgh reports in his diary of March 3 that Eden saw Nasser as Mussolini after the dismissal of Glubb (Schuckburgh 1987, 342). Others have commented on Eden's belief that Nasser was another dictator, either Mussolini or Hitler (see Rhodes 1990; Kyle 1991; Love 1969; Neff 1981). Eden was fundamentally shaped by his experience as a member of the Foreign Office during the 1930s. During this time he met with Hitler on two occasions as the official British representative, and with Mussolini a number of times as well (Eden 1965). His conversations with Hitler largely focused on German rearmament, the Rhineland, the Saar Valley, and Hitler's complaints about the constraints placed on Germany by the Treaty of Versailles. After both meetings, Eden believed he had some agreement with Hitler on these issues, but Hitler would inevitably break these agreements. Mussolini would also promise to moderate his position on various international issues when meeting with Eden, but, like Hitler, would rarely keep his promises. One issue to which Eden devoted much of his time was the Italian claims on Ethiopia. Eden sought to have an oil embargo imposed on Italy because of its aggressions in Ethiopia, but Samuel Hoare, the British Foreign Secretary, and Pierre Laval, the French Foreign Minister, gave Mussolini complete control over Ethiopia in December 1935, leading to vigorous opposition from Eden and others. Eden saw this abandonment of Ethiopia to Italian aggressions as one of the first steps towards the policy of appeasement that led to his resignation three years later.

It is important to note here that Eden did not formulate his objections to Hitler or Mussolini based on their domestic politics. While he spoke eloquently about the Holocaust in the midst of World War II (Eden 1965, 415), he wrote very little about this aspect of Nazi domestic policy. What did offend Eden were the violations of international morality that both Hitler and Mussolini seemed intent on committing. This is not to say that Eden did not object to the Holocaust, nor that he did not find fascism abhorrent ethically and politically. What is important is that these aspects of Nazi politics did not seem to effect Eden in the same way that the violations of international norms did. And the most important of those norms, especially for a Foreign Secretary, was the honoring of international obligations and promises. This concern with the ordering of international society, and not necessarily domestic societies, constitutes a fundamental element in the colonial ethic, especially as it was practiced by Great Britain.

We find this concern in Eden's discussion of dictators, which occurs in the midst of his explanation of Nasser's nationalization of the canal. He argues that "There is a redemptive type of dictator, whose rule is comparatively mild and beneficial" (Eden 1960, 480). But Nasser clearly did not fit that role. And while Eden does link Nasser to Hitler in a passage where he describes Egyptian officers as familiar with *Mien Kampf*, Eden focuses more on the violations of international order that Nasser has committed.

Claiming that "an international agreement was at stake" (473) in the seizure, he argues that:

From the start, the Suez crisis was never a problem between two, or even three, powers only; it concerned a very large part of the world. We realized that the repercussions ranged wide and naturally took heed of the advice offered. (Eden 1960, 548)

For Eden, then, there was a parallel between Nasser and the dictators, but the parallel focused more on the tendency of dictators to violate the norms of international society. He stresses this point in his letters to Eisenhower. On September 6, Eden wrote:

Hitler established his position by a series of carefully planned movements. These began with the occupation of the Rhineland. . . . Similarly, the seizure of the canal is, we are convinced, the opening gambit in a planned campaign designed by Nasser to expel all Western influence from Arab countries. (Eayrs 1964, 106)

Eden continues by questioning whether or not the Arabs are really willing to follow Nasser:

Will the Arabs not be prepared to follow this lead? Can we rely on them to be more sensible than were the Germans? Even if the Arabs eventually fall apart again as they did after the early Caliphs, the damage will have been done meanwhile. (ibid., 107)

Lloyd also believed in the Nasser/Hitler analogy, focusing on the similarities between the taking of the Rhineland and the seizure of the Canal (Lloyd 1978, 192).

Thus the British saw in Nasser a dictator whom they needed to defeat for the sake of a non-British, international society. In the same way the British had saved Europe from the Kaiser and Hitler, they also needed to save the Arab and African worlds from the dangers of Nasser. In so doing, the British were supporting the international norms that they believed protected the world order that they had worked so long to establish. These were the norms that gave Great Britain its moral, national purpose.

While they were trying to implement a set of normative goals, the British leaders were overwhelmed by the importance of the British political presence. Manifesting itself in the form of state agency, the British political presence prevented them from accomplishing any of the goals in the intervention and, in fact, contributed to its overall failure. This political aspect appears in three contexts: First, the British insisted that they were better able to order the Middle East than were the Americans, an insistence that led to their conflict with the Americans over the use of force. Second, part of the British ethic was a belief that they knew how to order international society better than the positive international law found in the UN. But in the Suez intervention this belief appeared only in the Conservative arguments for the action, while the Labour party sought to bring British policy back into line with the UN. This partisan difference, which can be partly ascribed to parliamentary tactics of trying to overthrow the opposition, can also be seen as an example of how the political presence of a state agent depends on a unified political community. Thus the resistance at this point comes not from outside of the British political context but from within it, a resistance that derives from a conflict over the definition of the political presence, or national purpose, of the British state. Third, the politics of the intervention can be seen in the "collusion" between the British, French, and Israelis. In fact, it was the British who insisted on secrecy, largely because of their need to appear as defenders of the Arab world. Thus, the British would not allow themselves to be seen as allies of Israel, but insisted on portraying themselves as peacekeepers. This portrayal led to a number of clashes with both the French and the Israelis, and hampered the conduct of the intervention at a number of key points.

So how did all these normative concerns with international order and morality translate into political action? During the course of the intervention, and in later histories of it, a number of commentators have pointed out the importance of "prestige" in the conduct of British foreign policy. Robert Menzies, the Australian Prime Minister who was sent by the 18 power conference to Nasser in September, and who was a strong supporter of Britain throughout the crisis, pointed out in a broadcast on August 13, 1956 that:

> The fact remains that peace in the world and the efficacy of the UN Charter alike require that the British Commonwealth, and in particular its greatest member, the United Kingdom, should retain power, prestige, and moral influence. (Eayrs 1964, 56)

Shuckburgh makes a similar point in 1954, in describing the failure of Great Britain to achieve peace in the Middle East with Project Alpha:

> Great nations, no less than individuals, must have pride, and never was British pride more sorely tested than in those years after victory when we found we were not victors at all. (Shuckburgh 1986, 214)

And Harold Macmillan told Robert Murphy, the United States special envoy to Great Britain, that if Britain did not accept Egypt's challenge, "Britain would become another Netherlands" (Murphy 1964, 380).

Clearly the British felt that their presence on the international stage meant a great deal in the resolution of the crisis. To allow an upstart dictator to violate the international norms that Great Britain and others had worked so hard to construct struck hard at the British position in the world. Lord Beloff, writing about the consequences of the intervention for the Conservative Party, argues:

> Anthony Eden thus takes on a new image—that of the last British Prime Minister who believed in common with the majority of the citizens of the country Britain was still a world power, only temporarily weakened by the impact of the war years. His diplomacy in the Middle East, whether attempting in Project Alpha to design a settlement of the Palestinian problem or, as at Suez, colluding with Israel and France to bring down Nasser as an obstacle to his designs, reflects the illusions of a passing age. In that sense his tragic fall was more significant than some of his chroniclers would have us believe. (Beloff 1990, 334)

Beloff is correct in arguing that Eden's downfall was more significant than just his own personal tragedy; it demonstrated to many in the British political community that their prestige was not the same as it was when Disraeli and Gladstone were able to dictate to Egypt its financial and political future. Prestige is presence, the presence of a Great Britain that matters, one that has an effect on the course of world politics. Even President Eisenhower recognized this political aspect of Suez: "France and Britain considered Suez as something of a symbol, a symbol of their position in the entire world" (Eisenhower 1965, 34).

As the British tried to accomplish the ethical goals outlined in the previous section, they tried to accomplish these goals through an entity that required a clear, strong, historically secure presence in relation to other countries. And the conflict between this presence and the ethical norms contributed in a number of important ways to the failure of the intervention. The clash between Great Britain and the United States, a clash over political presence and not over ethical norms, played a key role in this failure. For while the United States wished to prevent Nasser from holding the canal, and had interpreted his actions in ways quite similar to the British, they did not feel that their reputation as defenders of decolonization could survive participation in an action that looked very much like traditional gunboat diplomacy. The British believed that the United States simply did not understand the threat, the Arabs, or the importance of Great Britain's place in the Middle East. The conflict between these two political visions led to one of the most conflictual periods in relations between the two Anglo-Saxon allies.

Both the British and the French, and most others, believed that the United States provided the spark that resulted in the Suez conflagration. On July 19, 1956, John Foster Dulles, the United States Secretary of State, issued a statement informing the Egyptian government that the United States and the World Bank were withdrawing funding from the Egyptian project of constructing the Aswan Dam (*Documents on International Affairs* 1956, 69–70). Nasser learned of the action while on a plane with Nehru returning from Yugoslavia after meeting with Tito; he claimed that he expected the renege, but that the manner in which it was abruptly delivered to the Egyptian ambassador, with little advance warning, demonstrated the "arrogance of these people," as Nehru put it (Heikel 1973). Heikel claims that the decision to nationalize the canal was made soon thereafter; in his speech nationalizing the canal, Nasser claimed that the revenues from the canal would be used to finance the canal. Indeed, in that same speech, Nasser stressed that the actions of the World Bank and the United States had irreparably harmed Egyptian pride, demonstrating at the very beginning of the crisis that the issue of state presence would play a key role. Nutting's biography of Nasser also stresses this point, arguing that "dignity" was a key to Nasser's reactions throughout the crisis (Nutting 1971).

The nationalization of the canal was not perceived in the United States community as a justifiable action, nor were their interpretations of Nasser any more enlightened than the British. Herbert Hoover, Under Secretary of State, and an engineer with experience in the Middle East, argued at a White House meeting on July 27 that "Nasser's actions are not based on reasoning, but are irrational and emotional" (*FRUS The Suez Crisis* 1990, 7). The CIA profile of Nasser also stressed his irrationality and propensity to "lose his head" (Neff 1981, 87). Furthermore, important voices in the American foreign policy establishment stressed the strategic importance of the canal for the United States and for its European allies. Reports by the Joint Chiefs of Staff stressed the military value of the canal, "It is militarily unacceptable to the United States and N.A.T.O. for this [canal] to be controlled by a power which is hostile or potentially hostile to the Western Powers" (*FRUS The Suez Crisis* 1990, 265; see also 117–18).

Thus the Americans certainly did not see the nationalization of the canal as a positive development. Why, then, did they not fully support the British and French in their military response? Numerous answers to this question have been proposed, but the one that appears most convincing can be found in statements made by Dulles and Eisenhower on the United States position on decolonization. On June 1, 1953, returning from a tour of the Middle East, Dulles stated that:

I am convinced that the United States position has become unnecessarily ambiguous in this matter [colonialism]. The leaders of the countries I visited fully recognize that it would be a disaster if there were any break between the United States and Great

Britain and France. They don't want this to happen. However, without breaking from the framework of Western unity, the Western powers can gain rather than lose from an orderly development of self-government. I emphasize, however the word orderly. Let none forget that the Kremlin uses extreme nationalism to bait the trap by which it seeks to capture the dependent peoples. *Documents on International Affairs 1953*, 264.

In his address to the nation on October 31, 1956, Eisenhower put the difference between the United States and its allies in terms of the UN, stressing that the United States believed strongly in the rule of law (*Documents on International Affairs 1956*, 265–69). While the British, French, and many others questioned the United States commitment to the UN, especially in light of its bypassing of it in other contexts, Eisenhower's belief that the British and French were acting outside the bounds of internatinal law played an important role in the United States' refusal to act with its traditional allies (Bowie 1974).

But, the British believed that the UN was not necessarily the place through which international norms should be protected.[6] And this refusal to act along with the United States led to some of the more serious complications of the intervention, and, in fact, was the major factor in the failure of the intervention as a whole. This failure to act together was surprising for a number of reasons: Eden and Eisenhower had been friends prior to the intervention, and even remained so after; the United States had similar strategic concerns as the British; and the United States believed that the British process of decolonization was working well, unlike the French process. How then does such a failure come about?

It is based on the clash of the two political visions found in the leaderships of the two states. We find a hint of this clash in the following passage from Eden's memoirs, in which he describes the American style of guidance for the developing world:

In her [United States] judgment, there is nothing wrong in expending large sums of capital on the development of a country and deriving much gain from the process, the American companies or individuals accepting no responsibility for the administration of the country. . . . This practice can also have unexpected consequences which seem less laudable. It remains a fact that two of the more backward countries in the Middle East and Africa, Saudi Arabia and Liberia, are also two where American interests play a conspicuously large part. Much of the sparing between the United States and Great Britain on colonial issues could certainly be removed if more was understood of the record of this country in the colonial sphere, especially since the beginning of the century. But the orderly development of self-government in an important territory, like Malaya or Nigeria, is not sensational news; a riot in Cyprus is. As a consequence, understanding grows slowly. (Eden 1960, 559)

Eden tried to make a peace offering to the United States in this statement, but it reveals quite clearly his view on American policy toward the developing world. Like the French (cf. Luethy and Rodnick 1956), Eden believed that the Americans were more interested in the economic benefits to be gained from the developing world than in the moral duty of leading them to self-government. Eden is critical of Saudi Arabia throughout his story of Suez, claiming that, thanks to American weapons and money, the Saudis were able to spread opposition to the Baghdad Pact and any form of British influence in the Arab world (Eden 1960, 649).[7]

Lloyd also stresses the difference between the United States and Great Britain. He claims that Robert Murphy, the United States special envoy who first came to London for the tripartite talks, was unable to understand the gravity of the situation. Lloyd argues that the United States failed to act promptly in either of the world wars and the failure to act here was a further example of how the British had to act on their own to create an orderly world. Others agree with this evaluation of the United States, especially in parliament. Even before the crisis began, one member of parliament was lamenting the existence of "Anglophobe American Ambassadors" in the Middle East who were undermining Britain's political position in the area (*Documents on International Affairs 1956*, 62). In the debate of September 12, one member argued that the United States government was under the influence of certain "economic interests" in its failure to support British action (558 H. C. Deb. 50). Richard Crossman, an influential member of the Labour Party, pointed out that "Nasser watches America very carefully" and that the lack of American support will allow him to ignore British demands (90). And one Conservative member stated quite baldly on September 13 that "I am very suspicious of United States diplomacy in the Middle East. I am not against Anglo-American cooperation, but I do not want to see our great country, for which I have an undying affection, made a pawn of in American diplomacy" (192).

But did this conflict between the United States and British visions of the Arab world and Nasser have an effect on the intervention? Quite clearly it did. The Americans used their financial power to dissuade the British from their course in the Suez, since "Sterling was dependent on the dollar as Britain was dependent on the United States. Neither the currency nor the country could go it alone" (Kunz 1990, 218). Because the British had sought to make the sterling convertible in order that it might be the currency of the Commonwealth, it was now victim to American financial and economic power. As Kunz explains, the American financial position of 1956 was far more powerful than it is today, since at that time it controlled the only international currency, the dollar. Thus, when the British saw dollars rapidly being drained from the Bank of England to fund the operation in the Suez, they had no other recourse but to go to the United States for aid. When the Eisenhower administration refused this aid, the British had no where else to turn.

The United States also blocked the British in the United Nations. On October 31, the British and French had sent messages to both the Egyptians and Israelis asking them to withdraw from a ten-mile zone around the canal, which they had discussed earlier with the Israelis. On November 2 the United States introduced Resolution 997 into the General Assembly, asking that all parties halt hostilities and that "all Member states refrain from introducing military goods" into the conflict (*Documents on International Affairs 1956*, 271). In so doing, the United States officially distanced itself from the joint British and French action, a course they had been recommending against for the past three months. The combination of the economic threats and the lack of public support prevented the British from continuing their actions, and on November 6 Eden told Eisenhower that he would end the intervention; that same day, Eden convinced Mollet to halt the operation.

Clearly, then, the American resistance to the action led to its abrupt end. But what caused the American resistance? The Americans had similar strategic, and even moral, concerns about Nasser's seizure of the canal. They did not believe that allowing Nasser to control the canal on his own was in accordance with the interests of the Western Powers. I have argued thus far that part of this resistance came from a clash between the American and British national purposes. But a further element contributed to the resistance, one that reveals how actions from within the target state contribute to the failure of an intervention.

That further element was Arab opinion, which the United States took very seriously at the time. In a White House meeting of July 31, Allen Dulles, the head of the CIA and brother of John Foster Dulles, argued that while opposition by the Egyptian military would be light in an intervention, "the problem of pacifying the area would be extremely difficult," (*FRUS The Suez Crisis* 1990, 65). This comment might not indicate much about American views of Egyptian opinion, except for the fact that the CIA had two agents working closely with Nasser, Kermit Roosevelt and Miles Copeland (Copeland 1969). These agents had become an important pipeline of information between the Egyptians and the CIA, and they had informed Allen

Dulles of the importance of Egyptian opinions about Western control of the canal. Dulles' advice played an important role in the development of United States policy, due to his institutional position and relationship with his brother, and such advice would undoubtedly have played a key role in the American decision to seek a peaceful resolution to the crisis.

On October 19, the two Dulles brothers, along with Kermit Roosevelt, met to discuss the "situation in Egypt" (*FRUS The Suez Crisis* 1990, 745–6). Undoubtedly at this meeting Roosevelt informed the Secretary of Nasser's beliefs and attitudes concerning the French and British provocation. Such information would obviously play an important role in the development of the American attitudes, demonstrating the importance of Arab political opinion in the creation of American resistance. As Eisenhower himself asked in a meeting at the White House after the British and French had begun bombing Egypt, "How could we possibly support Britain and France if in doing so we lose the whole Arab world?" (910).

Finally, one of the most important influences on American policy in the Arab world came from Saudi Arabia. Discussions not revealed in most histories of American participation can be found in the FRUS volume published in 1990 which detail the American-Saudi discussion. On August 20, the American ambassador in Saudi Arabia was informed that King Saud had certain views on the situation that may help in its peaceful resolution (*FRUS The Suez Crisis* 1990, 246). The Administration felt this message important enough to send a special envoy to the Saudis, and on August 21 Robert Anderson began meetings with various Saudi officials in an attempt to gauge their opinion. In conversations over the next five days, it appears that the Saudis played an important role in revealing to the Americans that an attempt to develop a Users Association would not be acceptable to the Egyptians, or to the Arab world (287–94). As Prince Feisal said in response to a question of who would be on the advisory commission charged with operating the canal:

> Even if operation of the Canal is separate and independent [from the sovereignty of Egypt], the mere fact of putting foreign states on this Board I believe would be considered intervention in the affairs of Egypt. (294)

Thus, at the moment when the first London Conference was taking place, in which the users were trying to put together a formula to run the canal, the Saudis were playing an important role in indicating to the United States that such a commission could not simply be run by "foreign states," but would have to respect Egyptian control of the canal.

Clearly the concern of the American policy makers with Saudi opinion relied on the oil investments held by American companies in Saudi

Arabia. But this does not diminish the fact that the Saudi ability to speak for the Egyptians and to convince the Americans of their mistake in pursuing the Users Association played an important role in the American resistance to the British action. Arab politics, especially in the 1950s, was not separated into discrete state entities, but was awash with the Arab nationalism of which Nasser was the champion. And even though the Saudis were never strong supporters of Arab nationalism, at this time they did believe that an infringement on the sovereignty of one Arab country was an infringement on the sovereignty of them all. In other words the Saudis, the strongest opponents of Nasser in the Arab world, came to his defense by convincing the Americans to abandon attempts to force the Egyptians to conform to Western ideas on how to run the canal.

The American resistance to the British action played a key role in ending the intervention. That resistance derived from two sources: the clash between the American and British political presences, and the clash between the British political presence and a more general Arab resistance. Each of these forms of resistance contributed to the American decision to block the British in financial markets and in the UN. And in these forms of resistance, we see how the politics of an intervention can prevent its ethical goals from being realized.

Linked to the belief that only Great Britain could properly understand and defend international norms, the British did not believe that the United Nations should play a role in resolving the conflict. As noted in the previous section, the British had developed an ethic of international affairs that held that the UN was not the place in which international morality would be best protected because it had been taken over by the "bacillus of nationalism," in the words of Eden. Thus the government did not see the UN as a vehicle that could successfully remove Nasser from the canal. Part of that concern was one that returns in debates over the United States intervention in Somalia; that the UN simply is unable, due to its lack of a military force, to accomplish any police actions. But a more important part of the refusal to use the UN derived from the British belief that only a country that had fought to preserve the peace in Europe and had been leading the developing countries to self-government understood enough about world affairs to know how to handle a dictator like Nasser. Thus, the British government used the UN, especially the Security Council, as a forum in which to argue for their position, but not as a means by which to solve the conflict.

But in Great Britain itself, the UN was not only seen as the home of developing countries' nationalisms. In fact, many saw in the UN a means by which to solve exactly the type of conflict that the Suez Crisis had created. Great Britain had been one of the leading countries in the development of the League of Nations, and many of the strongest proponents of collective security had been prominent intellectual and political figures in Great Britain, such as Gilbert Murray, Alfred Zimmern, and David Davies. These "idealists," along with Americans like James Shotwell and Nicholas Murray Butler, had helped develop the League of Nations, which, after the American refusal to join, had largely been supported by British leadership (see Smith 1986, 54–67). Thus there remained in Great Britain a rich vein of support for international organizations, and the UN was given the same kind of support that had been given to the League. More importantly in the context of the Suez crisis, the Labour Party had become one of the strongest supporters of the UN. Hugh Gaitskill's speech on August 2, in which he seemed to support the Eden government's initial reactions to the nationalization of the canal, and in which he had compared Nasser to Hitler, ended with the following:

> While force cannot be excluded, we must be sure that the circumstances justify it and that it is, if used, consistent with our belief in, and our pledges to, the Charter of the United Nations and not in conflict with them. (*Documents on International Affairs* 1956, 137)

This last sentence was to become a point of contention between Gaitskill and the Conservative members of Parliament in mid-September, when the Labour Party had become much less enthusiastic about the line of aggressive action the Eden government had been pursuing. Gaitskill sought to emphasize the final line of his speech, while the Tories sought to remind him of his comparisons between Hitler and Nasser and his seemingly tacit approval of the use of force (558 H. C. Deb. 1–159).

What the difference between Labor and Conservative parties really entailed was a disagreement about what constitutes the political presence of Great Britain on the world stage, a political presence that depended on divergent readings of the history of British support for collective security. For while the Labour and Conservative parties did have ideological differences, those differences did not seem to be part of the conflict; the socialist leanings of the Labour Party seemed to have very little impact with their insistence on British respect for the UN Charter. Thus the difference between the two parties was about politics, in the sense I have been using that term throughout this book; a difference over what constitutes the political presence of a state agent in world politics. For the Labour Party that presence equaled a Great Britain that remained true to its traditional support of collective security and support for international law even when it did not conform to British interests. For the Conservative Party that presence equaled a Great Britain that defined international law and morality, and that used the UN only in contexts in which it supported those distinctly British norms.

Eden believed that the "The United Nations today is steeped in anti-colonial prejudice. Colonialism is a subject on which it will neither hear reason nor act reasonably" (Eden 1960, 438). The point was perhaps best articulated by Julian Amery, leader of the Suez Group:

> I know that we did what we did against the Security Council, against the General Assembly, but I confess that I have never shared the view of the Archbishop of Canterbury that the Apostolic succession has somehow descended on the members of the Security Council. I was indeed a little shocked to find the fervour with which—in all sincerity I know—a number of hon. Members opposite have almost transferred their allegiance to the United Nations organization. It is the first time since the Reformation that a substantial body of opinion in England has believed it should take orders from an authority outside this country. I take the view that the spirit of the United Nations is very important, I think far more important than the Charter; and it seems to me that the spirit enjoined on us the responsibility to stop the war and to promote a settlement. The fact that we were an interested party only strengthened our right to do it. Interested parties, after all, have the greatest responsibilities. (560 H. C. Deb. 830–1)

The "greatest responsibilities" devolve upon certain countries, and Great Britain was certainly one of them according to Amery. Furthermore, and more importantly, the United Nations cannot be the "authority" that dictates to the state of Great Britain what its policies ought to be. In fact, the British must be able to help the United Nations interpret its own charter, in light of its traditional role as protector of international society. Another Conservative member pointed out that the world is "disunited as never before" and that this lack of unity requires a strong political presence like Great Britain (794). And one member held that only by means of the British and French action could the United Nations police force have been created (769). Finally, Harold Macmillan pointed out that the British violated a number of international laws in declaring war on Hitler in 1939, but that obligations to "literal" readings of international law are subordinate to the moral obligations of a country (689–90).

The Labour Party, on the other hand, sought to portray Great Britain as a defender of the type of international law found in the United Nations. Gaitskill in his speech of September 12, in which he gave the first public indication of the disagreement between the Labour and Conservative parties on this issue, said

I realise, of course we all do, that the United Nations is imperfect and not yet the world authority which we, at least, would like to see it become, but the real issue before us today is a fundamental one. It is whether we wish, as a country, to create that world authority or whether wish to relapse into international anarchy. Every motive—self respect, self-interest, our responsibility for world leadership, our membership of the Commonwealth, our alliances—all these we should stand by our pledges to the United Nations honestly and fairly and, by our restraint and our patience, set an example for the world. (558 H. C. Deb. 32)

For Gaitskill and the Labour Party Great Britain must be "an example for the world" in its support for the United Nations. Only by acting in accordance with the international community could the British political presence on the world stage fulfill its "responsibility for world leadership."

The lack of agreement between the Labour and Conservative Parties on the role of the UN and the responsibility of Great Britain to use the UN to solve the crisis contributed decisively to the failure of the intervention. Nasser himself told one journalist "But I do not intend to fight them. I intend to stand back and wait for world opinion to save me," (Moncrieff 1966, 45). Nasser further declared "How can I declare war against a nation, half of it backing Eden, and the other half in the streets and Trafalger Square objecting to him" (Hewedy 1990, 167). Clearly, Nasser's strategy worked, not only in terms of world opinion but also in terms of British public opinion. By not responding with angry rhetoric or hostile force, Nasser was able to present his position as a victim of colonialism, thus undermining the political presence of Britain and France as peacekeepers.

Furthermore, the British resistance to using the UN prevented the British from coming to an agreement with the Egyptians in mid-October when they brought their case before the Security Council. At those meetings, and more importantly, at meetings in the office of Secretary General Dag Hammerskjold, the Egyptian foreign minister, Mahmoud Fawzi had offered some important concessions to Lloyd and Christian Pineau, the French Foreign Minister. Robert Bowie reports that in these meetings, from October 9 through 12, Fawzi and Lloyd seemed ready to agree to a resolution of the crisis (Bowie 1974, 49). Lloyd himself believed that some agreement could have been possible, based on reports from American sources (*FRUS The Suez Crisis* 1990, 740–2). But instead, Eden, prodded by the French and supported by Tory backbenchers who refused to see the UN as a place where such conflicts could be solved, refused to deal with Fawzi and planned a war with the French and Israelis.

This conflict between the Labour and Conservative Parties undermined the intervention by preventing the Eden government from acting with the full force of the nation behind it. With rallies led by the Labour Party being held within earshot of the Cabinet meetings, and with public opinion equally divided, the Eden government could not assert itself against the resistance of the United States, United Nations, and combined Arab world. The belief that the UN was not the proper forum for solving this conflict also prevented the British and French from coming to an agreement with the Egyptians during the Security Council debates of mid-October, at a time when the Egyptian delegation seemed close to agreement. Thus debates over what constituted the British political presence, especially in relation to the United Nations, greatly contributed to the failure of the intervention. As General Sir Charles Keightley pointed out some years later

> The one overriding lesson of the Suez operation is that world opinion is now an absolute principle of war and must be treated as such. (Kyle 1990, 130)

As in the British intervention in Russia in 1918, the British actions against Egypt in 1956 provide us insights into the practice of intervention. The belief that the Egyptians were creating havoc in the Middle East, Africa, and the entire developing world led the British to believe that by destroying the Egyptian military and political presence they would truly be able to help the process of decolonization, to which they were at that time fully committed. But as they tried to help the developing world become a productive part of international society, they were unprepared to do this without playing a role that accorded with their prestige. Chester Cooper, the American liaison to the British Intelligence staff at the time of the intervention, perhaps best expressed this political aspect of the British intervention in the following quote:

> Men of influence in Britain during the 1950s were those whose early lives were fashioned in the knowledge certain that Britain was *Great* Britain. Everything they had learned and experienced and fought for convinced them that their nation still had a responsibility, indeed a destiny, to play a major role in shaping the course of the twentieth century, just as had the 19th. With the passing of the Empire, it now fell to the Commonwealth, with the British at its head, to lead the way. (Cooper 1978, 263–4)

The norm of intervention that drove the British was a sense of responsibility not just for the Egyptians, but for the whole world, a world that they felt they needed to order. But as a state agent, it was essential that that order was British, and that it revealed the presence of *Great* Britain.

FRENCH INTERVENTION IN EGYPT

French actions in Egypt sprang from and reflected many of the same normative concerns as the British. But the French actions were shaped by their distinct national history and purpose. That distinct history gave to the French intervention more of a humanitarian cast than the British actions. This is not to say that the French are more humanitarian than the British in their history or foreign policy; rather, it reflects the specific understanding of humanitarianism that manifests itself in a military intervention. As we shall see, that humanitarianism did not mean feeding the starving or halting a civil war but was an attempt to save what the French saw as a victimized community—the Jews who had suffered through the Holocaust. The French belief that Israel was surrounded by hostile Arab states and had been abandoned by the United States and Great Britain, coupled with their belief in themselves as the defenders of the oppressed around the world, led them to believe that they needed to rescue Israel. Mollet told one author that "Et en 1956, j'ai sauvé Israël" (Bar-Zohar 1964, 163). This conception of saving a beleaguered state is further explored in the next chapter, which details the United States intervention in Somalia, and how the notion of humanitarianism does not just involve saving people but also includes saving states. A similar conception can be seen in the French construction of its action as an attempt to save a state from destruction.

Moreover, the colonial norms that motivated and sustained the French intervention diverged in a number of important ways from the British ones. The French relationship to Algeria was qualitatively different than the British connections to Jordan and Iraq; the French believed, as an editor of one of France's leading newspapers at the time of the crisis described it, that Algeria was "the only part of the empire which is French soil; a part of metropolitan France." Thus, when Nasser stirred up the rebels in Algeria, many in the French community saw it as "if our frontiers were invaded again" (Luethy and Rodnick 1956, 64). The colonial norm that supported the French intervention, then, had a much different set of moral and political connotations.

La Mission Civilisateur

Many factors entered into the decision to topple Nasser. One of the most important, however, was the belief that Nasser, and the pan-Arabism he helped create, was behind the rebel actions in Algeria. But why did they see Nasser as the font of all their troubles in the area? The threats to Algeria and the Middle East in general were part of a larger French notion of its role as a colonizer. That notion revolved around a particular French understanding of the relationship between its culture and foreign policy; that is, the foreign policies of the French nation were focused not just on achieving a set of strategic goals but also on spreading the wisdom and culture of France. To save the Middle East and Algeria from Nasser was to demonstrate the advantages of French culture and government over the challenges posed to it by Arab nationalism.

French colonial policy revolved around two key themes: assimilation and culture. One theorist, comparing British and French colonial policy, writes, "The French, in contrast to the British, and all other nations in Europe, actually tried in recent times to combine *ius* with *imperium* and to build an empire in the old Roman sense. They alone at least attempted to develop the body politic of the nation into an imperial political structure . . . " (Arendt 1967, 128–9). That is, the French sought not simply to administer territories for the benefit of the people within them, as the British did, but instead sought to incorporate those territories into the French nation, to create a worldwide body politic that would manifest the ideals of French civilization and culture. This included making colonial peoples into citizens of France, as long as they would accept the French language and culture as the norm in their communities.

The policy of assimilation created two tendencies. On the one hand, it led to a greater equality between the peoples of the metropole and those of the colony, both the natives and the *colons*. The French were particularly proud of the fact of their conceptions of political equality, conceptions that led one French Minister of Colonies to write:

> Do most people realize that in Senegal, just as in the Antilles, all the Negroes vote? In Algeria, an Arab who renounces certain of his special privileges can become a French citizen; a few years later he can be elected to office just like a citizen of Paris or Marseilles. . . . No discrimination exists between the white Frenchman and the colored Frenchman. Perhaps the unknown soldier who rests under the *Arc de Triomphe* is a colored Frenchman. (Stern 1944, 12)

This sense of equality between the natives of France and the natives of the colonies created in the French colonial ideology a strong sense that their empire was truly for the benefit of its subject races. But the flip side to this conception was that any alternative culture could not compete with the French. The French may have come to learn about past civilizations in their colonial efforts, as Napoleon discovered in Egypt, but they certainly did not believe they would find any living culture which could stand with their own. This particularly French colonial ideology served to diminish any sense of dialogue between the French and their colonies. As Victor Hugo wrote in 1847 "Nous ne sommes pas venues en Afrique pour en rapporter l'Afrique mais pour y apporter l'Europe" (Rey-Goldzeiguer 1991, 405). Thus the French colonial ideology strove to create an equality between the colony and the metropole by assimilating those communities it had colonized. The second important theme of French colonial ideology was that of spreading French culture and civilization, that is, *la mission civilisateur*. The following quote perhaps best expresses that norm in its different manifestations:

> The main, moral, goal [is] to liberate populations subjected for centuries to the Black Flags, the Siamese despots, Turkish domination or the slave merchants of Central Africa, and to raise them to the civilization of Pascal, Claude, Bernanr, Pasteur, Branly, . . . The economic goal is to bring the raw materials buried for centuries in the African or Asiatic soil and complementary to those of European France to the outside world. . . . The French political goal is to create a homogeneous body of one hundred million people capable of resisting all the forces of aggression to which France has been exposed since the time of Charlamagne. . . . The philosophical goal is to enable free thinkers and the faithful of all religions—the Gospels, the law of Mahomet, the books of Confucius—to live under human laws, in an atmosphere of concord and respect for all peoples. (Stern 1944, 263–4)

This quote, written in the midst of World War II, is revealing on a number of counts. First, it reveals the French conception of its role as colonizer as freeing previously subject populations by incorporating them into the French political system. Second, it reveals the French belief that its technological and economic wisdom is a moral boon to the people of the colonies; without French knowledge, these populations could never develop their own natural resources. And third, a point that is explored as follows in the analysis of Algeria, there is the sense that by defending the colonies, the French are not simply defending helpless others, but are in fact defending France itself. By implicitly linking threats to the colonies to threats to France, this conception of its empire reveals how an attack on the colonies was not unlike an attack on France itself.

French colonial history began in the Renaissance and encompasses a vast territory (see Meyer et al. 1990). This section focuses in particular on French actions in Algeria and Egypt. Not only were these the two most important historical legacies operating during the intervention, they also display some of the important aspects of French colonial policy. In 1798, Napoleon Bonaparte, at that time a rising general in the French army, acting under the authority of the French Directorate, embarked on an expedition for Egypt. The general proposed the expedition as a means to "defeat England by seizing Egypt, thus seizing the direct route to the Indies" (Tarrade 1990, 297). He landed at Alexandria on June 1, 1798 and conquered Egypt in only six weeks. But the British soon struck back, and the French lost their control of Egypt by August 1801. Despite the military defeat, the French effort in Egypt was seen as a success. For in undertaking the expedition, Napoleon had prepared it

> à la manière des derniers voyages d'exploration maritime avec la participation d'environ deux cents savants, écrivains, artistes et techniciens et elle apportera aux pays conquis les progrès administratifs et techniques de la France révolutionnaire. (Tarrade 1990, 296)

In bringing "scholars and artists" he hoped to uncover the secrets of Egypt; but in "carrying to the country the techniques of the French revolution" he also hoped to spread the wisdom of the French civilization. It was this dual cultural policy that underlined French colonial policy; on the one hand, drawing forth from the colony information and new insights (largely about ancient history), but on the other hand spreading the "modern" knowledge of France around the world. The French emphasized that their establishment of the *Institut d'Egypte* contributed to the study of Egyptology and the modernization of Egypt (Stern 1944, 103–6). While the British may have used Egypt as a base to advance into India, France sought to create a cultural and moral presence in Egypt that would benefit not only the Egyptians, but the entire world as well. For in fact the dual nature of French colonial policy in regards to culture, both drawing from colonies and giving them French culture, allowed the French to claim that their colonial policy not only benefited the conquered lands, but also allowed them to believe that they were providing a service to the world by uncovering the wisdom of these ancient societies.[8]

In accordance with this point, the French believed that not only did their discoveries in Egypt contribute to a greater understanding of ancient civilizations, they also believed that their presence in Egypt provided the world with one of the most important engineering feats of all time, the creation of the Suez Canal. Napoleon's engineers had considered a canal, but did not believe it was possible due to technical problems. But in 1855, Ferdinand de Lesseps, a French civil servant, proposed the idea of a canal, encouraged by the belief that such a canal would lead "à une union de forces entre l'Occident, principe mâle, selon eux, et Orient, principe femmelle" (Azeau 1964, 20). The idea soon caught on throughout France, where it was seen as an example of French ingenuity and brilliance, a means by which Western knowledge could advance the cause of civilization throughout the world. Lesseps founded a public company in 1858, and work began in 1859. Halted at times by political hindrances from within both Egypt and France, the canal was completed in 1869. Celebrations ensued, in which most of the European powers were invited to Egypt to memorialize "the most beautiful ditch in the world" (Azeau 1964, 30). Lesseps was honored as the man who brought civilization to Egypt, and the canal came to be seen as a centerpiece of international cooperation and development. Again, France was seen as a power that brought to the world a great advancement, due to its ability to draw forth from the colonial world riches that the natives would have been unable to extract themselves.

Thus, while the French political presence in Egypt was limited after 1801, it certainly saw itself as playing an important role in the scientific and technological development of both Egypt and the world. The second French colonial possession that plays an important role in this narrative is that of Algeria. Algeria also demonstrates the second main theme of French imperialism, the belief in assimilation as the way to truly provide the proper French benefits to its colonies. In the beginning of the nineteenth century, French merchant vessels in the Mediterranean were being harassed by pirates from the North African Coast. The French, British, and even newly established Americans sought to control these pirates, but to no avail. In 1830, the French attacked and began fighting to take over Tunisia, Morocco, and Algeria. The conquest was not at first welcomed by the French parliament, and from 1830 through 1840 the battle was waged in both Northern Africa and France itself. But, once the area was more securely in French control, the debate within France itself subsided. Furthermore, the conquest of Algeria came to be seen more as a means by which to overcome the humiliation of the defeats at Waterloo than as a strategic or economic move (Rey-Goldzeiguer 1991, 346). From 1840 through 1850, led by the army of General Bugeaud, the French subdued Algeria and established a colonial presence there. Up until 1871, Algeria was run by the army, but after that date it became a part of France, coming under the jurisdiction of the Department of Interior. Numerous attempts were made to further integrate Algeria into the French nation, including a bill brought by Leon Blum before the parliament in 1936 that would have given all Algerians automatic French citizenship (Gordon 1966, 34). But in 1954, Algerian Arabs sought to break away from France, leading to a civil war from 1954 through 1962, when France officially granted Algeria its independence (Agernon 1990, 507–32).

French public opinion and leaders at the time of the Suez intervention continued to exhibit remnants of both "*la mission civilisateur*" and assimilation. In relation to Egypt, the French believed that their role in creating the Suez canal gave them a special concern with both it and Egypt itself. Abel Thomas, a defense ministry bureaucrat whose history of the intervention provides some key insights into its inception and execution, argued that France has always had the best interests of Egypt at heart in its Middle East policies:

> Depuis que Bonaparte avait exterminé les janissaires turcs qui maintenaient l'Egypte en esclavage, la France avait envoyé Monge et Champollion dans Vallée des Rois, l'ingénieur Jubin qui implantait le coton, Ferdinand de Lesseps qui trouvait l'isthme de Suez à la demande du government egyptien, et les lycées français de la Maison laïque qui s'implantaient à Alexandrie, au Caire, à Heliopolis. (Thomas 1978, 264)

Providing engineers, schools, and archeologists, France had greatly improved Egyptian society, according to this understanding. Furthermore, the French believed that Nasser was undermining not only their presence in Northern Africa, but was hurting the Egyptian people themselves. Douglas Dillon, the United States ambassador to France, reporting on a conversation with Louis Joxe, the Secretary General of the French Foreign Ministry, claimed that the:

> French felt that western action should be directed as much as possible against Nasser as an irresponsible individual dangerous to his own people as well as to the rest of the world. The West should make a real effort to differentiate Nasser from Egypt and the Egyptian people . . . (*FRUS The Suez Crisis* 1990, 31)

While such comments do not evidence a strong humanitarian concern for the Egyptian people on the part of the French, they do indicate that there was some sense among leaders that the French had helped Egypt in the past and that it was Nasser, not the "people," who were the enemies.

But even more important than the aid that had been provided to the Egyptian people themselves, the French believed that their presence in Egypt had contributed much to the world. One Socialist deputy argued that the canal was a "French creation" (Luethy and Rodnick 1956, 67). An editor of one of the leading journals argued that "It was a great French achievement which France gave to the world. She was right in making a hero of Lesseps. He created something truly noble, and something France could be very proud to present to the world as one of the contributions of French civilization" (63). In his speech before the first London conference, Christian Pineau, the French foreign minister, reminded his audience that ". . . c'est la France qui a conçu et réalisé le Canal contre tous les scepticismes," (*Documents Diplomatiques* 1956, 255). And while the thrust of the

French arguments during the crisis centered around the international status of the canal, they would often revert to the claim that the canal was a French creation, a creation that contributed greatly to the improvement of both the Middle East and the world as a whole.

The French colonial ethic in Egypt, then, exhibits the sense of "*la mission civilisateur*," a sense that without the French presence the colony and the world would be greatly impoverished. The French presence in Algeria, however, exhibited another aspect of that ethic, that of assimilation. In terms of the Suez intervention, this aspect of the ethic manifested itself as a belief that a threat to Algeria was a threat to France itself. In November 1954, Algerian rebels, with both moral and financial support from Egypt, began a more aggressive campaign to remove France from Algeria. When Guy Mollet came to power in January 1956, he stressed that he wished to bring an end to "cette guerre imbécile" (*Documents Diplomatiques* 1956, 316). Mollet, a socialist, appointed a moderate governor of Algeria in January 1956, but when he visited Algeria in February of that year, Mollet was attacked by the white colons who believed that the appointment was intended to signal a French pullout from Algeria. Sufficiently chastened by "l'affaire des tomates" Mollet appointed Robert Lacoste instead, a more hardline administrator.

Thus, in the beginning of 1956, the Mollet government was faced with a rebellion in France that was being supported by Nasser. What was the nature of this threat to Algeria? Why, having just allowed both Morocco and Tunisia to gain their independence (cf. Agernon 1990, 402–8), did the French leadership believe it should fight to hold on to Algeria? The French clearly believed that their presence in Algeria had helped create a better society. Perhaps the best expression of the sentiment that drove this belief comes from a scholar who had close ties to Mollet and other important socialists:

Tunis and Morocco were independent states when France took them under her wing as protectorates. There were sovereigns there going back centuries. There were institutions and local government and local officials receiving their orders from the Bey or the Sultan. But what was there in Algeria when the French took over in 1830? Nothing. No sovereign. No laws. No institutions of any kind that united the anarchist and chaotic conglomeration of villages and poverty-stricken peasants that France united and built up into a territorial unit under the guidance of France. It was France that gave borders to this territory, gave it existence and spirit. Algeria is a monument to French ingenuity. It was France and only France which raised it from the dust and gave it life. France fathered it and mothered it. Without France there

would have been nothing. And more than one million Frenchmen have gone there to make their homes and to raise its economic level to that of France. Algeria is not a partisan, political
affair; it is a national one; and interference in Algerian affairs by
any one is considered grave interference in French domestic
affairs. (Luethy and Rodnick 1956, 79–80)

Guy Mollet himself, explaining the benefits of French colonialism in
Northern Africa, wrote:

Nos ingenieurs, nos specialistes, se sont adaptés aux techniques du
désert, ont créé des techniques nouvelles, ont montré au monde le
visage d'une France jeune et dynamique. (Mollet 1958, 52)

Algeria, then, was not simply another colony; it was an example of what
the French could do, a moral example of how the French could turn a place
without borders or life into an economically viable and politically strong
state. Once again we hear echoes of different types of interventionary
ethics in these sentiments: colonial, in the discourse of parenting (recall
Eden on Jordan and Iraq); and humanitarian in the sense of saving a community from chaos. Even more interesting, just as Somalia was an attempt
to save not only a starving people, but also a "failed state," so the French
in Algeria believed they had saved a territory with no sovereignty.

As in the case of the British attitudes toward the region, these colonial
norms do not seem to be truly "norms" with positive valence we have of
this term. But if we view them as positivist facts that somehow influenced
the decision to intervene and the course of the intervention, calling them
norms does have some validity. As the intervention approached, these sentiments were to be found in a number of places. When they met on June 18
in Washington, Christian Pineau emphasized to John Foster Dulles that
Algeria was part of France in the same way that the states in the United
States were part of the American nation; "l'Algérie constitue pour la
France un problème d'ordre interieur" (*Documents Diplomatiques* 1956 I,
1021). Furthermore, prior to the nationalization and the onset of the crisis,
the French had been authorized by NATO to send troops to Algeria to
quell the rebels, in March and April 1956 (328–9). The circulars and memos
from these diplomatic documents reveal a belief on the part of the French
Foreign Ministry that a threat to Algeria was not simply a threat to a
colony, but a threat to France itself, thus justifying a movement of troops
away from Europe into Africa. Jean Chauvel, the French Ambassador to
Great Britain, said to the British and Americans, "If Egypt's act went without response it would be impossible for France to pursue the struggle in
Algeria" (Vaïse 1991, 137).

Pineau claimed in his account of Suez that Algeria was not the main reason for the French action. Despite this claim, he, along with others in the Mollet government, continued to stress Nasser's support for the rebels (see August 17 statement by Pineau in London, *Documents Diplomatiques 1956* III, 255; also the meeting between Lloyd and Pineau on August 24, Vaïse 1991, 138). As Maurice Vaïse notes, Pineau himself had been to Egypt in March 1956, where Nasser had given him his word of honor that he would not support the Algerian rebels; "Given such flagrant lies, why not turn the nationalization weapons against Egypt and kill two birds with one stone, eliminate a budding dictator and settle the Algerian affair?" (Vaïse 1991, 137). And before the intervention was launched, Pineau sent a memo to the French representative at the UN, pointing out that a ship had been intercepted by the French on the way from Alexandria to Algiers, loaded with weapons, "Whereas the link between the Algerian war and the Suez intervention had long been known, here it appears as a subject of formal discussion: a striking confirmation" (138).

While Nasser's support for the rebels in Algeria gave the French reason enough to want to topple him, they also believed that his pan-Arabism was contributing to the elimination of the Western presence in the Arab world, especially the French presence. As noted, the French had previously granted independence to Morocco and Tunisia, but Nasser's radio broadcasts were hindering the development of relations between the newly sovereign states and the French. On July 31, soon after Nasser had nationalized the canal, the ambassador in Morocco reported that this action will clearly threaten "l'interdependence" between France and Morocco, especially if the challenge is not met (*Documents Diplomatiques 1956* II, 198–99). In conversations between Pineau and Dulles on August 1, Pineau claimed that:

> According to the most reliable intelligence sources we have only a few weeks in which to save North Africa. Of course, the loss of North Africa would then be followed by that of Black Africa and the entire territory would rapidly escape European control and influence. (Vaïse 1991, 137)

In a letter to President Eisenhower explaining the diplomatic notes sent to both Egypt and Israel, Mollet points out that:

> This demand is but too well justified by a long experience with failures to honor international agreements and with provocations by the Arab states in the Near East. To mention only what touches us directly, I will point out that again yesterday the Embassy of France in Amman was stoned while the French Consulate General

in Jerusalem and French cultural institutions in Aleppo were set on fire. (*FRUS The Suez Crisis* 1990, 869)

For Mollet and Pineau, these threats to French positive moral influence were emanating from Cairo.

These particurlarly French colonial attitudes were important in creating a certain amount of conflict with the British. In so doing, the political presence of the British and French, and the conflicts between them, played a key role in undermining the success of the intervention. The French were well aware of the fact that Great Britain did not look with favor upon aid from Israel as a means to defeat Nasser; when the idea of including Israel was first broached by the French to Great Britain in the early days of August, Eden refused to even consider it (Neff 1981, 289). Pineau points out that Lloyd thought the creation of Israel itself was a mistake, making cooperation with them appear unlikely (Pineau 1976, 47). And as the French assiduously courted the Israelis to include them on terms that would be beneficial to both in the actual intervention, the British only officially became part of the meetings at Sèvres.

The moment at which the British refusal to treat the Israelis as equals became a problem for the French was in the actual conduct of the operations. I have already described how this British political position helped to undermine the possibilities for cooperation early on. What I want to stress here is the French interpretation of this resistance to cooperate. The French believed that the British political position *vis-à-vis* the Israelis prevented the actual military operation from succeeding. By this stage, much of the joint British and French military plans had already been put in place, and the introduction of the new role as "peacekeepers" severely hampered the well-developed plans of the participants. André Martin, Deputy Chief of Operations for the French during the intervention, argued that:

> There was especially a quasi-morbid hostility to the Israelis in the British High Command on Cyprus. These factors inhibited making the only logical decision: putting aside the prepared plan in order to respond to the unstoppable Israeli advance towards the Canal. . . . On the evening of November 3 we could have been in Ismailia, but the operations plan, concocted so scientifically, had not taken into account the difficulties of the diplomatic situation and the limited room for maneuver. (Martin 1990, 57)

Jaques Baeyens, the diplomatic liaison at Cyprus for the French, also attributes many of the problems of the military operation to the anti-Israeli attitude. He notes that the British appointed a military leader who had fought the Haganah in Palestine, making him unlikely to cooperate with the Israelis in battle (Baeyens 1976, 62). He also argues that the British commanders "ignored the Israelis" (76). He concludes that this lack of coordination between the British, French, and Israelis fundamentally undermined the operation as a whole, just as a similar lack of cooperation had led to the fall of Dien Ben Phu in Indochina (89–90). And Thomas argued that the French could have succeeded better with the Israelis alone than with the British (Thomas 1978, 116).

Finally, the British not only refused to cooperate with the Israelis, they appeared to hesitate throughout the operation, at least in the French interpretation of events. In a telegram to Pineau on October 1, Jean Chauvel, the French Ambassador to Great Britain, claims the British, especially Lloyd, were wavering in their support for action against Egypt (*Documents Diplomatiques* 1956 II, 483). This impression was only reinforced when Lloyd appeared close to a compromise at the United Nations when he met with the Egyptian Ambassador and the Secretary General. All these impressions were confirmed for the French when Anthony Head, the British Minister of Defense arrived on Cyprus only days before the launch of the intervention. Head attempted to alter the battle plan to avoid civilian casualties, "précaustions humaintaires" that the French viewed with a certain amount of skepticism (Azeau 1964, 289). More importantly, Head's attempts to alter the plans at the last minute further confused the operation and helped to unsettle both the French and British military leaders (Martin 1990; Baeyens 1976).

The British, while allied with the French in the overthrow of Nasser, demonstrated a hesitation and lack of cooperation that contributed to the French view of them as part of the reason for the failure of the overall operation. That hesitation was linked to the traditional antagonism between the British and French in the Middle East in the official French version of the events at Suez:

> La Grande-Bretagne a longtemps joué contre nous dans le monde arabe. Elle s'est montré hesitante dans l'action, maladroite dans l'exécution et de propos peu fermes à l'heure de l'épreuve. (*Documents Diplomatiques* 1956 III, 272)

Thus the conflicting political policies of Great Britain and France hindered the operation of the intervention at its moment of proof, and those policies derived from the conflicting political presences of these two powers in the world.

Comment Israël fut sauvé

Abel Thomas entitled his book about the Suez intervention *How Israel was Saved*,[9] indicating the second overarching norm behind the French action in the Suez. It was in fact the French who first pursued the connections with Israel over a joint intervention, based on contacts already in place between the two defense ministries. Despite British resistance to working with Israel, the French actively pursued these contacts, resulting in meetings in September and October between French and Israeli defense officials, and culminating in the meeting at Sèvres on October 22, which finally brought the British together with the French and Israelis. Based on this meeting, it was decided that the Israelis would attack Egypt on October 31 and the British and French would impose themselves as peacekeepers soon thereafter.

While this collusion between the three parties tended to construct the Israelis as aggressors and the British and French as peacekeepers, there did exist a real sense in the French community that Israel deserved aid, and that the destruction of Nasser was necessary for Israeli survival. Although Charles de Gaulle, whose presidency inaugurated the Fifth Republic and sent France in a number of new directions in terms of foreign policy, moved French policy away from an alignment with Israel, there existed at the time of the intervention a number of factors that drew France and Israel close together. Nor were those ties all, or even mostly, strategic ones (although strategic reasons certainly existed); rather, the French were drawn to the defense of Israel for a number of ethical reasons, reasons that drew on the shared historical experiences of Jews and French citizens, at least in the eyes of French leaders. The French also tended to see Israel as a representative of humanity's atonement for its sins of anti-Semitism, and to see it destroyed would be to deny many of the ideals for which France stood. Finally, these normative links enabled the French support of Israel in the Middle East, and contributed in a number of ways to their joint attempt to topple Nasser.

One historian of the intervention, Michel Bar-Zohar, argues that the intervention could not have taken place without the links between Israel and France. And while he admits a bias in writing his account, being a "friend of both countries," he also reveals a number of important moments in the construction of their relationship. One of the most important is the story of the ship *Exodus*. In July 1947, a group of Jews from Germany wished to set sail for Palestine to help establish the new Zionist state. In their attempt to set forth from France, however, Ernest Bevin, in Paris for talks on the Marshall Plan, argued vigorously that they not be allowed to go to Palestine, since it would upset the delicate balance the British were trying to maintain between the Arab and Jewish populations. Despite these British objections the ship set sail on July 10, but the passengers were returned to France on July 20 aboard two British warships. The French, however, refused to allow them to land, leaving the passengers stranded offshore. As the British, French, and Jews argued, public sympathy for the stranded passengers built up in France. The British refused to surrender, and as a result the Jews were forced to disembark in Hamburg, Germany, on September 8, 1947.

So while the conflict did not lead to the Jews attaining their goal, it did contribute to a strong current of feeling in France in favor of the establishment of a Zionist state in Palestine. More importantly, it was the first time that the French and British had publicly disputed over Palestine, especially over Jewish immigration to Palestine (Bar-Zohar 1964, 26). Further, the French government's resistance to the British policy brought together public sympathy and French policy. For prior to this event, the Zionist cause in Palestine had already been aided by French officials, but only in a secret context (ibid.). The French refusal to recognize Israel in the UN might have appeared to undermine these links, but Bar-Zohar argues that this refusal can be attributed to the Quai d'Orsay's traditional pro-Arab policy, along with the influence of the Vatican, which sought to keep Jerusalem an international city (Bar-Zohar 1964, 36–7), and that it did not reflect the official thinking in France at the time of the intervention.

There clearly existed divisions in the French government over support for Israel (Dayan 1976, 149). The Ministry of Defense was the strongest advocate of support, while groups in the Ministry of Foreign Affairs tended to be in favor of stronger support for the Arab states. Maurice Mourgès-Manoury, the Minister of Defense, became a strong supporter of Israel, as did his deputy Abel Thomas. Thomas, whose history of intervention is dedicated to his brother who died in the resistance during the war, also links the initial French sympathy for Israel to the *Exodus* incident. He sets the context of the relationship in terms of France needing to establish a "balance of power" in the Orient through its relationship with Israel (Thomas 1978, 24). But his argument stresses the historic and moral bonds between the two countries. Thomas was instrumental in establishing contacts between the Israelis and French military leaders, including meetings in late June over arms deals and the initiation of meetings in the beginning of September to begin talks on joint action against Egypt. Meeting with Shimon Peres, Thomas describes him, and the Israeli people, in the following way:

> C'etait tout Israël qui parlait par la voix de Shimon Peres. Un peuple montrait sa formidable volonté de viver après avoir subi le plus formidable, la plus atroce holocauste d'Histoire. (Thomas 1978, 58)

Clearly, this was not just a strategic relationship.

Nor was Thomas the only French leader affected by the Israeli connection. As noted previously, Mollet argued that he had "saved Israel." In his only written account of the intervention, Mollet emphasizes the threat faced by Israel, and the importance of protecting a country created to allow escape from "des ghettos d' Europe" and "des camps de la mort" (Mollet 1958, 32). Pineau also emphasizes the fate of Israel in his published account of the intervention. Claiming that he was undecided on the intervention even up until the meeting at Sèvres, Pineau writes that it was his "concern over the fate of existence of Israel" that led him to finally decide in favor of the intervention (Pineau 1976, 131). And in describing the "tacit alliance" between Israel and France prior to the intervention, one historian points out that the French allowed the Haganah, the Zionist defense force, to establish a base in Paris in 1946 when the British forced them to leave Palestine (Crosbie 1974, 29).

But was this link that these actors felt a moral one? Or could it be explained in terms of the strategic interests that both Thomas and Pineau cite (Thomas 1978, 24; Pineau 1976, 11)? While Pineau and others claim the intervention can be explained by "l'ordre strategique," that strategic order derives in a number of important ways from the moral links between Israel and France. I have already noted the role of the Exodus in the shaping of those links. But the sympathy the Exodus plight aroused was not simply the result of an abundance of Zionists in France; rather it derived from a fundamental belief on the part of many French citizens that the Holocaust demanded the creation of a safe haven for Jews. Mollet claimed that Israel was created to save the Jews from "camps of death." And Pineau claimed that:

> Or, je reste convaincu que la destruction de l'Etat d'Israël réservait aux juifs un sort semblable à celui qu'ils ont subi à Aushwitz et autres camps d'extermination. (Pineau 1976, 133)

And in a memo sent to the French ambassador in the United States, Pineau insists that Israel cannot be allowed to disappear "pour des raisons tant humaines que politiques," (*Documents Diplomatiques* 1956 I, 316).

While many world leaders saw the creation of Israel as a means to save the Jews, why did the French feel the need to transfer that feeling into military action? For one thing, the French felt a certain amount of guilt over their participation in the Holocaust. When Moshe Dayan was presented with a military decoration in August 1954, some interpreted it as a sort of compensation for the Dreyfus affair (Bar-Zohar 1964, 69). As Andre Fontaini pointed out in a BBC interview in 1966:

> But for the public in France at large, a feeling of solidarity with Israel was explicit. Maybe we had more or less a feeling of responsibility for what happened to the Jews during the war, you know, and we felt that something was due to them. (Moncrieff 1966, 65)

But the link between the French and the Holocaust did not just revolve around guilt. Many socialists participated in the resistance, and were instrumental in saving Jews during the war. The socialist government of Guy Mollet, then, had a certain claim to being defenders of the Jews, a belief that helped sustain their actions in Suez. Bar-Zohar describes the "common past" of the Resistance and the Zionists:

> Pour les Français, cette guerre évoque toujours la Résistance, les F. F. I., les camps de concentration. Et chaque Français qui a lutté contre les nazis, qui a partagé la misère des Juifs dans les camps de concentration, qui a connu dans les F. F. I. les brigades juives combattant aux côtes des Alliés, éprouve une certaine camaraderie, une amitié envers les Juifs et leurs aspirations nationales. (Bar-Zohar 1964, 28)

In fact, many French believed that the Jews had helped them defeat the Nazis, creating not only a sense of guilt, but thanks (ibid.). Finally, this sentiment was not limited to a small group of socialists. Herbert Luethy, writing just months before the intervention, argued that the French constructed their World War II history as really being in favor of the de Gaulle government, even when they supported the Vichy during the war (Luethy and Rodnick 1956, 12). Thus the French public tended to recreate itself as supporters of the victims of the war, and actions to aid Israel were construed as a continuation of this theme. As Pineau explained "From a spiritual and political point of view the principles of the government of Israel were for us much more sympathetic than the Nasser principles" (Moncrieff 1966, 63).

Thus France found in Israel not just a strategic ally, but a moral presence in the Orient that they believed France had a responsibility to support. Indeed, many of the arguments that surrounded the intervention and later interpretations of it stress the moral responsibility France had in coming to the aid of a "young" state bound in so many ways to the traditions, ideals, and history of France itself. And while de Gaulle moved France away from such a close bond with Israel in the 1960s, there was clearly in operation at the time of the Suez intervention a belief on the part of most French leaders and citizens that Israel was a state that needed and deserved to be saved. While few Arabs or Egyptians would consider them as such, these attitudes of France toward Israel are very much ethical norms. They are grounded in a conception of France as a country that has a moral responsibility to do good for the downtrodden, in this case the Jews. Thus this element of the colonial norm has a clear ethical dimension.

The final aspect of the French ethic of intervention in the Suez concerns the link between Nasser and Hitler, a connection also made in the British context. For the British, however, the ways in which Nasser resembled

Hitler had more to do with their flagrant disregard for the norms of international society. The French, on the other hand, saw in Nasser an anti-Semitic dictator, similar to Hitler in terms of his ideological beliefs and domestic policies. Thus the French creation of Nasser as Hitler did not rely on protecting international society, as did the British, but rather on the need to save both Israel and the Near East in general from a demagogic dictator.

French parliamentary debates after the Suez nationalization roundly condemned Nasser and gave Mollet full support. Except for a few communist members, the French parliament provided much stronger support to its government than did the British parliament. One speaker, noting that Nasser was a dictator, further solidified the analogy by linking the crowds in Alexandria for Nasser's nationalization speech with the crowds of Nazis who cheered on Hitler. Nasser spoke in a voice of "fanaticism and xenophobia" leaving little doubt that he was leading a country by means of sheer demagoguery (_Documents on International Affairs_ 1956, 144). While denying that Nasser was like Hitler, one editor of a French newspaper spoke disparagingly of Arab nationalism as "nihilistic" rather than constructive (Luethy and Rodnick 1956, 69), a common description of Nazism. Another intellectual made the link more explicit:

> . . . we must use force against evil dictators if we are to expiate our past. We are convinced that Nasser is an evil dictator, and that the longer we wait, the more difficult it will be to overthrow him, as it was Hitler in 1938. Concessions to Hitler; no concessions to Nasser! That is the reasoning, which you must understand. Nasser is the symbol of all France's enemies. He stands for the actual manipulator of all France's humiliations in the past. This is why the MRPs, the Radicals, the Mendesistes, the Socialistes and a good part of the Moderate Right want a preventive war against Nasser. Our reaction to Hitler-Nasser is so great that we look upon the Israeli as the victim of the Hitler-Nasser. This we must never permit. (Luethy and Rodnick 1956, 80)

Nasser has become here a direct link to Hitler, and assumed the form not just of Hitler but of all France's past enemies! Furthermore, the threat to Israel becomes a threat to the Jews of Europe during the war, giving the French even more reason to strike back at him.

Nor were these comparisons limited only to popular culture or intellectual circles. Mollet makes the comparison to Nasser explicit, both in his public and private statements. He notes that Nasser incited the "miserable" Egyptian masses in much the same way Hitler had incited the Germans in their poverty. He also admitted that the reaction to Hitler was part of an anti-Munich sentiment, that it was "un bon reflèxe" (Mollet 1958,

31–2). In a discussion with Douglas Dillon, Mollet further argued that, although the comparison of Hitler and Nasser might appear to be banal, "he had to admit that the parallel was extremely close."

He then picked up a copy of Nasser's book "The Philosophy of the Revolution" which he had on his desk and said that he felt that all leading officials in the Dept. of State should read this book promptly if they had not done so already. He considered it a perfect parallel with "Mein Kampf." (*FRUS The Suez Crisis* 1990, 75)

In their news conference before French television in August, both Pineau and Mollet brandished Nasser's book, and continued to highlight the similarities between them. Dillon also heard a comparison between Hitler and Nasser from Louis Joxe, a French Foreign Ministry official (31).

But perhaps the clearest picture of Nasser-Hitler comes from Abel Thomas. Recall that Thomas was an important player in bringing together the Israelis and French for the joint intervention. In his history of the intervention, Thomas devotes 16 pages to drawing parallels between Nasser and Hitler (Thomas 1978, 124–39). He points out that Europe had been fooled by the "socialism" of Hitler and Mussolini, just as the Arab world was being fooled by Nasser (126). Nasser assassinated fellow leaders (127), employed former Nazis (127), and used anti-Semitism to incite the crowds (128). All these factors, according to Thomas, further encouraged the French to act against Nasser once he tipped his hand by intervening in the Suez.

As one of the first victims of Hitler, the French saw themselves as one of the few countries that could recognize a dictator and act against him accordingly. Thus the toppling of Nasser would not simply save the canal from Nasser, nor simply save the Arab world; it would, more importantly, save the world from the scourge of a dictator, a task only France could fulfill.

This view of their history, especially in their relationship with the Jews and Israel, differentiated the French from almost all other actors, at least from their perspective. One of the most important differences was with the most powerful actor in the system at that time, the United States. Herbert Luethy's essay on French foreign policy, written only months before the intervention, reveals some important aspects of the French attitude toward the United States. Many of these attitudes stem from the different roles played by the United States and France during World War II. Because of the establishment of two French governments during the war, the Vichy in France and de Gaulle's National Committee in London, the French have been forced to interpret their role in the war along two divergent tracks. Luethy argued that in 1956 the French emphasized that they were all aligned with de Gaulle, thus creating themselves as part of the resistance to the Nazis. While Luethy sees this as "myth" and "fiction" (Luethy and Rodnick 1956, 9), it is in fact part of the process of a national purpose being constructed through the reading of a particular national history (see Morgenthau 1965). Only by constructing the French nation as being in alignment with de Gaulle could France regain its role in world affairs as a representative of the "rights of man."

Even more importantly for our purposes here, the de Gaulle government-in-exile sought to recreate the French empire, especially in its colonial aspects. This included a reassertion of its rights in North Africa, the Levant, and South Asia. But because de Gaulle and his government were not considered equal partners in the war-time alliance, they had no say in many of military policies of the United States and Great Britain. And a number of the those policies infringed on what many considered to be France's traditional colonial rights. In 1943 Roosevelt met with the Sultan of Morocco and the allies accepted the "Algerian manifesto." This kind of direct interference in French colonial possessions created hostilities not only in the de Gaulle government, but among many French as well. In the Levant, the British prevented the French from having any role in the creation of the Syrian and Lebanese governments, while in Indochina the British and American victory over the Japanese prevented any French role in deliberations over the future of that area. As Luethy notes "French publications on postwar affairs in Indochina have laid particular stress in this connection upon the hostility shown by America to the re-establishment of French sovereignty in this area" (Luethy and Rodnick 1956, 4).

These events led many French leaders and citizens to paint the United States as hostile to any of their aims in foreign affairs, but especially in relation to their former colonies. Even though de Gaulle did not become president until 1960, most French leaders inherited the ambitions and hostilities formed by the period in exile. Combined with the decimation of French industrial and military power, this created a situation in which French foreign policy relied less on power calculations and more on "juridical rights, traditional claims, and historical precedents," (Luethy and Rodnick 1956, 8). While I would argue that most foreign policies are based on these historical and juridical claims, such a policy orientation in 1956 led to clashes with the United States as the most powerful victor of that war. As one French official declared, "It is no longer Perfidious Albion that we fear, but Perfidious Uncle Sam" (83).

A further important point made by Luethy concerns French "cultural policy." The French interpreted their influence in world politics through their culture. While culture plays an important role in the implementation of foreign policy of most states, the French consciously sought to create French cultural centers in their former colonies. The establishment of

"Friends of France" groups in countries around the world was part of an effort to demonstrate to the world the benefits of French political presence. This was especially true in places like Egypt and Algerian, where there persisted a belief that the French culture far surpassed the native cultures. Thus French policy was judged by its ability to spread its presence throughout the world, and the growing dominance of the United States in Africa and Asia was seen as the intrusion of a culture without the same heritage and importance as the French. Notes Luethy:

> For French intellectuals, these adverse tendencies of the modern world are summed up especially in the terms "Americanism" and "Americanization"; and are exemplified by such slogans as "coca-colonization," "Hollywood barbarity," "America degrades the mind," etc. . . . The profound "anti-Americanism" of many French intellectuals . . . is an expression of the feeling that a war is in process between hostile civilizations. The defense of French cultural influence and prestige thus becomes an important factor in the way relations with the outside world are seen. This is true not only in the case of the specialized personnel of the Foreign Office; but also for the bulk of the intellectuals—and consequently for public opinion generally, which in France is unusually sensitive to currents of thought in intellectual circles. (Luethy and Rodnick 1956, 26)

Furthermore, the French were chaffing under United States military control. They had refused to place their forces under a NATO umbrella at this time, and did not wish to appear as conforming to United States defense policy in relation to the Soviet Union or Eastern Europe. While the Mollet government also viewed the Soviets as an enemy at this time, they believed that the there were ways to deal with Russia that did not necessarily imply a complete lack of dialogue. Their resistance to NATO and policies in relation to Germany all manifested a desire to free themselves from American tutelage.

These sentiments played an important role during the Suez crisis. Christian Pineau, on meeting the United States Secretary of State for the first time in March 1956, believed that Dulles was consumed by "Chrétienté et libre entreprise" (Pineau 1976, 34). Further, Pineau saw these tenets as ones that made up American foreign policy more generally; unlike the nuanced influence of France, America exercised only its brute force in pursuit of goals that are undeveloped and even inimical to the small and medium powers (35). Abel Thomas also castigated the United States, mainly for not supporting Israel, but also more generally for failing to live up to its responsibilities to help develop the world (Thomas 1978,

52). Finally, Mollet, in an implicit criticism of the United States, argued that France was interested not only in the political independence of African and Asian states, but in their social and economic independence as well (Mollet 1958, 48).

How did these sentiments manifest themselves in the planning and execution of the intervention? In fact they manifested themselves more in terms of what the French did not do than in what they did. As noted in the previous section, Dulles had sought a number of means by which to bring about a peaceful resolution of the crisis; the holding of the August meetings, the Users Association, and the use of the United Nations. At each of these stages the French refused to conform to the policy of the United States. While the August meetings were taking place in London, the French had already begun the process of planning for military operations with both the British and the Israelis, although on separate tracks. And while Eden readily agreed to their plans, it was the French who came to London in early October and laid before Eden the plans for the tripartite action (Nutting 1967, 95). Finally, at the meetings between the French, Americans and British during the Security Council debates in October, Pineau appeared uninterested in the discussions taking place, undoubtedly because he was already aware of the joint military action about to take place, but also because he did not see the plans hatched by the United States to be of any value in solving the crisis (Bowie 1974, 49).

A further manifestation of anti-Americanism that may have played a role in the intervention concerned the French focus on Europe. While Mollet was concerned with how the intervention would affect relations with the United States, one of the more important planks of his government was the creation of stronger unity among Europeans. Both Mollet and Pineau listed this as one of the goals of their administration, and the possibility of acting alongside of Great Britain, the one holdout from European union, undoubtedly appealed to their European sense. When it became clear that the United States would not act with the two powers, rather than try to compromise with the leader of the Atlantic Alliance, the French sought to tighten the connections with Great Britain, excluding the United States from important meetings on strategy (*Documents Diplomatiques* 1956 II, 367–73).

Finally, the official French account of the Suez crisis places blame for its failure clearly at the feet of the United States. Noting that the United States has failed France in Indochina, in Algeria, and in Suez, the French concluded that "Au cours de cette crise, ils ont choisi de nous faire échoue" (*Documents Diplomatiques* 1956 III, 272). Although they sought afterwards to repair those relations, the French continued to believe that they had been betrayed at a critical stage in their relations with the United

States. And that betrayal had more to do with the conflicting presences of the United States and France than it did with any divergence in ultimate goals. We have already seen that the Americans believed that Nasser's actions could not be allowed to stand, and were not adverse to his removal. But in terms of the Suez, they refused to use force, while the French insisted upon doing so. And this clash can be attributed more to the clash of political presences than to any French propensity to use force or increased security concerns.

CONCLUSION

An argument that the intervention in Egypt in 1956 has normative components stands in stark contrast to most interpretations of it. The resistance to finding any normative elements in this action results not just from the obviously immoral aspects of this intervention—collusion, great power use of force, and lying among allies—but from the more general view of politics as being about interests and power rather than about ideals. Those who have studied the Suez intervention see it as a great power move to secure access to Canal and the oil that flowed through it.

The analysis I have presented here, however, puts the normative issues at the forefront. I do not argue that the British and French acted in a morally good way; from almost any perspective, their actions violated standard notions of moral goodness. Rather, I have argued that a set of distinct norms motivated their actions, what I have called a colonial norm. British manifestations of this norm appeared in both the Middle East region, where they felt obligated to aid Jordan and Iraq, and in the global system, where they felt obligated to uphold certain norms of international society. The French manifestation of the colonial norm existed regionally in their responsibility to protect Algeria and save Israel and universally in their belief that dictators must be stopped at all costs. Importantly, the norm of colonialism differed in these two cases primarily because the differing national histories (or, more accurately, differing interpretations of those histories) of the two states. In other words, the colonialism of each agent grew out of the way in which its leaders, writers, and citizens narrated domestic and international histories.

Yet, as in the Russian intervention, the very norms that played such a key role in generating the interventions contributed to the conflicts that led to its failure. Because these colonial norms grew from conflicting political ideals, they caused conflicts between the two states embodying them. Great Britain, with its history in Palestine, refused to cooperate with Israel, while the French, with their narration of a past as one of resistance to the

Nazis, naturally turned toward the Israelis. The lack of British support for the key local ally in the intervention played a key role in undermining it. The British interpretation of their history as the primary creator of international society might have led to the use of the UN as a means to solve the conflict; instead, their narration of themselves as superior to the UN perhaps played a role in Eden abandoning Lloyd's negotiations at the last minute. The British political presence also conflicted with that of the Americans, whose failure to support the intervention was one of the most important reasons for its failure. As I noted earlier, a part of this American resistance derived not just from its own political history, but from resistances generated by the Arab political community. The French refusal to cooperate with the Americans grew out of their belief that the United States represented the most important challenge to a strong French cultural and political presence in the international system.

In the end, the intervention at Suez failed for many reasons, including those of power politics. But, as I have tried to argue here, some of that failure can be attributed to clashing normative visions of agents whose competition on the international stage represents a version of Arendt's agonal politics.

CHAPTER FOUR

Intervention in Somalia

INTRODUCTION

This chapter continues with the themes articulated thus far with an analysis of the intervention in Somalia from 1992 to 1993. While the normative elements of this intervention are more well-known, the political ones will also be explored here. This chapter also expands the book's arguments beyond the liberal democracies that have been the focus of the other case studies. The final section examines how the UN's role in Somalia also contains normative and political aspects. If it is the case that the UN somehow represents the "sense of the international community" then its role in this intervention can be scrutinized to discover a meaning for intervention that is more broadly shared than simply among the liberal democracies. While it is true that the liberal democracies were instrumental in the foundation of the UN, it is also true that the Soviet Union played a key role in its formation, and that the role of developing countries in the General Assembly and in the various economic and social bureaucracies has been important in the development of its role in world affairs. The UN does not simply reflect liberal democratic values, it also reflects more wider ranging values and beliefs. Thus its role in the intervention in Somalia should reveal some of these more global values.

Even more importantly, using the UN to make my argument demonstrates that political agency should not be limited only to states. The UN is composed of its member states. The UN has, however, taken on a form of agency that has transcended those states. Institutionally, this can be seen in the growth of influence of the Secretariat's Office and in the work of social and economic councils. More importantly for my analysis, however, is how the UN has narrated itself a form of political agency. At one level, this can be seen in the body of international law and norms generated by the Security Council and the General Assembly. These laws, passed by member states, have given the institution a normative presence that differs from the sum of its parts. At another level, writers both from within the institution and outside of it have constructed the UN as an agent that represents the best in the international community. Not only does it represent certain values, it puts them into action.

On the question of intervention, the agency of the UN has vastly increased. As I have argued, intervention is one of the most direct manifestations of global political agency. While certainly constrained by the wishes of the member states and rarely going beyond the mandate of peacekeeping, the UN has in both actions and words pushed its political agency in these missions. The current Secretary General, Kofi Anan, who also served as Under Secretary for Peacekeeping Operations, has recently published his thoughts on intervention. In one of those speeches, he clearly presents the UN as its own political agent within the context of its normative role as a defender of human rights:

> And let me therefore be very clear: even though we are an organization of Member States, the rights and ideas the United Nations exist to protect are those of peoples. As long as I am Secretary General, the UN as an institution will always be a place where human beings are at the center of everything we do. (Anan 1999, 24)

In an even more striking passage from the same publication, Anan hints at a form of agency completely removed from its member states. In reviewing the UN's failure in Rwanda, Anan suggests that perhaps the UN would have been better served in Africa by one of the many new private security firms: "[I] even considered [as Under Secretary for Peacekeeping Operations] the possibility of engaging a private firm. But the world may not be ready to privatize peace" (Anan 1999, 13). If the UN had taken such a step, it would have been more than just "privatizing peace"; it would have meant a qualitative change in the UN's political agency by giving it an independent military force for engaging in peacekeeping operations.

Two other documents reveal the political agency of the UN, an agency that arises, in part, from narration. A key element of political agency is responsibility (Lang 1999). In two recent reports, the UN qua institution has taken responsibility for failed interventions. In its special report on the massacre at Srebencia in July 1995, the institution notes "there is an issue of responsibility and we in the UN share that responsibility as the assessments at the end of this report records" (*UN Report to the Secretary General* 1999, 5). In a similar report on the failure of the international community to stop the genocide in Rwanda, an Independent Inquiry concluded that the response of the UN before and during the 1994 genocide failed in a number of fundamental respects. The responsibility for this failure lies with a number of different actors, in particular the Secretary General, his office, the Security Council, and UNIMAR. "This international responsibility is one which warrants a clear apology by the Organization and by Member States concerned to the Rwandan people," (*UN Report of the Independent Inquiry* 1999, 12). These statements of responsibility, which distribute that responsibility across the organization, do not lay the blame only at the door of the member states. The UN bureaucracy takes on responsibility for the failure, a responsibility that gives it greater political agency both now and into the future. This chapter explores how the UN took on a certain amount of agency in its actions in Somalia. It is important to note, however, that the intervention in Somalia was not an isolated act by the UN, attributable to the whims of the Secretary General. Rather, as a political agent, the UN has and will continue to advance this agency in its pursuit of normative ideals that it further seeks to construct through its narration of itself.

In analyzing the intervention in Somalia, it is also important to recognize the changed international context that made this action possible. As I noted in the introduction, this book examines military intervention in three very different structural contexts: a pre-Cold War, a Cold War, and a post-Cold War international context. Certainly, the bipolar competition between the Soviet Union and the United States is not the only element of twentieth century international political structure. It did, however, structure the way we think and act politically at the global level. The end of the Cold War also created the possibility for new political actions, such as the intervention in Somalia. Indeed, a general euphoria emerged with the collapse of the Soviet Union, one not simply focused on the disappearance of a communist power. Rather, many saw in the collapse of the bipolar world an opportunity to put into place the ideals of the UN and other global institutions. It was this rush of goodwill that many argue made the intervention in Somalia happen.

Importantly, however, my argument will demonstrate that while the initiation of this intervention may well have been facilitated by the new international context, it also reflected elements similar to what were found in the other two interventions. In all three cases, normative concerns generated part of the rationale for the intervention. And, in all three cases, a denial of the politics of presence decisively contributed to its failure.

This chapter rests on less firm historical grounds than the previous two. Events in 1918 and 1956 are more historically accessible to us than events in 1992, largely because of the inability to obtain documents from the United States government, the lack of secondary source material, and the necessity of relying on media accounts. This paucity of historical information, however, does not fundamentally undermine the argument. For if the argument constructed so far, both in the theoretical chapter and in the previous two historical chapters, has any validity it ought to reveal aspects of precisely those interventions that have yet to be historically verified. Recall that the innovation of this book's method is not so much the discovery of new historical evidence in the traditional sense of that word, but rather the use of ethical and political registers to explore what have been traditionally seen as strategic actions.

Somalia, located on the Horn of Africa, had been a colony of Great Britain, Italy, and France at different times up until 1960. From 1960 through 1969 it was ruled as a parliamentary democracy with a broad array of political parties competing for power. When the president was assassinated in 1969, Mohammed Said Barre, a military officer, took power and proceeded to rule the country for the next twenty-one years. Said Barre's rule began as a reflection of traditional Somali norms, Islam and clan authority but soon moved to what he called "scientific socialism" (Omar 1992). As his rule became more totalitarian, Said Barre utilized not only the patronage of the Soviet Union but also clan divisions to sustain his rule. The clan system in Somalia had functioned as a way to create lines of authority based on lineage (not ethnicity, as some mistakenly called it during the intervention), but Said Barre turned the clan system into a means of assuring his power by rewarding those from his sub-clan.[1]

The existence of the Ogaden peoples in neighboring Ethiopia who had lived in Somalia, and a *coup d'état* in Ethiopia, led Said Barre to attack Ethiopia in 1977. This attack eventually led to the evaporation of Soviet support for Somalia as the Soviets turned to their newest patron, Colonel Halie Mariam Mengistu of Ethiopia. Said Barre then turned to the United States as a patron, which led to an influx of weapons, a buildup of military bases, and increased joint military exercises between the United States and Somalia in the 1980s. But as this superpower competition increased the amount of weapons in Somalia, Said Barre's rule increasingly agitated a number of different sub-clans, many of which began to arm themselves in opposition. Not only the sub-clans, but also intellectuals, women, and religious leaders protested his rule. On July 14, 1989, after Friday prayers, a group of Muslims organized a spontaneous protest, leading to a clash with security forces resulting in numerous deaths. This, and other events, prompted a group of Somalis to issue from Italy on May 15, 1990, a manifesto seeking the resignation of Said Barre and fundamental restructuring of the political system. When these protests led only to increased oppression, the country broke out in civil war, leading to Said Barre's escape from Somalia in January 1991.

In place of the previous totalitarian rule, a number of competing leaders tried to assert themselves. The two leading contenders were Mohammed Ali Mahdi, one of the signers of the Manifesto, and General Mohammed Farah Aideed, who had played a key role in the military defeat of Said Barre. Ali Mahdi and Aideed were to become the leading contenders in the ongoing civil war. But what brought the attention of the world to this conflict was the famine it helped to create. Throughout the winter and spring of 1992, as almost all diplomatic missions left Somalia, only a few correspondents remained to report on the worsening conditions. Nongovernmental organizations (NGOs) also remained, but their attempts to deliver food and provide medical aid were continually hampered by the warring sides. NGOs were forced to pay protection money to the various factions in order to ensure their safety. In July 1992, articles by Jane Perlez in *The New York Times* and trips to Somalia by United States Senators Nancy Kassebaum and Paul Simon focused worldwide attention on the famine and conflict. Meanwhile, the newly appointed Secretary General of the UN, Boutros Boutros-Ghali, sent a special representative to Somalia to bring the two main factions, Ali Mahdi's and Aideed's, to some sort of political reconciliation (*UN and Somalia* 1996, 121–33). But the attempts at reconciliation failed and as media attention continued to focus on the country, the UN failed to bring about any substantive change in the situation.

Official United States government involvement had remained limited until late July 1992, when President George Bush agreed to provide air transport for food aid. After having initially watered down UN Security Council Resolutions attempting to provide a "military guard" for the delivery of food, the Bush administration agreed to increase its food aid and to transport a Pakistani troop contingent of 500 guards in August. The Security Council, prompted by Boutros-Ghali, authorized a greater troop contingent for what became known as UNOSOM, later to be known as UNOSOM I. But those greater levels of troops were never deployed, due to resistance from the Somali leaders, whose suspicions of UN intentions were now growing. Frustrated by the inability of the UN guards to make any real dent in the power of the military factions in Somalia, the United States approved a massive deployment of troops in November 1992 to provide humanitarian relief. While Bush officials tried to limit the "Thanksgiving" decision to a simple protection of relief distribution centers, the Secretary General sought to increase the mandate of the mission to disarmament and political reconciliation. As these debates continued, approximately 28,000 United States and allied troops were deployed in Somalia on December 8, 1992, under the glare of television lights with little resistance. UNITAF, the newly named mission, quickly established control of Mogadishu, the Somali capital, and began to spread out into the surrounding countryside. When President Bush arrived in Somalia in January 1993, on a final whirlwind tour as president, he witnessed the powerful United States military accomplishing what the UN could not; the provision of food aid and the beginning of institution building.

When Bill Clinton took over the presidency, having previously given his support to the deployment, he inherited a process that seemed well on its way to success. Very little media or congressional coverage of the mission took place in the early spring of 1993. On March 26, 1993, the Security Council passed Resolution 814, which expanded the mandate of the mission to include "nation-building" a decision which had the full support of the United States.[2] On May 4, 1993, the mission was formally handed back over to the UN, under UNOSOM II, although the United States forces, now greatly decreased from their high point of 28,000, still played a key role, with a Quick Reaction Force of 1,800 Marines and logistical support of approximately 3,000 more. These troops, however, did not report to the UN commander, but remained under United States command, although they were to serve in support of the mission.

The mission was radically changed on June 4, 1993, when a group of Pakistani soldiers in search of weapons were attacked by Aideed forces at the radio station he controlled. This attack galvanized the world community, including the Security Council and the Clinton Administration, leading to Security Council Resolution 837 calling for the arrest and prosecution of all those "responsible" for the attack. With little discussion of the utility of employing military forces on a police mission in a country without a judicial system, the Clinton Administration sent in a contingent of Army Rangers and Delta Commandos to capture Aideed, along with undercover agents to track his movements, placing a $20,00 bounty on his head.[3] Aideed, a former police chief in Mogadishu, easily evaded his captors. On October 3, 1993, in a raid on a hotel in Mogadishu, eighteen United States soldiers were killed and one was taken hostage. To add insult to injury, the bodies of the Americans killed were dragged through the streets of Mogadishu and the hostage was paraded before cameras. Only four days later, President Clinton announced that all United States forces would be withdrawn by March 31, 1994, leading a number of European countries to also announce their withdrawal. The UN forces were eventually withdrawn in March 1995, without having resolved the political conflict and without having built any institutions that remained, although relief agencies were able to provide food more easily.

This history has been interpreted in a number of ways, and will continue to be the source of numerous "lessons" concerning peacekeeping, peacemaking, the role of United States military forces in the new world order, multilateral action, and humanitarian action (Allard 1995, Bolton 1994, Clark 1993, Clarke and Herbst 1996, Clarke and Herbst 1997, Crocker 1995, Farer 1996, Hirsch and Oakley 1995, Morales 1994, Stevenson 1995, *UN and Somalia* 1996). Some point out that the intervention, while problematic in a number of ways, was not a complete failure; as Chester

Crocker points out, over 250,000 lives were saved (Crocker 1995, 3). Others are more critical, highlighting the missed opportunities and unrealistic expectations. A number of works recognize the point being made in this book, that military interventions cannot ignore politics (Farer 1996, Clarke and Herbst 1996, Sahnoun 1998). The lack of clarity on the meaning of "politics", however, makes the analysis presented here all the more useful. Rather than being a catchall phrase that can encompass any element of the intervention that was not taken into account, politics in this book means the importance of presenting a narrated agent, either *qua* person or political community, in a competition with other agents. This political element comes to the fore in the Somali intervention in the competition between the United States and the UN and the conflicts between the intervenors and the Somali people and leaders.

Two normative elements predominated in the intervention: First, the stated aim of providing humanitarian aid, mainly by protecting the distribution centers and routes for the delivery of food supplies, was the overriding concern in the early United States intervention. While the military forces did not themselves engage in the delivery of such supplies, they did protect the NGOs who were. Second, the loosely defined mission of "nation building" became an important part of the intervention when the Security Council redefined the mandate of the intervention in Resolution 814. This ethic manifested itself in three different ways: political reconciliation, institution building, and "saving a failed state." The first, political reconciliation, occurred from the very beginning of the operation, including the Bush administration's initial role; this point will become important in the following discussion, especially because some commentators argued that the Clinton administration altered the mandate. The second manifestation involved the creation of police and judicial systems. The third aspect, seen more clearly in some of the theoretical literature on the intervention, was an attempt to fix a more prevalent problem in world politics—the collapse of sovereign authority.

The politics of the intervention, as in the other two instances, revolved around an attempt to establish the presence of an agent in the course of an intervention. The state agents in this case were the United States and the UN. The first political aspect was the assertion by the United States that it alone could do the job and that it must act alone to do the job correctly. This led to the United States seeking to define the mission according to the Weinberger-Powell doctrine, a military doctrine which posits that only quick, decisive, and publicly supported actions can succeed. It also meant that the United States refused to place any of its troops under UN command, preferring a separate line of command. These two aspects of the intervention contributed to its failure, especially in the June and October attacks by the Aideed forces and the subsequent withdrawal of United States forces.

The second political aspect of the intervention was the political presence of the UN. While nominally composed of its member states, the UN clearly exhibited a political presence in this intervention at odds with the United States and other members of the organization. This political presence conflicted with both the United States and the Somali people during the intervention contributing to its failure at a number of key points. The final political aspect of intervention was the strong political resistance offered by the Somali people, especially the Aideed faction. While he was branded an outlaw and criminal by many involved in the intervention, some evidence demonstrates that his actions appealed to a larger group of Somalis during the intervention, especially after he was declared an outlaw. This resistance challenged the political presence of both the UN and the United States.

This intervention, like the previous two, exhibits a number of normative aspects. But it also exhibits a number of political factors that contributed to the overall failure of the mission. What makes this intervention perhaps most interesting is the role played by the UN, which, as a quasi-state agent, may force us to reexamine the role of states and state agency in world politics.

THE NORMS OF INTERVENTION IN SOMALIA

John Stevenson, in his book *Losing Mogadishu*, begins and ends his analysis of the United States intervention in Somalia asking what are the "moral duties of a nation" (Stevenson 1995, xvi). Indeed, much of the coverage, both media and historical, of this intervention places a particularly strong emphasis on this question. But what exactly are the moral duties of a nation, and how did this intervention fulfill those duties? While the image of starving children or victims of ethnic cleansing certainly aroused sympathies, why should one state rather than another be responsible for solving these problems? What is it about the United States in 1992 that made it responsible for solving these problems?

It may not be clear what the source of that responsibility is, but both the Bush and Clinton administrations believed it existed in the case of Somalia. In his speech to the nation on December 4 explaining the United States actions in Somalia, George Bush argued:

> The people of Somalia, especially the children of Somalia, need our help. We're able to ease the suffering. We must help them. We

must give them hope. America must act. . . . We come to [Somalia] for one reason only, to enable the starving to be fed. (Bush 1993, 2175–6)

The ethic here appears to be based on pragmatism; as the only nation that can act to solve this problem, the United States was bound to do so. Bill Clinton agreed with this characterization. In February 1993, he claimed that "I think we have a responsibility there" (Clinton 1994, 150). But as the mission evolved, so did the norm. On July 2, he argued that:

The ultimate purpose of our presence in Somalia is to restore normal conditions of life and try to help build the nation there so that people can engage in self-government. (Clinton 1994, 1028)

Neither Clinton nor Bush ever clearly articulated a basis for the overall ethic of the intervention. But there appear to be two key aspects to the action: feeding the hungry and rebuilding a nation. Nor should these two ethics be seen as confined to the two different administrations. Bush and his administration built the foundations for the policy of nation-building, and Clinton emphasized the success of feeding the people as proof of the wisdom of the mission. These two aspects of the intervention play a key role in explaining its overall normative element.

By April of 1992, the UN estimated that 4.5 million Somalis, 65 percent of the population, were in need of external assistance (*The UN and Somalia* 1996, 21). The civil war had destroyed most of the water supply and electrical infrastructure in the country. It had also forced many from the grain producing southern regions to emigrate, thus preventing Somalis from having any domestic source of agriculture, never a large portion of their supply in any case. Their important export crop, livestock, had also been largely eliminated by the fighting. The UN had undertaken relief operations in April and September of 1992, which had begun to stem the tide of the famine. The fighting in Mogadishu, however, prevented a large portion of the supplies from reaching the needy, leaving them stranded on quays in the city (20–4). Thus while there was a certain amount of resistance to the provision of food from donors, the more pressing problem in the latter half of 1992 was that the civil war was preventing the delivery of food that was already in Somalia. Even more disturbing to many in the UN and the United States government was that much of the food was being hijacked by the warring factions for their own uses (168).

During 1992, Boutros-Ghali continued to agitate for more action to be undertaken in Somalia to solve the joint problems of famine and civil war. Coming to office in January 1992, he sought to promote the Somali cause in both the Security Council and before the public at large. On July 23,

1992, he argued that the West ought to focus just as much attention on Somalia as it was on the "rich man's war" in Yugoslavia (Hirsch and Oakley 1995, 37). His reports to the Security Council also helped prompt action; on April 21 he issued a report on the state of the cease-fire in Mogadishu, and called for an increased military presence. Along with the 50-member cease-fire observation team, Boutros-Ghali recommended an additional 500-member force. In his report he defined the mission of the force in the following terms:

> The UN security personnel will not have any law-and-order responsibilities *vis-à-vis* these armed elements. Their task will be to provide the UN convoys of relief supplies with a sufficiently strong military escort to deter attack and to fire effectively in self-defense if deterrence should not prove effective. (*The UN and Somalia* 1996, 138)

On April 24, the Security Council passed Resolution 751 which approved this recommendation. These forces, the foundation of UNOSOM I, were clearly intended for the provision of humanitarian relief and not for the larger project of "nation-building."

But the UN was not the only forum in which the issue of humanitarian relief was being addressed. Very few reporters had remained in Somalia during the civil war and ensuing famine. One reporter from *The New York Times*, Jane Perlez, however, did remain, and her reporting played an important role in presenting the image of starving Somalis to a larger audience. Her front-page story on Somalia on July 19, 1992, was central in bringing the famine to the attention of the United States public (Lyons and Samatar 1995, 31; Stevenson 1995, 37). In fact her reports had been covering the situation since December of the previous year (*The New York Times* Dec. 29, 1991, 4), but her stories in mid-July, coupled with the Secretary General's comments about Somalia and Yugoslavia, began to focus official American attention more acutely on Somalia. On July 23, *The New York Times* called for action in an editorial, advocating "an effective, mobile UN peacemaking force, strong enough to quell the warlords," something in which "the big Western powers have shown very little interest." The editorial also implicitly criticized President Bush for lack of action.

Nor were newspapers the only place where such agitation was beginning to take hold. The Democratic controlled Congress had been holding hearings on the famine and civil war since 1991. On January 30, 1992, the House Select Committee on Hunger held hearings on *The Humanitarian Tragedy in Somalia*. A number of officials testified at the hearing, from both NGOs and the United States government. Representative Alan Wheat noted in his opening statement that "we are here to put on record that the

Congress cares about Somalia and the United States cares about Somalia and we will not let the world stand by while Somalia destroys itself" (*Humanitarian Tragedy in Somalia* 1992, 2). The House Sub-Committee on Africa also held a hearing on September 16, 1992, which addressed many of the same issues (*The Crisis and Chaos in Somalia* 1992). In the Senate, Senators Nancy Kassebaum and Paul Simon played key roles in bringing the issue to the fore. The two co-authored an editorial piece entitled "Save Somalia from Itself" on January 2, 1992 in *The New York Times*, which helped draw attention to the famine, as well as chairing a hearing on March 19, 1992. Perhaps the most important role was played by Kassebaum, whose visit to Somalia in July 1992 drew world, and especially American, attention to the crisis. As one witness before a House hearing argued ". . . thank goodness for Nancy Kassebaum, because her visit kicked off a train of events that at last galvanized the world to respond, but not before a third of the country's babies are dead and the relief effort almost impossible because it has gone so long without the monstrously large international relief effort that is needed" (33).

The majority of these hearings and press reports focused on the famine, stressing the fact that children were dying, that relief was there but could not get through to the needy, and that much of the problem was being caused by the civil war. On July 27, 1992, Marlin Fitzwater, the Presidential Press Secretary, made a statement in support of UN efforts to provide aid through military force if necessary. Soon thereafter, on August 14, Fitzwater announced that the United States would transport more food and airlift the 500 Pakistani troops who would make up the bulk of the security guard for the food supplies. He also announced the appointment of Andrew Natsios as the Special Coordinator for Somali Relief (Bush 1993, 1194, 1354, 1360). Natsios himself described the decision to "ratchet up the mission" as prompted by Bush's reading of diplomatic cables about the civil war and famine, leaving him "deeply disturbed" (*The Crisis and Chaos in Somalia* 1993, 22).

As recently as April, the administration had been watering down Security Council Resolutions calling for military forces, but by July they were offering to transport the troops. And while such moves were certainly not the deployment of 28,000 troops, they did signal a change in the approach the American government was taking toward the conflict in Somalia. Throughout the early summer of 1992, the official foreign policy bureaucracy had been moving toward some sort of action in Somalia. In July, Acting Secretary of State Lawrence Eagleburger had been told by Bush that the administration needed to be more "forward leaning" on Somalia (Hirsch and Oakley 1995, 38). After the August decision to transport the troops, interagency discussions had proposed a number of different solutions for the crisis, including a massive aid program along with military forces; the majority of these suggestions, however, did not envision a large United States military presence in Somalia. But the August decision, according to Hirsch and Oakley, had brought about an "activist" concern in the administration (40). This point is important to stress, for some have argued that the Bush decision to deploy the 28,000 troops in November, after the election that he lost, indicates either an abdication of responsibility for the consequences of his action or even a Machiavellian curse on Clinton. The fact that the decision to transport the Pakistani troops was made in August indicates that the Bush administration saw the crisis primarily in terms of providing food relief, and that they fully expected to be responsible for the mission as a whole.

By mid-November, the situation in Somalia was clearly deteriorating. The UNOSOM troops were confined to the airport, and food was still not being transported to the areas in most need. At this point, it appears the Defense Department began to move in the direction of a massive military deployment. General Colin Powell, the Chairman of the Joint Chiefs of Staff, Defense Secretary Dick Cheney, NSC Advisor Brent Scowcroft and General Joseph Hoar, commander in chief of CENTCOM, were instrumental in the decision to act on a large scale (see Hirsch and Oakley 1995, 42; Oberdorfer 1992a; Oberdorfer 1992b; Blumenthal 1993). The Deputies Committee, a group of deputy secretaries from the Defense and State Departments who had been meeting on Somalia since the summer, met daily November 20 to 26. On November 21, Admiral David Jeremiah, Powell's representative, told the group that the military was ready to provide a massive intervention of troops for the delivery of aid (Oberdorfer 1992b). In a review of options on the day before Thanksgiving, November 25, Bush decided to send the troops (Hirsch and Oakley 1995, 43).

As Hirsch and Oakley argue, the November decision to deploy troops was directly linked to the August decision to transport the Pakistani troops. It appears from this evidence that George Bush and his military and foreign policy advisors believed that the reason to deploy troops was largely in response to the famine in Somalia. Cheney and Powell stressed that the mission was confined to providing a secure environment for the delivery of supplies and then handing the mission over to the UN. Powell described the mission in the following terms: "It's sort of like the cavalry coming to the rescue, straightening things out for a while and then letting the marshals come back to keep things under control" (Stevenson 1995, 51). The Bush address to the nation on December 4, quoted at the beginning of this section, placed strong emphasis on the provision of aid, comments that were seemingly directed at both the American public and the

UN bureaucracy. Boutros-Ghali sent a letter to Bush on December 11 arguing that the mission needed to be expanded to include a disarmament component, but Bush refused, arguing that the mission needed to stay focused on what it initially went there to do: provide the means to deliver relief supplies (Boutros-Ghali 1999).

This ethic of providing food for the hungry did not remain only a part of the initial decision-making process. It continued to play an important role throughout the course of the intervention, even after the ethic of nation-building came into play. In Congressional testimony on December 17, Representative Donald Payne of New Jersey argued that:

> for the first time in many years America is viewed as helping the powerless and homeless, and without a cold war agenda. We are helping women and children, literally too weak to speak for themselves, who have been the brutalized victims of the ruthless male warlords. (*The Crisis in Somalia* 1992, 49)

In a briefing by the Joint Chiefs of Staff before the Senate Armed Services Committee, Senator John Glenn asked if the mission had been a success thus far, and was told by Admiral Mike Cramer, Director of Intelligence, that the mission was successful in terms of its main goal, preventing starvation (*Joint Chiefs of Staff Briefing* 1993, 29). Especially after the October 3, 1993, firefight in which a number of United States troops were killed trying to capture Aideed, the Clinton administration reverted back to the importance of feeding the hungry as the main goal of being in Somalia; this is *after* they had been pursuing the goal of nation-building and capturing Aideed throughout the summer and fall of 1993. Peter Tarnoff, Under Secretary of State for Political Affairs, in testimony before the Senate Foreign Relations Committee, argued that the main goals were "humanitarian" (*United States Participation in Somalia Peacekeeping* 1993, 11). And President Clinton wrote in his message to Congress outlining the withdrawal of troops from Somalia:

> We went to Somalia on a humanitarian mission. We saved approximately a million lives that were at risk of starvation brought on by civil war that had degenerated into anarchy. We acted after 350,000 already had died. . . . We went to Somalia because without us a million people would have died. (*Military Operations in Somalia* 1993, 1)

To make the case that the intervention had as part of its ethic the provision of food to the hungry is not, in fact, that difficult. The majority of the coverage, both on the spot and more investigative, appears to confirm that the famine played a key role in the November decision (Oberdorfer

1992b). More importantly, the increased media and congressional coverage of the famine in July followed soon thereafter by the Bush administration decision to aid in the provision of food seems to indicate that the desire to help in providing food was an important part of the overall ethic of the intervention. And even after his administration had played an important role in moving the mission toward a "nation-building" role, Clinton and his administration continued to stress the provision of food as the most important part of the mission. Clearly, the United States sent troops to Somalia in large part to prevent the massive starvation that was threatening its people.

While the provision of food to the hungry clearly played a dominant role in the initial decision, and remained important throughout, a second norm soon became apparent. In Security Council Resolution 814, passed on March 26, 1993, the new mandate called for, among other things, political reconciliation, the reestablishment of police and judicial systems, economic rehabilitation, and:

> Creation of conditions under which Somali civil society may have a role, at every level, in the process of political reconciliation and in the formulation and realization of rehabilitation and reconstruction programmes. (*The UN and Somalia* 1996, 262)

This resolution, passed after UNITAF, the United States-led force, had achieved most of their goals and were preparing to hand over control of the mission to a largely UN-led force, indicated a subtle, but important shift in the mission's mandate. No longer was the main goal the securing of an environment for the delivery of food; it now also included the creation of a "civil society" that could bring about political reconciliation and rehabilitation.

Before exploring what this mandate meant for the intervention as a whole, it is important to clarify two points. First, in that Resolution 814 indicated what the mandate of UNOSOM II would be, and not necessarily that of UNITAF, did this resolution have any impact on United States policies in the intervention? Recall that on May 5, 1993, the United States-led task force which had been deployed on December 8, 1992, UNITAF, officially ended its mandate and turned the intervention over to a UN-controlled force, composed of approximately 22,000 troops. The United States, while significantly drawing down its forces under UNOSOM, still retained a Quick Reaction Force of 1,800 soldiers, and approximately 3,000 logistical and support forces. In terms of the United States role in the intervention after May 5, these troops continued to play an important role. The United States forces did remain under United States command (a point to which I return in the next section), but they were an integral part of the operation as a whole. Moreover, United States officials continued to identify with the mission, and played an important part in the formulation of Security Council Resolution 814. On its passage, Madeline Albright, then Ambassador to the UN, said "With this resolution, we will embark on an unprecedented enterprise aimed at nothing less than the restoration of an entire country as a proud, functioning, and viable member of the community of nations" (Bolton 1994, 62). And Clinton himself approvingly cited the task of nation-building throughout the spring and summer of 1993:

> The ultimate goal is to restore conditions of peace which existed before the Pakistanis were murdered. The ultimate goal is make sure that the UN can fulfill its mission there and continue to work with the Somalis toward nation building. June 16, 1993. The ultimate purpose of our presence in Somalia is to restore normal conditions of life and try to help build the nation there so that people can engage in self-government. July 7, 1993 (Clinton 1994, 862, 1028)

Such statements indicate a clear concern with more than just feeding the hungry; the United States was now involved in a project more akin to the colonial project of teaching peoples how to govern themselves. And even though its troop levels had been significantly reduced, the United States government continued to identify with the new mandate, even after the deaths of the Pakistani forces on June 5.

The second point of clarification concerns the accusations made by Bush administration officials and other commentators that the Clinton administration on its own had altered the mandate of what had originally been a humanitarian action. John Bolton, a former Bush administration official, wrote in *Foreign Affairs* in 1994 that the Clinton administration was pursuing its overall policy of "aggressive multilateralism" to the detriment of the more constrained original mission of UNITAF (Bolton 1994). Both Henry Kissinger and Jeane Kirkpatrick argued that the new policy in Somalia was the result of idealist Clinton administration officials who did not understand the constraints of power politics (*UN Peacekeeping: The Effectiveness of the Legal Framework* 1994, 229, 239). But, in fact, the Bush administration, when it set out its initial goals for the intervention, could not help but indicate that a greater role than just a simple relief operation might be necessary. Colin Powell and Dick Cheney refused to put a time limit on the action when it was first proposed, indicating that perhaps they saw a longer term mission than just feeding the hungry. While Bush and others tried to distance themselves from the nation-building aspect of the intervention, especially after the October 3 debacle, certain statements by administration officials in December and January indicate that this ethic played an important role in the mission from its very inception. On December 17, James Woods, a former official in the Defense Department, listed the fourfold aim of the mission:

> To conduct joint and unilateral military missions in Somalia under UN auspices; to secure major air and seaports, ground routes, and major relief centers; to provide a secure environment; to disarm, as necessary, forces which interfere with humanitarian relief operations; and to protect and assist UN and nongovernmental humanitarian relief operations. (*The Crisis in Somalia* 1993, 8)

The statement appears to support only humanitarian operations, traditionally understood. Yet the third and fourth aims, "to provide a secure environment" and "to disarm forces" hints that the mission might have been seen in a broader context than simply the provision of relief aid. And in a revealing statement on December 9 before the Senate Armed Services Committee, Lieutenant General Martin Brandtner, Director of Operations for the Joint Chiefs of Staff, argued that the first responsibility of the United States force was "peacemaking" and only later would it be "peacekeeping." In response Senator Sam Nunn asked "So we are really performing the role that the UN would ordinarily be expected to perform since they are a UN force?" (*Operation Restore Hope* 1993, 12). The difference between peacemaking and peacekeeping is central here. The former refers to Boutros-Ghali's new version of the UN role, which involves not simply interposing a force between two warring factions with their advance approval, but is the attempt to force warring sides to come to peace and to help recreate the civil society that existed prior to the outbreak of conflict (Boutros-Ghali 1995). Peacemaking is very much like the nation-building that Resolution 814 calls for, and it appears to have been a part of what the Bush administration conceived of as its original mission.

The Bush administration certainly did not envision the full-fledged nation-building role that the intervention eventually adopted. It is important to stress, however, that the seeds for such a continuation of the mission were certainly planted in the initial planning stages. In what ways, then, did the project of nation-building manifest itself during the intervention? I highlight three aspects of that norm here, although there certainly may be others that will be revealed when the relevant documents are released. The first is the project of political reconciliation. This task, which really involved the bringing together of Ali Mahdi and Aideed as the two most powerful players in the Somali civil war, began when UN Special Envoy James Jonah invited the two sides to New York in February 1992, long before there was any troop commitment. In fact, this initial meeting led to a tentative cease-fire, the original justification for the first fifty peacekeeping forces that were sent by the Security Council. But this cease-fire lasted only a few months, a fact that prompted Boutros-Ghali to begin formulating plans for a broader military mission in the spring and summer of 1992.

The next real attempt at political reconciliation came from the next UN Special Representative, Mohammed Sahnoun, an Algerian diplomat sent in April 1992 to try his hand at bringing the two sides together. Sahnoun did seem to be succeeding in bringing about reconciliation. But when in October 1992 he invited the two warring factions to the Seychelles, and openly criticized the UN bureaucracy, Sahnoun was replaced. It appears that the firing of Sahnoun may have fundamentally undermined the political reconciliation chances, as he had just ensured the compliance of Aideed when Boutros-Ghali announced an increase in the size of the UN force without consulting Sahnoun or Aideed, thus angering Aideed and creating distrust between him and the UN bureaucracy (Sahnoun 1994; Boutros-Ghali 1999).

When UNITAF was announced by Bush on December 4, it appeared that there might finally be the chance for a real political reconciliation. Not only the existence of 28,000 United States soldiers, but the role played by Ambassador Robert Oakley, a former ambassador to Somalia and seasoned negotiator, signaled to the players in Somalia that a new process might be under way. While Oakley's main role was to meet with the various faction leaders in advance of the military deployment to ensure a minimum of casualties, he also engaged in a certain amount of conflict resolution. When he met with Aideed and Ali Mahdi in December 1992, Oakley declared that "This is not a political meeting at all. It's a get-acquainted meeting to discuss some of these security related issues" (Lyons and Samatar 1995, 41). But his meetings were in fact designed to bring together the warring factions to see if any political reconciliation was possible. Oakley's own account of a meeting on December 11 between the two leaders describes how they met for two hours alone and produced a written agreement on a cease-fire:

> As far as possible, the goal would be achieved by dialogue and cooption, using the implicit threat of coercion to encourage the faction leaders to gain prestige by showing leadership at home and to the international community. Over a period of time, Oakley urged the Somali faction leaders to take a series of steps, first to allow for humanitarian activities and stop fighting and then to end the civil war and begin the process of national reconciliation. (Hirsch and Oakley 1995, 56)

Oakley's mission did produce a joint military committee formed from the two factions that persisted throughout December and January (58).

But Oakley and UNITAF did not concentrate only on the two main leaders. Seeking to "rebuild civil society" they organized meetings with intellectuals, elders, and women's groups throughout the early months of the intervention. These meetings were Oakley's attempt to downplay the importance of the factions and reemphasize the importance of other groups in the process of political reconciliation. In March the UN sponsored a national reconciliation conference in Addis Ababa, which resulted in the Addis Ababa agreements, outlining the basis for a new Somali political system. The agreement called for the creation of a Transitional National Council (TNC), composed of representatives from regional councils, various political organizations, and faction representatives (92–99). Signed on March 27, the agreement coincided with the new UNOSOM II mandate, adopted by the Security Council only one day before.

But the deaths of the Pakistani troops on June 5 put many of these projects on hold, largely because Aideed was no longer considered a legitimate partner. It was not until November 1993, after the deaths of the United States soldiers, that the political process of reconciliation once again became an objective. From June until October, the mission became much more focused: capture Aideed, who had come to represent the main obstacle in the path of nation-building.

In fact, the attempt to capture Aideed can be seen as part of the second manifestation of the nation-building ethic, that of creating social and political institutions. This process had been a part of the intervention from the beginning as well. Oakley describes the arrival of United States forces in Baidoa on December 16, part of Phase II of the mission. When they arrived, the Marines organized a "series of Somali-style "town-meetings" with community representatives of all kinds, in numbers that even exceeded 200" (70). These attempts to bring together local Somalis, outside of the framework of the warring factions in formal settings were an attempt to organize the types of regional councils that were to provide the representatives for the TNC in the Addis Ababa accords. Even more importantly, the mission called for the creation of police and judicial systems throughout Somalia. In fact, Oakley and General Robert Johnson, the commander of UNITAF, had to convince both the United States government and the UN bureaucracy of the wisdom of establishing a police force; clearly this was not a case of the UN advancing a proposal over the heads of the United States led intervention. Oakley argued that such a force would help establish a secure environment in Somalia, and provide an important source for the creation of institutions later on (87–92).

The pursuit of Aideed can be seen as a part of this attempt to create a functioning police and judicial system. True to its legal foundations, the UN bureaucracy immediately created a commission to investigate the circumstances of the deaths in June. Tom Farer, an international legal scholar, led a task force that published its report on August 12, indicating that Aideed's forces were clearly responsible for the attack (*The UN and Somalia* 1996, 296). On June 17, the Security Council adopted Resolution 837 calling for the arrest and trial of all those "responsible for the action" (272), and a bounty was placed on the head of Aideed.

Nor was the UN the only one interested in the arrest of Aideed. On August 22, Clinton ordered the deployment of 800 Army Rangers and Delta Force soldiers to Somalia for the explicit task of capturing Aideed. He had also put into place a team of undercover agents intended to track Aideed after the June incident. Without any sort of legal jurisdiction and without any functioning court system, the CIA organized a group of African judges who could try Aideed offshore on an American battleship (Sloyan 1994). The attempt to arrest Aideed and try him before a court, even if a fully contrived one, indicates that the United States and the UN were interested in preserving some sort of legal machinery in Somalia when they pulled out. The decision to prosecute Aideed, rather than just eliminate him as an enemy, recalls a liberal norm. This was not an attempt to simply eliminate obstructions to political reconstruction, it was an attempt to legally prosecute a criminal responsible for "murder," as Clinton called it, and thus help to create a liberal democratic society where there was only chaos.

The final aspect of the nation-building mandate is not really a part of the intervention itself, but involves the later interpretations of it. Much of the theoretical literature that resulted from the civil war and intervention in Somalia revolved around the concept of a "failed state." The concept had been used before (Helmen and Ratner 1992), and now it seemed to be coming true. The Brookings Institute's study of the intervention is subtitled "State Collapse, Multilateral Intervention, and Strategies for Political Reconstruction" (Lyons and Samatar 1995), and it focuses on how to respond to the collapse of a failed state, as does a number of others (Zartman 1995; Lyons and Mastanduno 1995). These analyses focus in particular on what it means for international relations practice and theory.

This ethic constitutes a slightly different aspect from what occurred on the ground in Somalia because these later interpretations rarely address the specific aspects of the state that they are trying to reconstruct. That is, the moral norm in some of these theoretical interpretations has less to do with helping individuals avoid starvation and anarchy, and more to do with filling a series of voids in the international system. For without sovereign states, it is unclear, at least to these analysts, what will be the future of the world; as "the end of history," the state must not be allowed to collapse, for without it, the project of modernity might be seen as a failure. The creation of Somalia as the most devastating instance of "state failure" has more to do with the normative concerns of international relations scholars than it does with the concerns of those who were actually engaged in the intervention. Depending on the way in which this new dilemma is framed, this last aspect of the nation-building ethic may be the most important element of all.

THE POLITICS OF INTERVENTION IN SOMALIA

It is not that difficult to identify the two normative components that justified and sustained the intervention in Somalia. The attempt to feed the hungry and rebuild the Somali political system were explicitly identified in the Security Council Resolutions that defined the mandates of the different interventionary forces. Less easy to identify are the political factors that played just as important a role in the intervention. The three on which this chapter focuses are the United States' belief that only it could accomplish the mission, and only by acting alone; the UN belief that only it should accomplish the task; and the Somali resistance to any political presence dictating the course of its political development. The conflict between these three competing political entities—a state, an international organization, and a series of unorganized political factions—both reveals how politics undermines an intervention and that not only states but other agents in world politics play a role that needs to be recognized. The previous two chapters have focused almost exclusively on how state agents create the political conflicts that lead to the failure of an intervention; this chapter demonstrates that politics, as I have defined it here, is not limited to the traditional nation-state but plays a role in the agency of a number of different players on the world stage.

United States as a political agent

With UNOSOM I in jeopardy of failure, Secretary General Boutros-Ghali began canvassing the members of the Security Council on ideas for a more concerted effort to solve the famine. On November 25 at an "informal" meeting of the Security Council, it was decided that more needed to be done. On that same day, Acting Secretary of State Lawrence Eagleburger met with Boutros-Ghali and informed him that the United States would be willing to provide troops to help alleviate the famine (*The UN and Somalia*

1996, 30). On November 29, Boutros-Ghali issued a report to the Security Council outlining five options for action in Somalia. Numbers four and five became the crux of the debate. Option number four called for a "country-wide enforcement operation undertaken by a group of Member States authorized to do so by the Security Council" (211). Option number five called for "a country-wide enforcement operation to be carried out under UN command and control" (212). While Boutros-Ghali recommended option number five, the United States chose option number four, thus creating UNITAF, a United States-led mission that acted in consultation with the UN but was not under its control.

The decision to act outside of formal UN control is perhaps the clearest indication of the political vision that animated the United States actions. As Colin Powell said, the United States would be the cavalry that would fix up the problem and then turn it back over to the marshals to restore law and order. United States officials in both the Bush and Clinton administration believed that only when the United States acted alone could it solve the problems of the New World Order. The descriptions of the decisions leading up to the November 25 visit of Eagleburger with Boutros-Ghali reveal this attitude.

Admiral David Jeremiah, the "alter-ego" of Colin Powell on the Deputies Committee, argued on November 21 that "the greatest chance of success lay in having the U.S. carry out the relief effort itself, with a division or so of troops," (Gordon 1992). But even after this green light from the Pentagon, the Deputies Committee still was hesitant to advocate full-scale military deployment; they recommended three options to the President, only one of which included a United States troop deployment, one much less significant than the 28,000 that eventually went. But when the recommendations came before the President and his advisors, they soon turned the decision into a much larger effort. Brent Scowcroft, the NSC Advisor, sought a large troop deployment: "Scowcroft was certainly strong on this option. He wanted to take very strong and decisive action. He didn't want incremental action . . . " (Gordon 1992).

This decision had been percolating up through the foreign and military policy bureaucracy for weeks. On November 12, Robert Galluci, an Assistant Secretary of State, had convinced Eagleburger that the United States should use "all necessary means" to accomplish the delivery of food. In a November 20 meeting of the Deputies Committee, Frederick Cuny, a humanitarian relief expert, had told the assembled deputies that about 2,500 United States troops might be needed, a "very bold proposal" at the time. But only a day later the Pentagon agreed to the use of United States troops, making the prospect of United States military action a real possibility (Oberdorfer 1992b).

The decision appears to be the result not just of the United States ethic of feeding the hungry or building a failed state; it also came out of an American vision of itself as the only state able to solve such problems. Eagleburger said "This is a tragedy of massive proportions and, underline this, one that *we could do something about.* We had to act." Another official said Somalia is a place where "only the U.S. can do something." Yet another said "there was never any doubt in anybody's mind that if you really wanted to be absolutely certain to deliver the goods on time, you go with the U.S. military." Summing these sentiments up, reporter Dan Oberdorfer argued that:

> As the U.S. feels its way toward new international roles in the post-Cold War world, the deliberations and decision of the past several weeks may have more than fleeting significance. Unlike previous large-scale military operations, there is not U.S. strategic or economic interest in the Somalia deployments, as the NSC deputies agreed at the very start of their discussions. The U.S. action in Somalia, which has startled many Americans, responds to a different set of priorities, including a growing belief in this country that only the U.S. is equipped to lead efforts to deal with some international crises and disasters. (Oberdorfer 1992b)

This conception of the United States as the only power capable of action, and of needing to act on its own, is one I have discussed in chapter three. When the Wilson administration intervened in Russia, it sought to act on its own and felt that only it knew how to change the world, and Russia, to create a peaceful international society. Here we have the United States embodying similar political sentiments, painting itself as the only power capable of successful action. But did this sentiment contribute to the overall outcome of the intervention? According to UN officials, it clearly did. In particular, some blame the lack of clear lines of authority for the October 1993 firefight leading to the deaths of the American forces and eventual pullout. Ironically, many U.S. foreign policy analysts argued that the deaths were the result of the United States placing its troops under UN command (see Kirkpatrick 1994; Bolton 1994). But the opposite seems to be the case.

After the June 5 killings of the Pakistani troops, the United States sought to arrest and try Aideed for their deaths. They immediately dispatched CIA undercover agents to Somalia to track his movements and a month later deployed 800 Army Rangers to capture him. The policy of capturing Aideed was taken after he increased his harassment of UN and United States soldiers. When the Rangers arrived they were placed under a completely separate command, reporting to Major General William Garrison (Hirsch and Oakley 1995, 122). But as they sought out Aideed, policy in Washington appeared to be changing. After the PLO-Israeli signing ceremony, Clinton and former President Jimmy Carter spent the night at the White House discussing the events in Somalia. Carter urged Clinton to abandon the manhunt for Aideed and return to the political reconciliation course (Blumenthal 1993). And it appeared that Clinton was taking his advice to heart. His statements on Somalia in the following week downplayed the search for Aideed, and argued on September 27, after a speech to the UN General Assembly, that the Somalis will have to begin to solve their own problems. In August, in a speech by Defense Secretary Les Aspin, the administration had also been indicating that it did not see the capture of Aideed as the key element (Hirsch and Oakley 1995, 125).

But the events on the ground, put into place by a United States belief that it alone could solve the problem in Somalia, ignored these tentative steps away from the mission of capturing Aideed. On October 3, 18 United States soldiers were killed, leading to the pullout from Somalia the following March. The story of that day has been described by Mark Bowden in *Black Hawk Down*, a book based on interviews with United States soldiers and Somali citizens. That work more than any other reveals how the belief that the United States political presence was unique was not confined to the upper echelons of government. The Army Ranger soldiers who flew into Mogadishu that day also believed that the United States was in Somalia on a unique mission, one that only it could accomplish. The United States forces, Army Rangers and Delta Force operators, were some of the best trained in the military structure. They believed themselves to be the very embodiment of the "calvary" to which Colin Powell had referred. While Delta Forcer soldiers generally do not talk to reporters about their views and missions, Bowden was able to interview one, Sergeant Paul Howe, at some length. Howe's comments on the reason that the United States and especially the special forces were necessary reinforces some of the attitudes to be found at the level of the Deputies Committee:

Civilized states had nonviolent ways of resolving disputes, but that depended on the willingness of everyone involved to back down. Here in the raw Third World, people hadn't learned to back down, at least not until a lot of blood flowed. Victory was for those willing to fight and die. Intellectuals could theorize until they sucked their thumbs right off their hands, but in the real world, power still flowed from the barrel of a gun. If you wanted starving masses in Somali to eat, then you had to out muscle men like this Aidid, for whom starvation worked. You could send in your bleeding-ear do-gooders, you could hold hands and pray and sing hootenanny songs and invoke the great gods CNN and BBC, but the only way to finally open the roads to the big eyed babies was to show up with more guns. And in this real world, nobody had more or better guns than America. If the good-hearted ideals of human kind were to prevail, then they needed men who could make it happen. Delta made it happen. (Bowden 1999, 33)

The belief that the "guns of America" could "make it happen" puts in much harsher terms the pragmatic attitudes of many of the principal decision makers. The fact that such beliefs existed at the level of the individual soldier reinforces the point made in chapter 1; understanding an intervention, especially its normative and political elements, requires looking not just at the initial decisions, but at the implementation of those decisions as well.

Boutros-Ghali's description of the events indicates that it may have been the belief that only the United States could solve the problems of Somalia led to the massacre:

The tragedy exposed weaknesses in UNOSOM II's complicated operational structure, in which the Rangers reported to their commanders in the U.S. rather than to the UNOSOM II command in Mogadishu. The 3 October operation was planned and ordered by the U.S. forces acting independently of UNOSOM and communicated to UNOSOM II staff, including my Special Representative and the Deputy Force Commander, only just before the Rangers set off in their helicopters. This weakened effective coordination between UNOSOM II troops and the Quick Reaction Force. (*The UN and Somalia* 1996, 55)

While Boutros-Ghali certainly had his own political agenda to advance (one explored in the next section), it does seem to be the case that the lack of a unified command structure led to the failed attack on the Aideed forces, and the failure to have support provided in time to prevent many of the casualties (51–55). Evidently, the cavalry could not do it alone.

There were certainly other manifestations of the American belief that only by acting alone could it solve the problems of Somalia. But the decision to capture Aideed, and the October 3 attack played a key role in the failure of the mission. The pullout of American forces led to the pullout of a number of European troops, thus undermining the strength of the mission. And while food deliveries were able to continue, the overall mission of rebuilding Somalia certainly was a failure.

UN as a Political Agent

But the United States government was not the only political agent involved in the intervention. To speak of the UN as having a political presence is complicated by two different sets of factors. First, the UN is divided into a number of different bodies. Roughly, these different parts can be grouped into four categories: the General Assembly, the Security Council, the Secretariat, and the various economic and social committees. In terms of agency, or being able to do something substantive, the Security Council and the Secretariat are perhaps the most important. Only the Security Council can authorize the deployment of troops under a UN mandate, and the Secretary General plays an important role in suggesting, and sometimes goading, the Security Council into action. But in speaking of the UN, one is never clear what is the point of reference, especially when the General Assembly makes pronouncements concerning affairs on which the Security Council may have a different position. To add confusion to this arrangement, the Security Council is composed of the five permanent members, but also a rotating group of eleven other states.

The second confusion about the UN is that it is formally composed of the states of the international system. Thus, in reality, it does not exist except as a means to coordinate the actions of member states. This confusion is, actually, one that all states share as well; a state is really only supposed to be the coordinating body of its citizens. But in the case of the UN this confusion is compounded because its members are not individual citizens, but states. Thus it is composed of collective bodies that may be at odds with its own policies. And this, in fact, was the case in the intervention in Somalia at a number of key points.

The previous section on the ethic of the intervention noted the role played by Boutros-Ghali in formulating that ethic and in advancing it before the various member states, either in the Security Council or outside of it. For the purposes of this essay, the Secretary General, along with the UN bureaucracy that he controls, is the entity that attempted to establish a political presence in Somalia. In the next chapter, I address what this means for the theory and practice of global political agency. In this chapter, I am mainly concerned with presenting the ways in which the Secretariat did establish a political presence in Somalia, and how that presence may have contributed to the collapse of the intervention.

One of the most important roles played by Boutros-Ghali was his use of Special Representatives who traveled to Mogadishu in advance of troop deployments, attempting to coordinate these actions with the various groups on the ground. His first envoy, James Jonah, played a pivotal role in bringing the various factions to New York in February 1992 for the initial cease-fire agreement. His next envoy, Mohammed Sahnoun, was also extremely important in bringing about some reconciliation between Aideed and Ali Mahdi. But it was Sahnoun's actions that brought him into conflict with the Secretary General. Because he was fired by Boutros-Ghali for acting outside of the UN mandate, Sahnoun's history provides some important insights into the politics of the UN Secretary General's office.

He reports several difficulties with the UN approach to the famine and conflict. First, even though NGOs had been providing aid throughout 1991 and 1992, the UN never seemed able to coordinate its food delivery efforts. They were hampered by the tendency of UN officials to stay confined to Mogadishu and rarely venture out into other areas of Somalia (Sahnoun 1994, 37). Second, the "bureaucratic approach of the UN headquarters in New York" undermined the ability of UNOSOM to accomplish its mission (38). The need to run every decision through the UN bureaucracy hindered the quick reactions that are so necessary in the midst of a famine and civil war. The most revealing indication of the UN political presence occurred in August 1992. Sahnoun had been working throughout the month to ensure the agreement of Aideed and Ali Mahdi to the deployment of the 500 Pakistani troops. He had finally received Aideed's formal approval on August 10, when, a few weeks later, both Sahnoun and Aideed heard on BBC radio that the UN would be deploying an extra 3,000 troops (Hirsch and Oakley 1995, 26). This decision, taken without any discussion with the Somalis on the ground, indicated the lack of respect for the political presence of the Somali factions in UN decision making. The decision led to increased hostilities by Aideed's faction and the prevention of any increase in the UN deployment, until UNITAF arrived in December. As Hirsch and Oakley describe the conflict between the UN and Sahnoun, the political presence of the UN becomes more clear:

> Sahnoun also tended to overlook much of Aideed's anti-UN posturing in the interest of obtaining his cooperation on the ground. This approach created friction with UN headquarters, where Boutros-Ghali and Jonah were disposed to take Aideed's criticisms personally and as an affront to the institution. They felt Sahnoun should defend the UN more vigorously, even if it complicated dealing with Aideed. (Hirsch and Oakley 1995, 30)

Sahnoun's departure from Somalia tended to worsen relations with the political factions. His replacement, Ismat Kittani, a more bureaucratically oriented UN official, did not help matters. In Somalia Kittani refused to go to the headquarters of the faction leaders to meet with them; instead, he demanded that they come to him. And that attitude, prompted by his belief that the UN deserved greater respect, clearly indicates the type of political presence that I have argued tends to undermine interventions. Kittani also sought to dictate who would be considered a legitimate player in Somalia, leading him to dictate to the factions rather then deal with them. Again, Hirsch and Oakley:

> Kittani was particularly concerned not to leave Aideed with the impression that the UN accepted his claim to future political

power, or to imply to self-designated acting president Ali Mahdi that he would be recognized as the future president. . . . By the end of November, Aideed and Ali Mahdi had virtually ceased their discussions with the UN—often dealing at a remove by communicating through lower-level representatives. (32)

The failure of the UN to play a constructive role in the months preceding UNITAF can largely be attributed to the bureaucratic hindrances to the mission of Sahnoun and the more colonial approach of Kittani. More importantly for the purposes of this essay, that bureaucratic hindrance derived from a desire on the part of the Secretary General to have a political presence, a presence that did not allow space for the concerns of the political factions in power in Somalia.

In his recently published memoirs, Boutros-Ghali argues that he was unclear why Sahnoun resigned and does not touch on the troubles encountered by Kittani in his work (Boutros Ghali 1999, 56–7). Indeed, throughout that work, which deals with the United States hostility to Boutros Ghali, the former Secretary General insists that the UN ought to remain independent and politically secure vis-a-vis the United States Moreover, the point being here is not necessarily a criticism of Boutros Ghali. Rather, the argument is that any Secretary General would seek to defend the political presence of the UN. Because it is a political agent, the UN will find itself more and more engaged in the types of actions described here, inherently political actions that may lead to conflict with state agents in the international system.

The Somali People as a Political Agent

The United States and UN conflicts certainly undermined the intervention. But the most important reason for the failure of the intervention came from the Somalis themselves. Obviously, the role played by the military factions in preventing the delivery of food and continuation of the civil war during the early 1990s was not directed against any outside interventionary power. But with the arrival of UN and United States troops in 1992, the factions began to agitate against the presence of foreign forces in Somalia. And even though those forces were ensuring the delivery of food aid, they remained the target of attack, both verbal and physical.

It is important to stress that while certain factions welcomed the intervention, more than just Aideed's offered resistance to it. Furthermore, Aideed's resistance was not the action of a single, hostile, power-hungry "warlord." Certainly, Aideed does not appear to be an admirable political figure, nor do I believe that his political presence deserves greater respect than any other faction leader. His ability, however, to articulate the reasons for resistance to the allied forces marshaled against the factions gave him a wider credence than he might have already had. And, even more importantly, when he became the object of the UN manhunt in June 1993, Aideed was transformed from a warlord into a martyr. For the purposes of accomplishing the mission, both of providing food aid and of bringing about political reconciliation, Aideed's role, partly constructed by United States policies, was fundamental to the withdrawal of United States troops in October.

Aideed's use of the radio played an important part in undermining the intervention. In fact, the capture of Aideed's radio station became one of the goals of UNOSOM II, especially after the hand-off from UNITAF. Aideed was suspicious of the UN, a suspicion fueled by a number of minor affronts to his political standing by UN officials and his distrust of Boutros-Ghali, whom he continued to see as the Egyptian Foreign Minister whose country had supported Said Barre. The June 4 Pakistani patrol, undertaken as a weapons search, included a search of Aideed's radio station. Although the UN officially denied its purpose was to overthrow the station, Aideed's inflammatory broadcasts against the UN undoubtedly played a role in the decision to include it on a search. After the attack on the UN forces, Aideed broadcast that the Pakistani soldiers had actually been firing on unarmed civilians.[4]

In Resolution 839, issued one day after the killing of the Pakistani soldiers, the Security Council "strongly condemned the use of radio broadcasts . . . to incite attacks against UN personnel" (*The UN and Somalia* 1996, 268). The UN also engaged in counter broadcasts with its own radio station (287). Radio Mogadishu, as it was called, was pinpointed in the official report as the source of anti-UN propaganda. But in describing how the radio station was in fact undermining the UN presence in Somalia, the official report reveals that Aideed was able to articulate his resistance to the intervention in terms that would resonate in just about any African or Asian country:

> This hostility is reflected in transcripts of broadcasts between 1 May and 4 June on the eve of the killing of 24 Pakistani soldiers. The broadcasts have a xenophobic tone, especially starting on 11 May, when they accuse UNOSOM II and the U.S. of being aggressors trying to colonize Somalia and to establish a trusteeship. They speak highly of Somalia's history of resistance to foreign domination and imposition. (374)

Appeals to a colonial presence, linked with recitations of Somalia's history of resistance to attempts at foreign imposition, were undoubtedly well-received in Mogadishu, filled at the time with foreign military troops. Thus Aideed was able to present his radio broadcasts as not simply the reactions of a disgruntled leader, but as the representative of Somalia's political aspirations.

In fact, the attempt to formally declare the radio station as the official voice of Somalia played a key role in UN action against it. The affront to Aideed was that the UN did not attempt to silence Ali Mahdi's radio station, furthering his already well-established belief that the UN favored Ali Mahdi. It appears that what prompted the UN to seize Aideed's station rather than Ali Mahdi's was not only the inflammatory broadcasts from Aideed, but also the fact that Aideed called his radio station the official Somali station, while Ali Mahdi claimed his was only a private station (Hirsch and Oakley 1995, 117, fn. 4).

This semantic distinction may seem unimportant at first glance, but upon further reflection, and in the context of the overall argument of this essay, it takes on new importance. What the UN refused to allow was the existence of any semblance of sovereignty where there was supposed to be a political void. The attempt by Aideed to speak for an official "Somali nation" struck a dissonant chord with the UN bureaucracy, mainly because of their belief that only an entity representing the "sense of the international community" could decide who or what was the sovereign in a failed state. Aideed's attempt to take on the mantle of Somali sovereignty not only challenged the other faction leaders, it challenged the ability of the UN to decide the status of Somalia.

Aideed's radio station, however, was silenced soon after the killing of the Pakistani troops. But he was able to continue in his quest to be a larger political presence than simply that of his own political faction when the Security Council officially blamed him for the deaths of the Pakistanis and the UNOSOM leadership placed a bounty on his head. Immediately, Aideed became a sort of hero, as the only one who was able to resist the presence of the intervening Western forces. ". . . Aideed and the SNA used their mastery of media relations well during this period, portraying themselves as victims and the United States and the UN as villains" (Hirsch and Oakley 1995, 120). John Stevenson argues that Aideed was transformed into a folk hero:

The prevailing image was of Aidid, a Third World underdog, scrapping gamely with the world's most powerful nation. He was able to capture a Nigerian soldier and an American helicopter pilot, kill eighteen Americans and wound seventy-seven others in a single engagement, and drag a dead and denuded GI through Mogadishu for his own video crew to capture for posterity—not merely with impunity but with the consequence of having his official status transformed from criminal to embattled statesman. (Stevenson 1995, 86)

By reacting to Aideed as a criminal, and treating him as such, both the UN and the United States contributed to Aideed's transformation. Indeed, the UN eventually took the bounty off Aideed's head, and even supported his talks with Ali Mahdi in Nairobi in February 1994, talks which resulted in an agreement that replaced the Addis Ababa accords, and actually gave more power to faction leaders like Aideed.

Finally, the events of October 3 indicate that support for Aideed, support shared by more than just his own clan, helped undermine the United States military action. The mission of October 3 was to capture two of Aideed's lieutenants who had been located in a house near the Mogadishu marketplace. In his description of that day Mark Bowden interviewed not just United States soldiers but Somalis as well. One Somali, reflecting on both the October 3 raid and one from July 12, pointed out that the United States was not just fighting Aideed:

> Didn't the Americans realize that for every leader they arrested there were dozens of brothers, cousins, sons and nephews to take his place? Setbacks just strengthened the clan's resolve. Even if the Habr Gidr were somehow crippled or destroyed, wouldn't that just elevate the next most powerful clan? Or did the Americans expect Somalia to suddenly sprout full-fledged Jeffersonian democracy? (Bowden 1999, 75)

Bowden describes a political meeting of Aideed's clan, which hardly conforms to the picture of hostile, unthinking warlordism and instead sounds like a participatory form of democratic governance (71-6). While such meetings may not have been customary and while leaders like Aideed did engage in autocratic policies, they also represented a form of politics that could have recreated a functioning political community.

When the soldiers began landing on October 3, the Aideed militiamen yelled to people "Come out and defend your home," an appeal that resonated with those who had been victimized by raids and swooping Black Hawk helicopters (31). Bowden's book describes Somali women fighting just as much as militiamen, putting United States soldiers in the uncomfortable position of having to kill women and children (43–6). As Bowden points out, ". . . this fight had turned into something akin to a popular uprising. It seemed like everybody in the city wanted suddenly to help kill Americans" (230).

In the end, the Somali resistance to the intervention found its outlet in a general who had contributed to the civil war that brought about the intervention in the first place. But because the intervening forces refused to respect the political presence of the various political factions, and because they considered some of those factions, like Aideed's, to be criminal, they quickly fell into the role of colonizer. And resistance to colonizing powers had powerful resonance in a country that had been the victim of both nineteenth century imperialism and twentieth century superpower competition.

CONCLUSION

The humanitarian intervention in Somalia demonstrates that no intervention is really only humanitarian. When these ethics of colonialism and liberal reformism are forced onto political communities that are denied any voice in the decisions of their political futures, they quickly lead to political resistance. And political resistance, whether from within the country or from outside it, usually undermines the intervention, leading to its failure. In the case of Somalia, this meant that while NGOs were now able to deliver food more easily, the Somali political community was no closer to ending its civil war and no closer to bringing a modicum of peace and stability.

CHAPTER FIVE

The Dilemma of
Humanitarian Intervention

INTRODUCTION

This book has been an attempt to explain the failure of intervention by means of a deductive analysis of the practice of intervention supported through three case studies. This chapter uses the theoretical framework and the three case studies to move toward some alternative conceptions of humanitarian aid, political agency, and global politics. Specifically, I explore the dilemma of international humanitarianism; that is, the conflict between the recurrent need to provide aid in times of civil war and famine, and the inability of armed intervention to accomplish these aims without trampling the political rights and freedoms of those being aided. I conclude by returning to the works of Hans Morgenthau and Hannah Arendt which provide possibilities for some alternative notions of global politics.

I began this book arguing that the failure of intervention can be understood by focusing on its normative and political aspects. This emphasis does not imply that strategic or economic reasons do not play a role in intervention; indeed I draw on a number of classical realist arguments in the construction of my theoretical framework. But the method employed here leads to the realization that intervention is not simply a defense of the national interest or the result of "power asymmetries" in the international system, but is, perhaps more importantly, an action designed to accomplish an ethical purpose (e.g., provide food to starving people, eradicate chaos, create a functioning government, enforce international norms). Simultaneously, it is a political action that presents the state agent in a public forum.

The three case studies all present failed interventions. They failed because of a clash of political presences, or a clash of state and nonstate agents. That clash was either between the allies undertaking the action or between the intervenors and the target community. Wherever it occurred, the clash between two or more competing political agents undermined the success of the overall intervention; that is, it prevented the initial ethical goals from being realized. In fact, the conflicts between agents were the result of the clash between their different normative visions of the intervention—normative visions that were important for defining not only the actions but also the agents themselves.

These failures lead to a deeper, and more interesting, question: how can we accomplish ethical goals in a world of competing state agents? My answer strikes at the heart of not only IR theory but international political practice as well: the dilemma of humanitarian intervention is really a dilemma of state agency. That is, the root problems of humanitarian intervention are to be found in the construction of the primary political actors, states, that prevail in international politics. This analysis has highlighted how the agency of these states is the basis of the problems of humanitarian intervention. Intervention, while it violates sovereignty, also reinforces and constitutes state agency. More importantly, as the practice of intervention demonstrates, state agency is detrimental in a number of ways to these forms of political agency. Interventions attempt to provide aid to the starving and create peace in the midst of civil wars. But in accomplishing this end, an intervention, even a humanitarian intervention, becomes a way to protect and strengthen sovereign statehood. More importantly, those sovereign states are not constructed simply as spaces within which politics can flourish. In the realm of international politics, the sovereign state is an acting state, and that fact of agency, because it occurs in a competitive contest with other states, leads to an increase in arms and a tendency toward war that in fact undermines whatever political practices might be taking place within its boundaries.

What is it about state agents that causes them to focus more on other state agents in an intervention rather than on the people who need assistance? And what possible alternatives are there to this form of international politics? Because state agents competing on the international level seem to be the cause of the failure of intervention, this chapter begins by proposing two alternative means to resolve humanitarian emergencies, nonstate agents and diplomatic means. But I find neither of these options resolves the dilemmas raised because neither of them eliminates the fundamental political element of competition in the public space. Finding nonstate agents and diplomacy unable to resolve the humanitarian dilemma, I return to the lessons of the case studies, especially the norms that motivate and sustain intervention. Rereading these norms—liberalism, colonialism, and humanitarianism—I seek to find in them ways in which to both retain state agency and resolve humanitarian dilemmas. While my conclusions are certainly not the only ones, they do build upon the lessons of these case studies and the insight that neither politics nor ethics can be removed from the practice of international relations.

NONSTATE AGENTS?

If state agents cannot provide aid because they engage in a competitive politics of presence, perhaps nonstate agents can accomplish those ends.[1] Indeed, such agents are very much a part of the global political system and have played an important role in the provision of aid in numerous international crises. Nonstate agents can be divided into two separate categories: international organizations (IOs) and nongovernmental organizations (NGOs). The former refers to organizations that have states as members, act as coordinating bodies for state action, and constrain state aggression by compelling multilateral action (Claude 1963; Ruggie 1993). Examples include the United Nations, the League of Nations, the European Union, and the World Bank. The latter are groups that exist and operate outside of state boundaries, dedicate themselves to specific political purposes, and often bring pressure to bear on state governments in pursuit of human rights or environmental action (Walker 1988); examples include Amnesty International, Greenpeace, the International Red Cross, and Catholic Relief Services.

Although such organizations have played an important role in the resolution of international crises and in the provision of humanitarian aid, they are unable to resolve the humanitarian dilemma of the modern world system. IOs, especially the United Nations, have become the favored choice among theorists of a new global order since the end of the Cold War; one recent report has argued that the United Nations can "serve as the principal mechanism through which governments collaboratively engage each other and other sectors of society in the multilateral management of global affairs" (*Our Global Neighborhood* 1995, 6). But Chapter 4 demonstrates that the UN, while playing an important role in prodding its member states to act, and in providing aid itself, failed to resolve the crisis in Somalia for precisely the same reason the states did. The UN as a collective presence on the global stage developed a political presence that it sought to defend in its interactions with states and NGOs. In other words, the dilemma of a state, that its political presence overwhelms its ability to deliver aid, plagued the UN as well. Secretary General Boutros-Ghali replaced Mohammed Sahnoun, the Algerian diplomat who was close to achieving some political reconciliation among the combatants, because

Sahnoun was not adequately defending the reputation of the UN NGOs may have less difficulty in this regard, especially if they are focused on particular political problems. But they will, in the competitive atmosphere of global politics, be forced to adopt a position similar to the state. Indeed, the classical realist dilemma of the collective applies just as much to the IO as it does to the state. Niebuhr argued that any political collective would engage in a competitive politics that generally does not lead to peace. When collectives interact on the global stage they pursue a political presence that rarely contributes to the peaceful resolution of humanitarian crises (Niebuhr 1932).

Furthermore, NGOs and IOs do not have the type of historical and political presence necessary for politics. As Michael Walzer argued in response to those who claimed that the protection of the state against intervention could lead to serious abuses of human rights, politics can only really take place within the confines of the nation-state:

> Rights are only enforceable within political communities where they have been collectively recognized, and the process by which they come to be recognized is a political process that requires a political arena. The globe is not, or not yet, such an arena. Or rather, the only global community is pluralist in character, a community of nations, not of humanity, and the rights recognized within have been minimal and largely negative, designed to protect the integrity of nations and then regulate their commercial and military transactions. (Walzer 1985, 234–5)

While Amnesty International or the United Nations has an important role to play in terms of protecting persecuted individuals or bringing together diplomats, neither of these groups provide the space for politics. As Hannah Arendt pointed out "Nobody can be a citizen of the world as he is a citizen of his country" (Arendt 1968, 81).[2]

DIPLOMACY?

Another possible means by which to moderate the competitive nature of international politics may be found in a practice that includes moderation and negotiation. Rather than turn to more traditional writings on diplomacy, I want to return briefly here to the work of Morgenthau, who, surprisingly, sets diplomacy up as a key element of his theory.

In his most influential work, *Politics Among Nations*, Hans Morgenthau constructs a moral theory in which the concept of rule or norm serves as a limit on power. These norms operate in three spheres: ethics in individual conscience, mores in social interaction, and law in the polity (Morgenthau 1986, 243–7). He argues that while these norms do not play a key role in limiting power in the international sphere, they certainly do impinge on those interactions.

Morgenthau recognized that moral discourse plays a role in international politics, but he did not look upon that role positively in every context. He argues that rather than acting as a constraint on power and political action, the moral discourse most prevalent in international politics actually serves to justify power politics. In fact, morality, controlled as it is by nation-states, has become a set of self-centered proclamations that do not create the possibility for dialogue but instead hamper it. He posits that nations see their moral discourse as applicable worldwide when they in fact only serve to advance the interests of the individual nation. He writes:

> [Nations now] oppose each other as the standard bearers of ethical systems, each of them of national origin and each of them claiming and aspiring to provide a supranational framework of moral standards which all the other nations ought to accept and within which their foreign policies ought to operate. . . Thus the stage is set for a contest among nations whose stakes are no longer their relative positions within a political and moral system accepted by all, but the ability to impose upon the other contestants a new universal political and moral system recreated in the image of the victorious nation's political and moral convictions. (Morgenthau 1986, 271)

Chastened as he was by the experience of World War II, in which the most extreme version of nationalism, fascism, led to some of the worst abuses in human history, Morgenthau sought to limit the link between moral discourse and nationalism.

There is a dissonance in Morgenthau's work on this point, if we recall the concept of the national purpose. The national purpose does exactly what Morgenthau warns against in *Politics Among Nations*: justify a policy of moral extremism based on a myth of national history. This tension within Morgenthau's work points to a possible resolution of the dilemma of humanitarian agency. For what is at the foundation of Morgenthau's concern with the nation is its lack of rationality. On this point, Morgenthau drew directly from Niebuhr: "In other words the nation is a corporate unity, held together much more by force and emotion, than by mind" (Niebuhr 1932, 88). Morgenthau, Niebuhr, and many other classical realists worried about the lack of moderate, rational leaders who could prevent the excesses of nationalism gone wild, that is, Nazi Germany. This caution about moral discourse in the international realm is a seriously neglected aspect of the classical realist scholarship. Recent theories of international ethics have sought to uncover moral "norms" that influence "decision making." Morgenthau (along with Niebuhr and George Kennan) realized that morality is always part of politics. They argued that statesmen continually abuse that moral discourse and, in so doing, create situations of irreconcilable differences. When such differences are coupled with the destructive power of the nation-state, the classical realists were well justified in trying to place international politics on a less emotional and more rational, self-interested plateau.[3]

How to reintroduce rationality into international relations became one of the guiding concerns of Morgenthau's work. His attempt to recreate the rational statesman as the key to understanding, and simultaneously critiquing, international relations was one step in this process. More importantly, he advocated a reinvigoration of a political practice that introduced a modicum of rationality into international relations. *Politics Among Nations* concludes with two chapters on diplomacy, something Morgenthau considered to be the only means of ameliorating the excesses of both the pursuit of power and the dangers of nationalistic moral discourse.

Morgenthau notes that when international relations was the province of diplomats answerable only to their "conscience," there was a clear set of limits on the exercise of political power. It is the rise of nationalistic power politics that has led to the world wars and the Cold War. Diplomacy is important for Morgenthau because it is the only means by which collectives can speak to each other while avoiding the competitive aspects that have been the focus of this essay. Diplomats speak to each other under the constraints of a set of rules and guidelines that control the more excessive expressions of political presence. It does not force changes on other communities, but instead seeks change through persuasion. It treats all state agents as equal, giving to each the respect that its political presence demands.

Can diplomacy, then, be the means by which humanitarian crises are addressed? Each of the interventions explored in this essay reveals moments at which diplomatic negotiation could have brought about some resolution of the crisis, and perhaps prevented the revolution, anarchy, or famine that prompted the intervention. In Russia, Wilson and Lloyd George's idea of the Prinkipo Conference foundered on the resistance of the White forces, and also on the inability of both leaders to convince their fellow diplomats, especially the French, that the Bolsheviks deserved a place at the diplomatic table. In the Suez crisis, the discussions at the UN in late October were nearing a solution when the British abruptly pulled out. Eden's insistence on solving the crisis without impinging on the rights of the British state undermined the chances of Selwyn Lloyd's discussions in the Secretary General's office. In Somalia, the "missed opportunities," as Sahnoun calls them, all revolved around diplomacy. Negotiations to peacefully end Said Barre's rule, negotiations between the political factions, and negotiations with the factions and NGOs about the delivery of food, were all aborted before they could have had any real effect.

Diplomacy does provide a space within which conflicts can be resolved. Its private nature tends to diminish the posturing in which state agents usually engage when in public forums. And the creation of a cadre of diplomats who share certain norms of behavior and expectations allows a sharing of perspectives rare in the international political realm. In terms of intervention, diplomacy appears to prevent its need from arising. The use of diplomatic conferences could encourage the resolution of humanitarian crises by bringing together not only state agents but NGOs and IOs that might be able to target specific aspects of the crisis.

But diplomacy remains problematic, especially if we recall the underlying problem of intervention, that it tends to reinforce state agents rather than protect individual persons. Diplomacy by its very nature relies on state agents, and its formalities and protocols revolve around the official granting and revoking of the right of states to act in world politics. The ability of the UN to grant certain political parties the official status of a state is not simply rhetoric but plays a key role in the practices of international politics. One need only consider the early Cold War years in which Nationalist China occupied the UN seat for China, even while the Communists controlled the mainland. Thus diplomacy may emphasize state agency in ways that are detrimental to the resolution of crises. In the historical cases of this study, diplomacy, while providing possible avenues for the resolution of the crisis, also may have exacerbated them. Both the British and the Americans in Russia were often more offended by Bolshevik dismissals of diplomatic protocols and traditions than by their domestic policy; the intervention was justified by these breaches of diplomatic practice just as much as by the dangers of Bolshevism. In Egypt, the diplomatic *faux pas* of John Foster Dulles in announcing the refusal of the Aswan Dam loan prompted Nasser's seizure of the canal; by refusing to admit Egypt as a legitimate player, the United States and other states used diplomatic practice to exacerbate the tensions. And in Somalia, the UN and United States's refusal to accept Aideed as the representative of the Somali people exacerbated the crisis there as well.

In other words, diplomacy, while providing a space in which state agents might resolve their differences through dialogue rather than conflict, still relies on competitive agents. And even when those state agents are separated from the excessive nationalism of the communities they represent, they cannot fully escape the dilemmas of state agency. Diplomacy allows the most powerful states to decide which states are legitimate and which are not. The use of IOs by the most powerful states further hinders cooperation; such organizations are used to justify the dominance of some political agents over others, thus preventing the development of any alternative communities. Diplomacy may be a possible means of moderating international politics, but by constituting some agents as more important than others, it cannot fully resolve the crises that lead to humanitarian emergencies.

THE FAILURE OF INTERVENTION

Neither IOs nor NGOs nor diplomacy seems capable of resolving the dilemma of humanitarianism raised at the beginning of this chapter. Perhaps within the histories of the interventions explored in this book there is an alternative solution. Chapter 1 developed the argument that intervention involves both ethics and politics. More specifically, most interventions have a normative element that involves not only a set of precepts but also an epistemological and ontological grounding. This ethic does not simply provide a cause for an intervention, but informs the decision, the action itself, political debates, and later historical accounts. But this ethic, in manifesting itself through a military intervention, becomes a political action as well, as a particular agent presents itself as representative of a corresponding set of ideals. The agent must display those ideals in a way that conforms to its unique history. Intervention, an action undertaken by a state, becomes an attempt to display publicly the moral and historical presence of a political community. Finally, the conflict between the alternative moral visions embodied by different agents usually undermines its success. This failure results from the fact that other groups, especially the group against which the intervention takes place, also demand a political presence and so will refuse any humanitarian or political aid that might be part of the intervention. This failure only becomes evident, however, when we see intervention as something that is both ethical and political.

The normative visions that informed these different interventions have been categorized into a three-part typology: liberalism, colonialism, and humanitarianism. These three terms allow us to see the different ways in which state agency manifests itself in the international system. They also demonstrate how positive normative ideals can be translated into conflicting political presences. As the case studies demonstrate, these three terms should not be limited to any one intervention, but can be found in all three. More interestingly, the description of these three normative types also reveals how the politics of state agency tends to negate the normative visions that are contained in an intervention.

Liberalism and International Society

In an intervention liberalism manifests itself in a domestic and international context. On the domestic level, the intervenor seeks to reshape the internal politics of the target state. In the Russian intervention, Ambassador David Francis' supported only those White leaders who were sufficiently liberal in their approach to domestic order during the attempted *coup d'état* in Northern Russia. General Graves refused to allow prisoners of war to be executed by White leaders in Siberia without a trial. On the international level, liberalism is the assurance that norms of international law and self-determination are respected. In Russia the Allies supported the Czech forces stranded in Russia because the support of a nascent political community was an important step in the construction of a Wilsonian, liberal world order.

What do these attempts to create liberal order, both domestically and internationally, have to do with state agency? The answer can be found in liberalism's emphasis on freedom. At the heart of liberal political philosophy is freedom (Locke 1980; Mill 1975; Sandel 1984; Flathman 1992). That freedom can manifest itself in the protection of individual rights or in the freedom to choose a form of government. In each of the interventions explored here, but especially in the Russian one, we see a desire to create a liberal domestic order; that is, an attempt to create a society in which individual rights are protected and representative government is able to flourish. The documents reveal that Wilson, Lansing, House, and the others involved in the Russian intervention sincerely sought to create a liberal democratic order. The ethic of liberalism was an important part of the Russian intervention.

But the historical chapters also reveal that the practice of intervention is not amenable to freedom. An intervention, as the use of force to implement a change in a political community, severely restricts the freedom of individuals to choose their own form of government. How can the initial ethic of support for freedom become a political practice that actually restricts it?

The answer lies in the politics of state agency. As an intervention moves from the ethic of helping others to become free toward a political practice in which state agents contest each other for political presence, the power of the state agent overwhelms the freedom of individuals. Ironically, the freedom of individuals is lost to another version of liberalism, what I have called international liberalism. Called by some neoliberalism, as a theory of international relations it emphasizes the ways in which economic interactions and international norms ameliorate the conflicts that would otherwise arise from international anarchy (Baldwin 1993). This differs from the liberalism of some, like Charles Beitz, who explicitly emphasize the benefits of domestic liberal theory for individuals in contrast to traditional emphases on state concerns (Beitz 1979). In terms of political practice, the international economic policy of the Clinton administration reflects the former sort (Reich 1991), while that of global commissions, for example the Committee for a Just World Peace or the World Order Models Project, reflects the latter (Walker 1988). The international liberalism to which I am referring is the former, a belief that the construction of state agents who respect international norms will bring peace.[4]

International liberalism, or neoliberalism, manifests itself in an intervention in its focus on creating a state agent that not only protects its individual citizens but, more importantly, can become a member of international society. And, as the historical chapters demonstrate, this construction of liberal state agents tends to undermine the construction of liberal domestic society. The Americans justified their support for the Czech forces more on the grounds that the Czech army represented the first step in national self-determination than on the grounds that they were contributing toward the creation of a liberal Russian political order. In fact, the Czech forces actually undermined the creation of a liberal society by supporting White reactionaries in their fight against the Bolsheviks. As for British actions in Russia, the attempt to create a Russian state that could continue the war against Germany, rather than supporting liberal forms of order, also demonstrates how international liberalism overwhelms domestic liberalism.

In other words, the politics of state agency overwhelms the politics of domestic liberal society. While this is a pervasive aspect of international relations, intervention reveals it in its clearest light. Interventions, while they may begin with an ethic of creating a liberal society, become attempts to create liberal state agents that will become members of international society. But, the historical instances of intervention explored here have also demonstrated that political communities that are the victim of an intervention do assert their freedom, often rather vigorously. In asserting this freedom, especially in the face of a political community presenting itself as protecting freedom, the target community plays an important role in undermining the success of an intervention. While the public presence of a state in an intervention prevents it from realizing its moral goals, that public presence also forces it to confront challenges to its vision of itself as representative of a certain way of life. The lesson to be drawn from the liberal meaning of intervention may appear bleak, but it may, in fact, have a glimmer of hope. For, on the one hand, it demonstrates that liberal forms of governance cannot be forced on a population by means of a state agent. But, on the other hand, it demonstrates that the public presence of the state agent helps to create the resistance that contributes to the development of forms of self-governance and political freedom. Thus while a state agent cannot accomplish the end of creating a liberal society, it may help plant the seeds of it for the future by generating forms of resistance to its rule.[5]

Colonialism and National Character

The second normative type is the colonial. Most interventions, while involving attempts to reform a domestic society, also revolve around a discourse of paternalism, the belief that this particular community is not quite prepared to undertake the tasks of governance. Again, we see this sentiment on a domestic and international level. Domestically the colonial intervention stresses the importance of proper administration and order; while the emphasis in the liberal intervention is freedom, the emphasis in the colonial is order. In the British intervention in Egypt in 1956, there was a belief, reinforced by memories of riots in Cairo and Alexandria from 1952, that Nasser and his cohorts ruled based on emotion and mass appeal and did not understand how to rule a society, as did the Iraqis and Jordanians.

Internationally, the colonial intervention is an attempt to prevent overly aggressive states from dominating an area. It usually includes the construction of a national community as somehow "naturally" inclined toward aggressive behavior, creating the need for a more permanent colonial presence. In 1956, both the British and the French believed that the Egyptian dictatorship was incapable of leading the Arab world, because of differences between Arabs and Egyptians (differences that, as conceived by the British and French, derived from a set of Orientalist assumptions about the Middle East) and because of the similarities between the aggressive behavior of Nasser and Hitler in their foreign policies. According to the Western powers, because the Egyptians did not understand how to govern themselves or how to be a good member of international society, the British had to lead them into the modern world.

Again, the question arises, what does this norm have to do with state agency? And how does it lead us toward a resolution of our humanitarian dilemma? The most important lesson to draw from the colonial meaning of intervention is that it relies not just on power but on knowledge. The British intervention in Egypt relied in a number of important ways on an Orientalist discourse; that is, the intervention found sustenance in quasi-scientific accounts of the differences between Egyptians and Arabs, and how the Middle East remained backward due to Islam or even to climate.

Intervention relies not just on power differentials but on interpretive strength. In the discourse and practice of international relations, that interpretive strength relies on being able to construct political communities in terms of "national character." Intervention, then, relies on concepts like "national character" or "national purpose." The colonial meaning of intervention reveals that what Morgenthau and other classical realists saw as a productive way to interpret world politics can also be deployed to limit the political presence of certain political communities. The colonial intervention demonstrates that both the ethical goals and the political practices often derive from intellectual discourses that construct the target peoples as helpless and pliant. The revolt prompted by an intervention must thus fight not only state forces but also state generated and supported interpretations.

Humanitarianism and Failed States

Finally, there is the humanitarian norm. In Somalia, American troops arrived to ensure the delivery of food to a starving and war battered community. American political leaders believed that the failure of the United Nations required action by a state agent, what they considered the most powerful state agent in the world at the end of the Cold War. And, again, there existed both a domestic and an international level to this humanitarian aid. On the domestic level there was the obvious need to provide food to starving peoples. As in most interventions, this attempt to deliver food also involved the attempt to halt, or at least mitigate a civil war. Indeed, this form of action can be found in interventions in both Somalia and Russia.

But the humanitarian project soon became humanitarian on an international level. What needed to be saved was not just individuals in a war-torn community, but states as viable actors in the world community. One can see this in Russia, where British and American leaders became concerned that communism did not advocate the creation of sovereign states, as did Woodrow Wilson's self-determination. Instead they believed that it sought to undermine the entire state system by drawing on different sets of political loyalties and economic needs. To stop communism, then, was to save not just the Russian people from its terrorism, but to save the newly forming world system. Similarly, the British and French action in Egypt was motivated by concerns that Nasser's Arab nationalism was undermining the state system that both the French and British had created in the Middle East. Thus to defeat Nasser was to defeat a force seeking to undermine the state system. Finally, the Americans in Somalia sought to create a state in the place of a political and juridical void so that this community could have the type of international presence necessary for it to interact with other state agents. The urge to fix "failed states" comes not just from the desire to solve a set of domestic problems, but also from the desire to make a certain group a viable player on the world scene.

The lesson to be drawn from humanitarian intervention is that humanitarian concerns do not exclusively, or even primarily, focus on individual persons, but, in an intervention, on the creation or protection of state agents. This means that while an intervening state may be able to provide some food for starving peoples, it will soon become more concerned with creating a state entity, usually in its own image. The desire to save failed states is to be found not only in interventions, but in the discourse that surrounds them. Arguing that certain political communities can no longer function as viable members of the world system, theorists of international relations are calling for ways to reconstruct such states, either through quick interventions (Goldman 1994) or longer term mandates (Jackson 1990). In any case, these humanitarian efforts end up focusing on creating state agents not on saving individual human lives.

Each of the three historical instances has been used to highlight one of the three aspects of intervention. But, as chapters 2, 3, and 4 reveal, these three aspects of intervention are to be found in all three. Indeed, they are to be found, to lesser and greater degrees, in most interventions of the twentieth century. In the American and British intervention in Bolshevik Russia, there is not only a liberal aspect, but also a colonial (in the British support for Kolchak in Siberia), and a humanitarian (in the American and British belief that their forces could provide the needed order to ensure the safe supply of food to the starving in Siberia). In the British and French action in Egypt, there is not only a colonial aspect, but also a liberal (in the construction of Nasser as a dictator who ignores liberal forms of political rule) and a humanitarian (in the French belief that their destruction of Nasser was a truly humanitarian action in support of the embattled state of Israel). And, finally, in Somalia, the intervention was not only humanitarian, but also liberal (in the stress on creating a "civil society") and colonial (in the belief that "warlords" do not know how to govern a society, thus requiring the long-term presence of United Nations observers to reconstruct the political system). Furthermore, the fact that, in the Somalia intervention, the United Nations, a body composed of all states and representing their collective views and interests (at least ideally), employed a discourse similar to that employed by the three liberal democracies indicates that these meanings have a wider range than just the United States, Great Britain, and France. As international organizations like the United Nations begin to take on more of the responsibilities for resolving humanitarian dilemmas, we can suppose that these three aspects of intervention will apply to more and more interventions.

These norms of intervention teach some important lessons. I have only highlighted a few of them here, specifically those that will contribute to possible resolutions of the dilemma that I identified at the outset of this chapter. There are certainly others, and from the histories I have written, I believe that other insights can be drawn. The ones I have highlighted all revolve around the theme of state agency; whatever may be the initial ethical goals, the intervention results in a policy of creating a state agent. And, as the historical chapters have also revealed, the creation of that state agent does not always lead to succor or political freedom for the individuals living in that territory. The next section explores some possible means to provide aid in a world of competing state agents.

NARRATION AND THE HUMANITARIAN DILEMMA

The humanitarian dilemma remains. Nonstate agents, while capable of reacting to specific emergency situations, remain incapable of dealing with the root problems that give rise to interventions. They also succumb to the same competitive, agonal politics that states do, as exemplified by United Nations actions in the Somali intervention. Most importantly, such groups cannot replace the state as a space in which politics can take place; they may be able to provide aid, but they cannot provide a political presence. Diplomacy is a practice that uses state agents in a spirit of dialogue rather than competition. But diplomacy does not escape the dilemmas of state agency in that it is constructed around a discourse of the more powerful states granting and depriving political agency to the least powerful. So while it may provide a space in which dialogue can take place, it is a space determined and constituted by the most powerful, leaving no room for equality among political communities.

Hannah Arendt's work, and life, articulate alternative forms of political agency that both respect the political space of the nation-state but also provide outlets for nonstate political action. Arendt's revival of Greek political thought in *The Human Condition* gave this essay its theoretical foundation. The notion of agonal politics, a politics in which agents present themselves to each other in moments of competition within a bounded sphere, prompted an understanding of international politics as a place where states reveal themselves. In an intervention, states display themselves by revealing their political histories and purposes as they try to impose a political system on a community in the midst of a humanitarian crisis or political revolution. But the agonal competition between states undermines these state purposes, as competing allies or target states resist the imposition of a specific state agent.

The Arendtian framework reveals both the genesis of intervention and its reasons for failure.

But agonal politics is not the only sort that Arendt articulated. As chapter 1 demonstrated, the agonal can be reconsidered through its narrative elements. In other words, understanding the importance of how narration constitutes state agency may give new ways to address the humanitarian dilemma. At the conclusion of chapter 1, I suggested how an attention to the narrative element can lead to more cooperative and restrained military and foreign policies. In the few remaining pages, I want to suggest more concretely how the three norms of intervention found in the cases I explored earlier can be used to reconsider the narration of state agency.

I have concluded that the dilemma of humanitarian intervention requires us to rethink the national histories that give rise to agonal state agency, in the hopes that we might develop a narrative state agency. This narrative state agency requires us to reimagine the historical foundations of foreign policy. I have suggested a possible alternative form of national history that respects the nation-state as the site of politics but also attempts to mitigate its more aggressive aspects. The three normative elements of intervention provide us with some more practical solutions to the dilemma of agonal state agency.

Freedom

An intervention seeks to create a community in which freedom in terms of rights and representation is respected. But interventions are unable to provide these freedoms. Can political freedom come from some other source, especially in a global political setting? Arendt's life provides us with a possibility.

As a German Jew who emigrated to America, Arendt sought to understand her relationship to the United States, Germany, and Israel. As a political theorist who felt herself to be part of a number of different political contexts, she sought to straddle some of the boundaries that make state agency possible. But while she saw the dangers of these boundaries, she also realized their importance for political action and engagement. In a letter to Karl Jaspers from 1947, she writes

> What I would like to see and what cannot be achieved today would be such a change of circumstances that everyone could freely choose where he would like to exercise his political rights and responsibilities and in which cultural traditions he felt most comfortable. So there will finally be an end to genealogical investigations both here and in Europe. (Kohler 1992, 91)

Arendt envisions here a world in which persons could freely choose the political contexts in which they wished to act. She struggled along with Jaspers to understand the place of Jews, Germans, and Americans in the global context (Kohler 1992). But she also argued, in her critique of totalitarianism, that those bereft of a political community can easily become the victims of violence and persecution, for they have been removed from the "common world" (Arendt 1968, 300–2). So while nationalism and its associated "genealogical investigations" are dangerous for the construction of a free political community, there is also a danger in existing outside of a political community with no place to call "home." Arendt can be read as seeking a type of political freedom that does not necessarily rely on a single national community, but that requires political engagement as part of a tradition or historical narrative.

Arendt's tentative answer to this dilemma can be found, on my reading of her, in her speech on accepting the Lessing prize in 1959. She argued that Lessing exemplifies the type of political existence that might mitigate the tensions of the agonal political method. On Arendt's reading of him, Lessing sought to create a world for which he, and all of us, has a responsibility. But that responsibility did not derive from a national purpose, as we have seen in the discourse of the interventions explored here. Rather, it is to be found in the telling of stories and in the creation of friendships. Nor are these practices to be seen as naive attempts to avoid the world. In telling stories, or narrating history, we construct the world in a particular way. Lessing's stories constructed a world in which persons were respected not for their nationality but for their friendship. As Arendt says of him:

> Lessing was concerned solely with humanizing the world by incessant and continued discourse about its affairs and the things in it. He wanted to be the friend of many men, but no man's brother. (Arendt 1968, 30)

Brotherhood, too much like nationalism, creates links too visceral for dialogue and prevents us from seeing each other as legitimate political presences. Friendship, on the other hand, provides the space in which political discourse can productively take place. Indeed, it was Aristotle who included friendship as one of the key aspects of the *polis*; unless we are friends, we will not treat each other as equals.

Thus the creation of friendships across national boundaries can be an important part of constructing a world in which persons are free. Rather than an intervention that seeks to impose a free community, we might imagine the creation of links among persons that cross boundaries. Emigration, immigration, and movement across borders can play an important role in this process. Certainly, the creation of these types of freedoms is the responsibility of those who can afford to travel and move freely in the world.[6] But these same individuals are often the ones responsible for the narration of stories, either fictional or historical. By moving across borders and sustaining friendships, those who narrate the past must be aware not only of their own histories but the histories of the multiple traditions and backgrounds that create our political world. Perhaps the use of the Internet can also play a role in this process, a technological advance being made more available to nonelites in the developed countries. Thus, both those who travel physically and those who travel technologically have a responsibility to narrate their collective pasts in ways that respect and enhance the understanding of other communities.

Knowledge

The colonial norm of intervention relied on the construction of national characters that sustained interventions by envisioning some groups as requiring aid and governance. This knowledge, as Edward Said has argued, develops from a complex interplay of different literatures and media (Said 1979, 1981). This meaning points us toward the ways in which the media in particular present the world to us and how those methods need to be reconsidered

Said's account of how the media and "experts" interpret Islam provides a powerful example of how knowledge can provide justifications for political action in international politics. Begun as a part of his larger study of Orientalism, Said's book *Covering Islam* ended up as a response to the media coverage of the Iranian hostage crisis. He argues that while experts discoursed eloquently about the rise of Islamic fundamentalism as if it were a single coherent bloc, they ignored the historical construction of Iranian anger toward the United States for its support of the Shah's oppressive internal policies. Media outlets during the crisis refused to acknowledge the wide variety of Islamic communities, reducing everything to the Ayatollah Khomeini's version of Islam. Even Iran was reduced to whether or not it was "for or against the United States" (Said 1981, 50). Said demonstrates that "communities of interpretation" exist in the media, communities that tend to reflect the cultural norms of their own cultural and nationalistic histories. Instead, Said seeks:

> Respect for the concrete detail of human experience, understanding that arises from viewing the Other compassionately, knowledge gained and diffused through moral and intellectual honesty: surely these are better, if not easier, goals at present

than confrontation and reductive hostility. And if in the process we can dispose finally of both the residual hatred and the offensive generality of labels like "the Muslim," "the Persian," "the Turk," "the Arab," of "the Westerner," than so much the better. (Said 1981, xxxi)

The media plays an important role in the creation of our history of the present. Its agents must become more aware of the ways in which their own cultural backgrounds and histories shape their interpretations of events. Similarly, the creation of "experts" on various issues needs to be challenged as problematic; these individuals, while capable of providing valuable insights, must not be the only ones responsible for the creation of narratives about various parts of the world.

Finally, the media needs not only to be aware of the narration of the history of others, but also of the narration of the history of its own community. For the United States, a useful exercise might be to draw out points in its history, or present political context, in which religious groups clash and negotiate for space in the political realm, thus demonstrating that "political Islam" is not that much of an aberration from the American context. While differences should not be dismissed, the similarities among historical accounts of national communities can be an important step in undermining the type of colonial knowledge that makes intervention possible. Attempts by developing countries to gain control of their own political histories by means of a New International Information and Communication Order (NIIOC) are a step toward that alternative narration (cf. Hamelink 1994); an even more important step might be a greater accessibility to the media and literature from those countries in the more developed states. An awareness of how Egyptians and Somalis interpret American political events might constitute an important step in the creation of an alternative narration of the developing as well as the developed world.

Failed Histories

The final norm of intervention is the humanitarian. I noted in this chapter how humanitarian sentiments in an intervention focus more on saving the state than on saving persons. The sentiment that prompts humanitarian action, witnessing the collapse of authority, peace, and material well-being, will remain and should be encouraged. How that sentiment manifests itself in political action is what needs to be reconsidered.

Briefly, that sentiment must be redirected toward the persons who require it, not toward the construction of state agents. Such actions will certainly require the development of political communities that can govern themselves. But such actions should not be undertaken without the knowledge that the historical accounts of both the intervenors and the target communities will play a role in that process. What needs correction is not failed states, but failed histories. While attention to the narration of the past may not seem to be a way to help those in need, it can play an important role in preventing the crises from developing. By respecting the narrations of women, elders, religious leaders and others in communities whose histories are rarely acknowledged, we can begin to see ways of acting that might sustain and support alternative forms of humanitarian aid.

This book has sought to understand the ethical and political aspects of intervention. In exploring these ethical and political aspects I have argued that the narratives that enable state agency ought to be the focus of our analysis. The suggestions for alternative action I have proposed in this chapter—greater global dialogue, new historical narrations, and alternative media accounts of world politics—are only suggestions. These suggestions revolve around the themes of narration and the state, and, by means of these twin themes, they seek to place the human back into humanitarian intervention. This book has stressed that a possible resolution of the humanitarian dilemma can result from reconsidering the narratives that create states as the primary actors in world politics. The alternatives suggested here place the human person, rather than the state, at the center of these collective narratives. Only then can dialogue truly take place, a dialogue that might subvert the competitive power politics so prevalent today.

Notes

CHAPTER 1: INTRODUCTION

1. For the most hostile response, see Spitz 1959. For an analysis of the controversy, see McClure 1995.

2. For a representative sample, see Benyabib 1996, Bowen-Moore 1989, Bradshaw 1989, Canovan 1974, Gardner 1990, Hansen 1993, Honig 1995, Isaac 1996, May 1996, and Villa 1996.

3. Although she did not avoid thinking. Her work, *The Life of the Mind* (1978) is an examination of two aspects of human life, thinking and willing. Her lectures on Kant's theory of judging, published posthumously (1982) is the third element of what she considered to be the essential functions of the mind.

4. Interestingly, this "common world" does not only arise from action but also from work, which creates physical objects that persist beyond the individual lives of persons, giving the world a permanence necessary for us to live. But, although work creates this common world, it is also affected by political action.

5. Arendt herself wrote very little on international relations, at least as I am considering it here. Her writing certainly addresses many important themes of global politics, such as human rights, refugees, and political violence. But she does not, as far as I know, explore the parallels between persons and states as political agents.

6. See Morgenthau 1962 and Arendt's letters to Karl Jaspers in Kohler 1992. In both of these works the authors deal with the question of Germany after World War II, the role of Israel for Jews, and the superpower competition between the United States and the Soviet Union.

7. A Hegelianism shared by others in the classical realism school; see Liska 1990 for a good example.

8. In fact, Morgenthau concludes *Politics Among Nations* with an analysis of diplomacy. Rarely do interpretations of Morgenthau address this aspect of his work that I find to be the most important.

9. Arendt might have raised an objection to this characterization of the diplomat as the embodiment of certain national ideals. Her description of government by bureaucracy as part of totalitarianism (Arendt 1968: 244–45) raises important questions about the role of government representatives. My understanding of the representative is not the same as Arendt's bureaucrat, although there could well be some overlap. Rather than guess at how Arendt would read my ideas at this point, I prefer to leave this as an unresolved tension in the text. I am indebted to Paige Arthur for raising this issue.

10. See Pocock 1991 for a similar argument concerning Europe and its inability to act as a coherent agent without a narrative history to support such actions.

11. The national purpose serves a further role. By defining an action like intervention in terms of a moral vision derived from a shared historical experience, the national purpose gives meaning to the lives of citizens in a way few other articulations can. In domestic politics, the values and meanings of a country's purpose are constantly contested. But in foreign affairs, a nation is able to celebrate its identity and, in fact, assert that identity in relation to others. This celebration of national identity returns us to Rienhold Niebuhr's interpretation of international politics, for it is in such moments of assertion that Niebuhr saw the inability of the national community to coexist with other national communities (Niebuhr 1932). More recent work in international relations theory has also addressed the ways in which foreign policy founds and sustains the nation in various ways (Campbell 1992).

12. The concept of a language game is borrowed from Ludwig Wittgenstein (1958). For a more extensive use of Wittgenstein's ideas to understand intervention, see Lang 1996.

13. But see Isaac 1996 for an alternative view on Arendt as supportive of human rights.

14. See George 1979 and Eckstein 1975 for further explanation of the case study approach.

15. What I am calling "Wilsonian" here should not be seen as simply American. Many of the idealist notions that helped shape the League of Nations originated in Great Britain, especially the activities of Lord Robert Cecil.

16. Cf. Kratochwil and Lapid 1996 and Barkin and Cronin 1993 for attempts to address this failure.

17. I am indebted to William Connolly for this formulation.

CHAPTER 2: INTERVENTION IN RUSSIA

1. Two other powers involved in the intervention were the French and the Japanese. While their roles were significant in different theaters (Japan in Siberia and France in the Caucasus), my lack of access to their archives and the predominant role of the British and Americans explains my focus in this chapter.

2. A further, more obviously normative impulse also played a role in the Russian intervention, that of feeding those who had been deprived by the civil war. Led largely by Herbert Hoover, the feeding of the Russians only developed later as an important element of the intervention, that is, after the Peace Conference. I choose not to explore this element in this book because it does not seem to have played an important part in the failure of the intervention. For more information on this element of the Russian intervention see Fisher 1927 and McElroy 1992, 57–87.

3. British and Japanese troops had, in fact, already been in Vladivostock in response to the death of three Japanese merchants in Vladivostock, who were supposedly killed by Russian soldiers on April 4, 1918. Kennan and others believe the killings to be genuine, but many argue that the Japanese and British reaction was in no way commensurate with the initial deaths; Kennan 1956 II, 105–06.

4. See the following for a fuller discussion of this "sentimental element" and the feeling of responsibility it prompted in Lansing and others.

5. In later interpretations of the intervention, Kennan demonstrates a more pronounced realist appraisal. Significantly, these later interpretations arise out of debates with Soviet historians, who both review his first interpretation and begin to publish their own interpretations of the intervention. Kennan reviewed some of these initial interpretations in 1960, and then went on to write two later interpretations of the intervention. One is in the context of a larger work, composed of lectures given on Russian-Western relations under the reign of Lenin and Stalin. There Kennan stresses the influence of the war, and the need to win the war, as the most important reasons for the intervention. He notes that it is obvious that the Allied powers, including the United States, were clearly concerned about the war in their decision on Russia: "In both cases, his original decision was closely linked with America's wartime concerns. Had there been no great European war in progress, neither expedition would ever have been dispatched" (Kennan 1969, 60). The emphasis in this article and in his later overall interpretations of the Russian intervention put Kennan clearly on the side of a realist interpretation. More focused on the concerns of the war and issues of national security, Kennan's analysis in these later interpretations differs in emphasis from the earlier ones. While Kennan's work provides a well-documented analysis of

the early interaction between the Russians and the Americans, his need to refute the Soviet historians forced him to alter his initial interpretation of the intervention. The military community's resistance to the intervention demonstrates that the war was not the decisive reason for the intervention, but that Woodrow Wilson's desire to save the Czechs played a much more important role. Only a sensitivity to the ethical and political interpretations of the main policy makers can reveal this. Furthermore, this is not to say that the Soviet history of the intervention is preferable to Kennan's. In fact, the Soviet histories of the event flagrantly disregard most of the documentary evidence on the part of the British and the Americans. Kennan's desire to refute their history is an admirable one. What I am stressing here is how that desire to refute the Soviets led to an important alteration in his account that ignores some of the important elements of the intervention.

    6. Wilson to Frank Polk, the State Department officer in charge of distributing the instructions to the other allies: "The memorandum is of so confidential a nature that I have, as you will see, written it myself on my own typewriter" (PWW 48, 639).

    7. It is interesting to note that in the marginal comments accompanying the previous quote, Robert Lansing penned in a list of Latin American countries in which the United States had intervened: Panama, Nicaragua, Santo Domingo, and Haiti. What his purpose was in noting this is unclear; it does indicate, however, that both Wilson and Lansing were aware of the fact that the United States had intervened in the past.

    8. If George Kennan represents the realist historian of United States foreign policy, than William A. Williams represents the Marxist. Actually, Williams was not a Marxist in the classic sense of the term, but he did draw on the economic sources of American foreign policy in his interpretations. Williams contributed two important works concerning the American intervention in Russia. The first, *American Russian Relations, 1787–1947* (1971) interprets American foreign policy as the result of economic expansion. He offers a more sustained analysis of the intervention in a two-part article published in *Studies on the Left*, a journal started by Williams' students devoted to a reinterpretation of American history from a Marxist perspective.

    9. United States National Archives, Record Group 59, S 250, R 46; Box 1 Office of East European Affairs, General Records, 1911–1940; File 1130, Siberian Intervention and Russian Railroad Corps; Memo to Secretary of State, September 23, 1919.

    10. United States National Archives, RG 59, S 250, R 46, Box 2; File 1500 Intervention and the Allies, Memo from Major General W. G. Hann, General Staff (1919).

    11. See the editor's introduction to the letters as printed in *Canadian-American Slavic Studies*: "Cromie's judgment was obviously respected in

military circles, and the letters help explain the standpoint from which London viewed the November events in Russia," (Jones 1973, 499).

12. Public Records Office, Kew. Foreign Office 538/3 Vladivostock Consul. Misc: Correspondence on Political and Military Situation in Siberia, 1918–1921. Nor was this attitude confined to British representatives. A memo from United States Marine Corps Lieutenant Colonel Brekckenridge written on July 18, 1918, relayed the following sentiments: "I do not think that the expedition should be a purely military one; we must consider the Russian mentality, which is childish and immoral. The people are a cross between children and domesticated animals, and should be appealed to as such. Therefore, the expedition should contain a circus, with many slight of hand performers, so called magicians, clowns, etc., and some animals and moving pictures; there should be many of these things, so as to amuse and attract the attention of simple people; they should be treated as children, amused on the one hand and quietly and sternly punished on the other." United States National Archives. M316, 1910–1929, Soviet Union, Roll 16; 861.001/2618.

13. War Office 95.5420 Sanitation Office. Memo, May 17, 1919.

14. War Office 95.5419 General Headquarters; Northern Expeditionary Force; Memo on Liaison with Russian Officers, May 1919.

15. See note indicating that Lockhart's memo was circulated to the War Cabinet on January 4, 1919 in Foreign Office 371/3337 Russia; Political. 130845 165857–190425; item # 185499.

16. See memo by Poole, September 15, 1918, Foreign Office 175 Archangel Military Commission; Box 1, #518.

17. Cf. Morgenthau, for one of many examples of this view of Great Britain in relation to the rest of Europe; Morgenthau 1986, 214–217.

18. A proposal sent to the warring parties in Russia, asking them to come to the island of Principe to work out their differences.

CHAPTER THREE: INTERVENTION IN EGYPT

1. Israel also participated in this intervention, as the rest of this chapter will make clear. Indeed, Egyptian accounts of the action continue to refer to it as the "tripartite aggression." Nevertheless, my account will focus primarily on the reasons for the British and French actions and the politics thereof. The reason for leaving out the Israeli motivations has more to do with access to materials than to any substantive reason. In fact, I believe that the Israeli intervention could be usefully subject to the same analysis.

2. The other point of contention was whether or not the British technicians who would help run the base and the canal would be allowed to wear military uniforms.

3. On Eden's informing him of the appointment, one of Lloyd's first reactions was that he was not well-suited for the position because he "did not like foreigners" (Lloyd 1978, 4).

4. The myths surrounding Lawrence's role in the Arab revolt are too vast to recount here. To understand this role, the best place to begin is with Lawrence's own interpretation of those events, found in *Seven Pillars of Wisdom* (1935). Fromkin (1988) helps to put Lawrence's role into a larger perspective. And, of course, the film, *Lawrence of Arabia*, provides not only a historical documentary of his role, but also gives a glimpse of how that role was viewed in a larger cultural context.

5. The Labour Party was a consistently strong supporter of Israel in its foreign policy orientation. This created some dissonance in the House of Commons debates in the midst of the crisis, in which the Labour party sought to portray the Conservatives as acting in violation of the UN, while simultaneously trying to support Israel's right to defend itself against Egyptian attacks. See the diaries of Gaitskill (1983) and Richard Crossman (1981) for this internal party struggle.

6. At least the Tories believed this; the Labour Party dissented from the Government mainly on the grounds that it did not act through the UN. I return to this point in the following section.

7. See Kerr 1974 for an analysis of the competition between Saudi Arabia and Egypt for influence and control in the Arab world during the 1960s and 1970s.

8. See also Yousseff 1998, in which an Egyptian writer develops the theme of a French fascination with Egypt extending back to the crusade of Louis XII. Interestingly, while he does not analyze them as such, the historical instances of interactions between France and Egypt all revolve around military interventions.

9. *Comment Israël fut sauvé: Les secrets l'expedition de Suez.*

CHAPTER 4: INTERVENTION IN SOMALIA

1. It is important to stress that the clan divisions, while certainly playing a role in Somalia's political history, are not "age old divisions" that have somehow been let loose by the end of the Cold War. In fact, during the Cold War, Said Barre used such divisions to support his rule, leading to further polarization and division in Somali society. A similar process took place in the former Yugoslavia, Iraq, and Syria. Each of these countries had, or has, rulers who utilized sectarian divisions to support their autocratic rule.

2. In fact, the resolutions expanding the mission were written in collusion with members of the United States government, including members of the Pentagon. Clarke and Herbst 1996, 73.

3. Admiral Jonathan Howe, the UN Secretary General's representative in Somalia had been urging the United States government to send in the special forces in order to capture Aideed and his lieutenants. See Boutros-Ghali 1999 and Bowden 1999.

4. It was, in fact, the case that the UN soldiers had on occasion killed Somali civilians in the course of the intervention. Part of the reason for this, however, was that a number of the faction leaders would use civilians as human shields in their battles with interventionary forces; see *The United Nations and Somalia* 1996.

CHAPTER 5: THE DILEMMA OF HUMANITARIAN INTERVENTION

1. While this section assumes that international organizations and nongovernmental organizations are the only agents who can act instead of states, one needs to also consider individual persons as possible agents. This may be difficult to see because so much of the presence of individuals at the global level is that of rights bearers only and not necessarily active agents. But, individuals do make a difference at the global level, especially in their ability to act together in protest. See the recent work by Bleiker 2000 for an exploration of this idea as the person as an effective political agent.

2. See Connolly 1991 for a critique of this point, especially in relation to Walzer.

3. Unfortunately, this moral caution became the amorality of power politics in its neorealist versions (Waltz 1979).

4. This point can be seen as an important critique of the neoliberal argument. While much of neoliberalism is seen as a way to overcome the excesses of realism and neorealism, this argument in fact reveals that it succumbs to the same emphasis on the state as agent that is found in realist theories. Thus it may not be all that different from those theories it is trying to contest.

5. This last point puts an interesting spin on the argument of J. S. Mill concerning intervention. Mill argued that interventions are wrong because they do not allow communities to defend their own rights and freedoms. But the conclusion here might be that interventions could provide an important catalyst to the assertion of those rights and freedoms. See Mill 1859/1989.

6. But cf. Anderson 1994 for a discussion of the dangers of long-distance nationalism; that is, the ways in which expatriates tend to support aggressive nationalistic movements in countries of which they are no longer a part, as small groups of American Irish and Jews do in the case of Ireland and Israel. While the resolution of this problem would require a dissertation in its own right, suffice it to say that we must remain aware of this phenomenon as we move in and through different historical and national contexts.

Bibliography

Adam, Hussein. "Somalia: Militarism, Warlordism, or Democracy?" *Review of African Political Economy* 54 (1992): 11–26.

Adams, Sherman. *First Hand Report: The Story of the Eisenhower Administration.* New York: Harper and Brothers, 1961.

Adler, Emanuel and Michael Barnett, eds. *Security Communities.* Cambridge: Cambridge University Press, 1998.

Agernon, Robert-Charles. "De l'Empire à la dislocation de l'Union française" in Jacques Thobie, et al., *Histoire de La France Colonide, 1914–1990.* Paris: Armnd Colin, 1990: 309–408.

Allard, Kenneth. *Somalia Operations: Lessons Learned.* Washington DC: National Defense University Press, 1995.

Amery, Julian. "The Suez Group: A Retrospective on Suez." *The Suez-Sinai Crisis, 1956: Retrospective and Reappraisal.* Edited by Selwyn Ilan Troen and Moshe Shemesh. London: Frank Cass, 1990: 110–26.

Anderson, Benedict. "Exodus." *Critical Inquiry* 20 (1994): 314–27.

Annan, Kofi. *The Question of Intervention.* New York: United Nations Publishers, 1999.

Arendt, Hannah. "The Concept of History: Ancient and Modern." *Between Past and Future: Eight Exercises in Political Thought.* New York: Penguin Books, 1968: 41–90.

———. *Crises of the Republic.* San Diego: Harcourt Brace Jovanovich, 1972.

———. *Eichmann in Jerusalem: A Report on the Banality of Evil, Rev. and Enlarged Ed.* New York: Penguin Books, 1964.

———. *The Human Condition.* Chicago: The University of Chicago Press, 1958.

———. *The Life of the Mind.* San Diego: Harcourt Brace Jovanovich Publishers, 1978.

———. "Lying in Politics: Reflections on the Pentagon Papers." *Crises of the Republic.* San Diego: Harcourt, Brace, Jovanovich, 1972: 1–47.

————."On Humanity in Dark Times: Thoughts on Lessing." *Men in Dark Times*. New York: Harcourt, Brace, Jovanovich, 1968: 3–31.

————. "Reflections on Little Rock" *Dissent 6*, 1 (1959): 45–56.

————. *On Revolution*. New York: Penguin Books, 1963.

————. *The Origins of Totalitarianism*. San Diego: Harcourt Brace and Company, 1968.

————. "What is Freedom?" *Between Past and Future: Eight Exercises in Political Thought*. New York: Penguin Books, 1968: 143–72.

————. *Lectures on Kant s Political Philosophy*, edited by Ronald Beiner. Chicago: University of Chicago Press, 1982.

Aron, Raymond. *Peace and War Among Nations*. Trans. Richard Howard and Annette Baker Fox. Garden City: Doubleday, 1966.

Azeau, Henri. *Le piège de Suez (5 novembre 1956)*. Paris: Robert Laffont, 1964.

Baeyens, Jacques. *Un coup d' èpée dans l'eau du canal: Le Seconde Campagne d'Egypte*. Paris: Librarie Artheme Fayard, 1976.

Baker, Ray S., ed. *Woodrow Wilson: Life and Letters*. New York: Doubleday, Doran and Co., 1939. 8 vols.

Baker, Ray S. and W. E. Dodd, eds. *The Public Papers of Woodrow Wilson*. New York: Harper Brothers Publishing, 1927. 6 vols.

Baldwin, David, ed. *Neoliberalism and Neorealism: The Contemporary Debate*. New York: Columbia University Press, 1993.

Balfour, Arthur James. *Essays: Speculative and Philosophical*. New York: George H. Doran Company, 1921.

————. *Opinions and Arguments from Speeches and Addresses of The Earl of Balfour*. Garden City: Doubleday, Doran and Co., 1928.

————. *Philosopher and Thinker: A Collection of the More Important and Interesting Passages in his Non-Political Writings, Speeches, and Addresses, 1897–1912*. Edited by Wilfred M. Short. London: Longmans, Green and Co., 1912.

————. *Retrospect: An Unfinished Autobiography*. Boston: Houghton Mifflin and Co., 1930.

Barkin, J. Samuel and Bruce Cronin. "The State and Nation: Changing Norms and the Relevance of International Relations." *International Organization* 48 Winter 1994): 107–30.

Barnett, Michael. *Dialogues in Arab Politics: Negotiations in Regional Order*. New York: Columbia University Press, 1998.

Bar-On, Mordechai. "David Ben-Gurion and the Sèvres Collusion." *Suez 1956: The Crisis and Its Consequences*. William Roger Louis and Roger Owen, eds. Oxford: Clarendon Press, 1991. 145–60.

Bar-Zohar, Michel. *Suez: Ultra-Secret*. Paris: Fayard, 1964.

Beitz, Charles. *Political Theory and International Relations*. Princeton: Princeton University Press, 1979.

Beitz, Charles, et. al. *International Ethics.* Princeton: Princeton University Press, 1985.

Beloff, Lord. "The Crisis and its Consequences for the British Conservative Party." *Suez 1956: The Crisis and Its Consequences.* Edited by William Roger Louis and Roger Owen. Oxford: Clarendon Press, 1991: 319–34.

Benhabib, Selya. *The Reluctant Modernism of Hannah Arendt.* Thousand Oaks: Sage Publications, 1996.

Ben-Gurion, David. *Israel: Years of Challenge.* New York: Holt, Rinehart and Winston, 1963.

Betts, Richard. "The Delusion of Impartial Intervention." *Foreign Affairs: Agenda 1995.* New York: Foreign Affairs Press, 1995: 20–33.

Bierstecker, Thomas and Cynthia Weber, eds. *State Sovereignty as Social Construct.* Cambridge: Cambridge University Press, 1996.

Biondi, Jean-Pierre et Giles Marin. *Les anticolonistes (1887–1962).* Paris: Robert Laffont, 1992.

Bishop, James K. "Escape from Mogadishu." *Foreign Service Journal* (March 1991): 26–31.

Blumenthal, Sidney. "Why are We In Somalia?" *The New Yorker.* October 25, 1993: 48–60.

Bolton, J. "Wrong Turn in Somalia." *Foreign Affairs* 73 (1994): 56–66.

Boutros-Ghali, Boutros. *Unvanquished.* New York: Random House, 1999.

Bowden, Mark. *Black Hawk Down: A Story of Modern War.* New York: Atlantic Monthly Press, 1999.

Bowen-Moore, Patricia. *Hannah Arendt's Philosophy of Natality.* New York: St. Martin's Press, 1989.

Bowie, Robert. *Suez: 1956.* New York: Oxford University Press, 1974.

Bradley, John. *Allied Intervention in Russia.* New York: Basic Books, 1968.

Bradshaw, Leah. *Acting and Thinking: The Political Thought of Hannah Arendt.* Toronto: University of Toronto Press, 1989.

British Documents on Foreign Affairs: Reports and Papers from the Foreign Office Confidential Print. Part II From the First World War to the Second World War. Series A: The Soviet Union, 1917–1939. Edited by D. Cameron Watt. Bethesda: University Publishers of American, 1984. 3 vols. (Cited as BDFA in text.)

Brown, Chris. *International Relations Theory—New Normative Approaches.* London: Harvester Wheatsheaf, 1992.

Buchanan, George. *My Mission to Russia and Other Diplomatic Memories.* Boston: Little Brown and Co., 1920. 2 vols.

Buchanan, Meriel. *Diplomacy and Foreign Courts.* New York: J. H. Shears and Co., 1928.

Buckley, Thomas and Edward Strong. *American Foreign and National Security Policies, 1914–1945.* Knoxville: The University of Tennessee Press, 1987.

Bull, Hedley. *The Anarchical Society: A Study of Order in World Politics.* New York: Columbia University Press, 1977.

———. *Intervention in World Politics.* Oxford: Clarendon Press, 1984.

Bull, Hedley and Adam Watson, eds. *The Expansion of International Society.* Oxford: Oxford University Press, 1984.

Bunyan, James, ed. *Intervention, Civil War, and Communism in Russia, April–December 1918: Documents and Materials.* Baltimore: Johns Hopkins University Press, 1936.

Bush, George. *Public Papers of the President: George Bush.* Washington: GPO, 1988–1993.

Butler, Gregory S. "Visions of a Nation Transformed: Modernity and Ideology in Wilson's Political Thought." American Political Science Association Meeting. Chicago, 1995.

Callwell, C. E., ed. *Field-Marshall Sir Henry Wilson: His Life and Diaries.* London: Caswell and Co., 1927. 2 vols.

Campbell, David. *National Deconstruction: Violence, Identity and Justice in Bosnia.* Minneapolis: University of Minnesota Press, 1998.

———. *Politics Without Principles: Sovereignty, Ethics and the Narratives of the Gulf War.* Boulder: Lynne Rienner Publishers, 1993.

———. "Violent Performances: Identity, Sovereignty, Responsibility." *The Return of Culture and Identity in IR Theory.* Yosef Lapid and Friedrich Kratochwil, eds. Boulder: Lynne Rienner Publishing Co., 1996: 163–180.

———. *Writing Security: United States Foreign Policy and the Politics of Identity.* Minneapolis: University of Minnesota Press. 1992.

Canovan, Margaret. *The Political Thought of Hannah Arendt.* London: Dent, 1974.

Carlton, David. *Britain and the Suez Crisis.* London: Basil Blackwell, 1988.

Carr, E. H., *The Twenty Years Crisis, 1919–1939.* New York: Harper and Row, 1939/1946/1964.

———. *A History of Soviet Russia.* New York: Macmillan Co., 1953. 8 vols.

———. *The Twenty Years' Crisis, 1919–1939: An Introduction to the Study of International Relations.* New York: Harper Torchbooks, 1964.

Childers, Erskine B. *The Road to Suez: A Study in Western-Arab Relations.* London: McGibb and Kee, 1962.

Churchill, Winston. *The Aftermath: The World Crisis, 1918–1928.* New York: Charles Scribner's Sons, 1929.

———. *The Second World War: Vol. I: The Gathering Storm.* Boston: Houghton Mifflin Co., 1948.

Clark, J. "Debacle in Somalia." *Foreign Affairs* 72 (1993): 109–23.

Clarke, Walter. "Uncertain Mandates in Somalia: Can External Intervention Revive Failed States?" Learning from OPERATION RESTORE HOPE. Princeton University. April 1995.

Clarke, Walter and Jeffrey Herbst "Somalia and the Future of Humanitarian Intervention" *Foreign Affairs* (March/April 1996): 70–86.

Clarke, Walter and Jeffrey Herbst. *Learning from Somalia: The Lessons of Armed Humanitarian Intervention.* Boulder: Westview 1997.

Claude, Jr., Inis. *Power and International Relations.* New York: Random House. 1962.

———. *Swords into Plowshares: The Problems and Progress of International Organizations.* 2nd ed. New York: Random House, 1963.

Clinton, William J. *Public Papers of the President: Bill Clinton.* Washington: GPO, 1993–1995.

Cohen, Marshall, "Moral Skepticism and International Relations" in Charles Beitz, et. al., *International Ethics.* Princeton: Princeton University Press, 1985.

Connolly, William. "Democracy and Territoriality." *Millennium: Journal of International Studies* 20 (1991): 463–84.

———. *Identity/Difference: Democratic Negotiations of the Political Paradox.* Ithaca: Cornell University Press, 1991.

Cooper, Chester. *The Lion's Last Roar: Suez 1956.* New York: Harper and Row Publishers, 1978.

Copeland, Miles. *The Game of Nations: The Amorality of Power Politics.* New York: Simon and Schuster, 1969

Corbett, Percy E. *Law and Society in the Relations of States.* New York: Harcourt Brace Publishers, 1951.

Crocker, Chester A. "The Lessons of Somalia: Not Everything Went Wrong." *Foreign Affairs* 74 (May/June 1995): 2–6.

Cronon, Edmund David. *The Cabinet Diaries of Josephus Daniels, 1913–1921.* Lincoln: University of Nebraska Press, 1963.

Crosbie, Sylvia. *A Tacit Alliance: France and Israel from Suez to the Six Day War.* Princeton: Princeton University Press, 1974

Crossman, Richard. *The Backbench Diaries of Richard Crossman.* Edited by Janet Morgan. London: Hammish Hamilton and Jonathan Cape, 1981.

A Chronicler (aka Cudhay, John). *Archangel: The American War with Russia.* Chicago: A. C. McClurg and Co., 1924.

Cutler, Lloyd. "The Right to Intervene." *Foreign Affairs* 64 (1985): 96–112.

Dallmayr, Fred. *Beyond Orientalism: Essays on Cross-Cultural Encounter.* Albany: State University of New York Press, 1996.

Damrosch, Lori Fisler and David J. Scheffer, eds. *Law and Force in the New International Order.* Boulder: Westview Press, 1991.

Dayan, Moshe. _Story of My Life_. London: Weidenfeld and Nicolson, 1976.

Diehl, Paul. F. _International Peacekeeping_. Baltimore: The Johns Hopkins University Press, 1994.

Documents on International Affairs. London: Oxford University Press. 1953–1957.

Dorman, Andrew and Thomas G. Offe, eds. _Military Intervention: From Gunboat Diplomacy to Humanitarian Intervention_. Aldershott: Dartmouth Publishing Co., 1995.

Druckman, Daniel and Paul C. Stern, "Evaluating Peacekeeping Missions" _Mershon International Studies Review_ 41: 152–65.

Drakulic, Slavenka "Bosnia: Guilt by Disassociation?" _Partisan Review_ 61 (1994): 6–79.

Dupuy, R. Ernest. _Perish by the Sword: The Czechoslovakian Anabasis and our Supporting Campaign in Northern Russia and Siberia, 1918–1920_. Harrisburg: The Military Pub. Co., 1939.

Eayrs, James, ed. _The Commonwealth and Suez: A Documentary Survey_. London: Oxford University Press, 1964.

Eckstein, Harry. "Case Study and Theory in Political Science." _Handbook of Political Science_. Vol. 7 _Strategies of Inquiry_. Fred Greenstein and Nelson Polsby, eds. Reading: Addison-Wesley, 1975: 79–138.

Eden, Anthony. _Facing the Dictators_. Boston: Houghton Mifflin, 1962.

———. _Foreign Affairs_. New York: Harcourt Brace and Co., 1939.

———. _Full Circle_. Boston: Houghton Mifflin, 1960.

———. _The Reckoning_. Boston: Houghton Mifflin, 1965.

Eisenhower, Dwight D. _Waging Peace, 1956–1961_. Vol. 3. _The White House Years_. Garden City: Doubleday and Co., 1965.

Elgood, P. G. _Bonaparte's Adventure in Egypt_. London: Oxford University Press, 1931.

Epstein, Leon D. _British Politics in the Suez Crises_. London: Pall Mall Press, 1964.

Farer, Tom J. "Intervention in Unnatural Humanitarian Emergencies: Lessons of the First Phase" _Human Rights Quarterly_ 18 (1996): 1–22.

Feste, Karen. _Expanding the Frontiers: Superpower Intervention in the Cold War_. New York: Praeger Publishers, 1991.

Finer, Herman. _Dulles Over Suez: The Theory and Practice of His Diplomacy_. Chicago: Quadrangle Books, 1964.

Finnemore, Martha. "Constructing Norms of Humanitarian Intervention" in Peter Katzenstein, ed. _The Culture of National Security: Norms and Identity in World Politics_. New York: Columbia University Press, 1996: 153–85.

Fisher, H. H. _The Famine in Soviet Russia, 1919–1923: The Operations of the American Relief Administration_. New York: The Macmillan Co., 1927.

Flathman, Richard. *Willful Liberalism: Voluntarism and Individuality in Political Theory and Practice*. Ithaca: Cornell University Press, 1992.

Foglesong, David. *America's Secret War Against Bolshevism: U.S. Intervention in the Russian Civil War, 1917–1920*. Chapel Hill: University of North Carolina Press, 1995.

Forbes, Ian and Mark Hoffman, eds. *Political Theory, International Relations, and the Ethics of Intervention*. New York: St. Martin's Press, 1993.

France. Ministre des Affaires Etranges. *Documents Diplomatiques Français: 1956*. Paris: Imprimerie Nationale, 1988. 3 vols.

Francis, David. *Russia from the American Embassy, April 1916–November 1918*. New York: Charles Scribner's Sons, 1922.

Fromkin, David. *A Peace to End All Peace: Creating the Modern Middle East, 1914–1922*. New York: Holt Pub., 1988.

Gaitskill, Hugh. *The Diary of Hugh Gaitskill*. Phillip Williams, ed. London: Jonathan Cape, 1983.

Gambari, Ibrahim A. "The Role of Foreign Intervention in African Reconstruction." *Collapsed States: The Disintegration and Restoration of Legitimate Authority*. William I. Zartman, ed. Boulder: Lynne Rienner, 1995: 221–34.

Gardener, Reuben, ed. *The Realm of Humanitas: Responses to the Writings of Hannah Arendt*. New York: Peter Long, 1990.

Gellman, Peter. "Hans J. Morgenthau and the Legacy of Political Realism." *Review of International Studies* 14 (1988): 247–66.

George, Alexander. "Case Studies and Theory Development: The Method of Structured, Focused Comparison" in P. G. Laurent, ed. *Diplomacy: New Approaches in History, Theory and Policy*. New York: Free Press, 1979.

————. *Forceful Persuasion: Coercive Diplomacy as an Alternative to War*. Washington, DC: USIP Press, 1991.

Glubb, John B. *A Soldier with the Arabs*. London: Hodder and Stroughton, 1957.

Goldman, Steven. "A Right of Intervention Based upon Impaired Sovereignty" *World Affairs* 156 (1994): 124–30.

Goldstein, Judith and Robert Keohane, eds. *Ideas and Foreign Policy: Beliefs, Institutions, and Political Change*. Ithaca: Cornell University Press, 1993.

Gordon, David. *The Passing of French Algeria*. London: Oxford University Press, 1966.

Gordon, Michael. "Somalia Aid Plan is Called the Most Ambitious." *The New York Times*. November 28, 1992: A6.

Graves, William S. *America's Siberian Adventure, 1918–1920*. New York: Jonathan Cape and Harrison Smith, 1931.

Graubard, Stephen Richards. *British Labor and the Russian Revolution, 1917–1924.* Cambridge: Harvard University Press, 1956.

Great Britain. Foreign Office. File 538, Siberia 1918–1921. Public Records Office, Kew.

Great Britain. Foreign Office. File 175, Archangel Military Commission. Public Records Office, Kew.

Great Britain. Foreign Office. File 371, Russia. Public Records Office, Kew.

Great Britain. Foreign Office. *Documents on British Foreign Policy, 1919–1934.* Eds. E. L. Woodward and Rohan Butler. London: His Majesty's Stationary Office, 1949. First Series, Vol. III.

Great Britain. Foreign Office. *Blue Books on British-Egyptian Relations.* London. His Majesty's Stationary Office. 1921–1957. (Cited as Blue Books in text.)

Great Britain. War Office. File 95, War of 1914 to 1918, War Diaries. Public Records Office, Kew.

Great Britain. War Office. File 106, Directorate of Military Operations and Intelligence. Public Records Office, Kew.

Great Britain. Parliament. House of Commons. *The Parliamentary Debates: House of Commons. Official Reports.* 5th Series. Vols. 110–14. London: 1918–1919. (Cited as Vol. H. C. Deb. in text.)

Great Britain. Parliament. House of Commons. *The Parliamentary Debates: House of Commons. Official Reports.* 5th Series. Vols. 557–58. London: 1956. (Cited as Vol. H. C. Deb. in text.)

Grieco, Joseph. "Anarchy and the Limits of Cooperation: A Realist Critique of the Newest Liberal Institutionalism" in David Baldwin, ed., *Neorealism and Neoliberalism: The Contemporary Debate.* New York: Columbia University Press, 1993: 116–42.

Hamelink, Cees. *The Politics of World Communications.* Thousand Oaks: Sage Publications, 1994.

Hamrick, John. "The Myth of Somalia as a Cold War Victim." *Foreign Service Journal* (February 1993): 27–32.

Hansen, Philip. *Hannah Arendt: Politics, History, and Citizenship.* Cambridge: Polity Press, 1993.

Harriss, John, ed. *The Politics of Humanitarian Intervention.* London: Pinter Publishers, 1995.

Hehir, J. Bryan. "Intervention: From Theories to Cases." *Ethics and International Affairs* 9 (1995): 1–13.

Heikal, Mohammed H. *The Cairo Documents: The Inside Story of Nasser and His Relationship with World Leaders, Rebels, and Statesmen.* Garden City: Doubleday and Co., 1973.

———. *Cutting the Lion's Tale: Suez Through Egyptian Eyes.* London: Andre Deutsch Ltd, 1986.

"The Hell Called Somalia." Editorial. *The New York Times.* July 23, 1992: A22.

Hellman, Gerald and Steven Ratner, "Saving Failed States" *Foreign Policy* 89 (1992/3): 3–20.

Hempel, Carl. *Aspects of Scientific Explanation: And Other Essays in the Philosophy of Science.* New York: The Free Press, 1965.

Hewedy, Amin. "Nasser and the Crisis of 1956" in William Roger Louis and Roger Owen, eds. *Suez 1956: The Crisis and Its Consequences.* Oxford, Claredon Press, 1990: 161–72.

Henkin, Louis, et. al., *International Law: Cases and Materials,* 3rd ed. St. Paul: West Publishing Co., 1993.

Hirsch, John L. and Robert A. Oakley. *Somalia and Operation Restore Hope: Reflections on Peacemaking and Peacekeeping.* Washington: U. S. Institute of Peace Press, 1995.

Hoffman, Stanley. *Duties Beyond Borders: On the Limits and Possibilities of Ethical International Politics.* Syracuse: Syracuse University Press, 1981.

Honig, Bonnie, ed. *Feminist Interpretations of Hannah Arendt.* University Park, PA: Penn State University Press, 1995.

House, Edward. *Philip Dru: Administrator.* Upper Saddle: Gregg Press, 1969 (1911).

Huerwitz, J. C. "The Historical Context." *Suez 1956: The Crisis and Its Consequences.* William Roger Louis and Roger Owen, eds. Oxford: Clarendon Press, 1991. 19–29.

Ironside, Edmund. *Archangel, 1918–1919.* London: Constable, 1953.

Isaac, Jeffrey. "A New Guarantee on Earth: Hannah Arendt on Human Dignity and the Politics of Human Rights." *American Political Science Review* 90 (March 1996): 61–73.

Issaiev, V. I. *Bolshevism in Russia through British Eyes: Complied from the White Book on Bolshevism and Parliamentary Debates.* London: Russian Liberation Committee, 1919.

Jackson, Robert. *Quasi-States: Sovereignty, International Relations and the Third World.* Cambridge: Cambridge University Press, 1990.

James, Robert Rhodes. "Eden." *The Suez-Sinai Crisis, 1956: Retrospective and Reappraisal.* Selwyn Ilan Troen and Moshe Shemesh, eds. London: Frank Cass, 1990. 100–9.

Johnson, Paul. *The Suez War.* New York: Greenberger, 1957.

Jones, David, ed. "Documents on British Relations with Russia, 1917–1918." *Canadian-American Slavic Studies* 7–8 (1973–1974).

Kassing, David. *Transporting the Army for Operation Restore Hope.* California: Rand Corporation, 1993.

Katzenstein, Peter, ed. *The Culture of National Security: Norms and Identity in World Politics.* New York: Columbia University Press, 1996.

Keohane, Robert, ed. *Neorealism and Its Critics.* New York: Columbia University Press, 1986.

Kennan, George. *American Diplomacy, 1900–1950.* Chicago: University of Chicago Press, 1951.

———. "American Troops in Russia: Aid for the Czecho-Slovaks?" *American Intervention in the Russian Civil War.* Ed. Betty Unterberger. Lexington: D.C. Heath Co., 1969: 51–61.

———. *Soviet-American Relations, 1917–1920.* 2 vols. Princeton: Princeton University Press, 1956.

———. *Soviet Foreign Policy, 1917–1941.* New York: Robert Krieger Pub. Co., 1979.

———. "Soviet Historiography and America's Role in the Intervention." *American Historical Review* 65 (1960): 302–22.

Kerr, Malcolm. *The Arab Cold War: Gamal abd el Nasser and His Rivals, 1958–1970.* 3rd edition. London: Oxford University Press, 1974.

Kettle, Michael. *Churchill and the Archangel Expedition, Nov. 1918–July 1919.* New York: Routledge Pub. Co., 1992.

———. *The Road to Intervention: March–November 1918.* New York: Routledge Pub. Co., 1988.

Kirkpatrick, Jeane. "Where is Our Foreign Policy." *The Washington Post.* August 30, 1993: A19.

Kingseed, Cole C. *Eisenhower and the Suez Crisis of 1956.* Baton Rouge: Louisiana State University Press, 1995.

Knox, Alfred. *With the Russian Army, 1914–1917: Being Chiefly Extracts from the Diary of a Military Attaché.* London: Hutchinson and Co., 1921. 2 vols.

Kohler, Lotte and Hans Saner, eds. *Hannah Arendt/Karl Jaspers: Correspondence, 1926–1969.* Trans. Robert and Rita Kimber. New York: Harcourt, Brace, Jovanovich, 1992.

Krasner, Stephen. "Sovereignty and Intervention." *Beyond Westphalia? State Sovereignty and International Intervention.* Gene Lyons and Michael Mastanduno, eds. Baltimore: The Johns Hopkins University Press, 1995: 228–49.

Kunz, Diane B. "The Importance of Having Money: The Economic Diplomacy of the Suez Crisis." *Suez 1956: The Crisis and Its Consequences.* William Roger Louis and Roger Owen, eds. Oxford: Clarendon Press, 1991. 215–232.

Kyle, Keith. "Britain and the Crisis, 1955–56." *Suez 1956: The Crisis and Its Consequences.* William Roger Louis and Roger Owen, eds. Oxford: Clarendon Press, 1991: 103–30.

United Nations. *The United Nations and Somalia, 1992–1996.* Introduced by Boutros-Boutros Ghali. New York: United Nations Department of

Public Information, 1996. (Cited as The United Nations and Somalia in text.)

Lamb, Richard. *The Failure of the Eden Government*. London: Sidgewick and Jackson, 1987.

Lang Jr., Anthony F. "The Meaning of Intervention: The Politics and Ethics of Traditional and Humanitarian Intervention." Dissertation. Baltimore: The Johns Hopkins University, 1996.

―――. "The Responsible State: Hans J. Morgenthau on State Responsibility." Manuscript. Baltimore, 1996.

―――. "Responsibility in the International System: Reading US Foreign Policy in the Middle East" *European Journal of International Relations* 5, 1 (March 1999): 67–107.

Landrin, René. "Pélican: une opération humanitaire exemplaire" *Défense Nationale* (Mai 1995): 101–16.

Lansing, Robert. *Notes on Sovereignty: From the Standpoint of the State and of the World*. Washington: Carnegie Endowment for International Peace, 1921.

Lapid, Yosef and Friedrich Kratochwil, eds. *The Return of Culture and Identity in IR Theory*. Boulder: Lynne Rienner Publishing Co., 1996.

Laquer, Walter and Barry Rubin, eds. *The Israel-Arab Reader: A Documentary History of the Middle East Conflict*. New York: Penguin Books, 1984.

Lasch, Christopher. *The American Liberals and the Russian Revolution*. New York: McGraw Hill, 1962.

Lauterpacht, E., ed. *The Suez Canal Settlement: October 1956–March 1957*. London: Stevens and Sons, 1960.

Lefebvre, Denis. *L'Affaire de Suez*. Bruno Leprince Éditions, 1996.

Lefort, Claude. *Democracy and Political Theory*. Minneapolis: University of Minnesota Press, 1988.

Lennox, Lady Algernon Gordon. ed. *The Diary of Lord Bertie: Vol. II, 1914–1918*. London: Holder and Stroghton, 1924.

Levin, N. Gordon. *Woodrow Wilson and World Politics: America's Response to War and Revolution*. New York: Oxford University Press, 1968.

Lewy, Guenter. "The Case for Humanitarian Intervention" *Orbis* (Fall 1993): 621–32.

―――. *War Memoirs of Robert Lansing, Secretary of State*. Indianapolis: The Bobbs-Merril Co., 1935.

Link, Arthur S. *Woodrow Wilson: Revolution, War and Peace*. Arlington Heights: AHM Publishing Co., 1979.

Link, Arthur, ed. *The Papers of Woodrow Wilson*. Princeton: Princeton University Press, 1966–1993. 65 vols. (Cited as PWW in text.)

Linklatter, Andrew. *Men and Citizens in International Relations*. 2nd ed. New York: Macmillan Publishers, 1990.

Liska, George. *The Ways of Power.* London: Basil Blackwell Publishers, 1991.

Lloyd George, David. *Memoirs of the Peace Conference.* New Haven: Yale University Press, 1937. 2 vols.

———. *War Memoirs of David Lloyd George, 1917–1918.* Boston: Little Brown and Co., 1936. 5 vols.

Lloyd, Selwyn. *Suez 1956: A Personal Account.* London: Jonathan Cape Ltd., 1978.

Locke, John. *Second Treatise on Government.* Edited by C. B. Macpherson. Indianapolis: Hackett Publishing Co., 1980.

Lockhart, R. H. Bruce. *British Agent.* New York: G. P. Putnam's Sons, 1933.

———. *Retreat from Glory.* New York: G. P. Putnam's Sons, 1934.

Loughlin, John P. "The Algerian War and the One and Indivisible French Republic." *French and Algerian Identities from Colonial Times to the Present.* Alec G. Hargreaves and Michael J. Hefferman, eds. Lewiston: The Edwin Mellen Press, 1993: 149–60.

Love, Kennet. *Suez: The Twice Fought War.* New York: McGraw Hill Book Co., 1969.

Louis, William Roger. "The Tragedy of the Anglo-Egyptian Settlement of 1954." *Suez 1956: The Crisis and Its Consequences.* William Roger Louis and Roger Owen, eds. Oxford: Clarendon Press, 1991: 43–71.

Louis, William Roger and Roger Owen, eds. *Suez 1956: The Crisis and Its Consequences.* Oxford: Clarendon Press, 1991.

Luethy, Herbert and David Rodnick, eds. *French Motivations in the Suez Crisis.* Princeton: Institute for International Social Research, 1956.

Lyons, Gene M. and Michael Mastanduno, eds. *Beyond Westphalia? State Sovereignty and International Intervention.* Baltimore: The Johns Hopkins University Press, 1995.

Lyons, Terrence and Ahmed I. Samatar. *Somalia: State Collapse, Multilateral Intervention, and Strategies for Political Reconstruction.* Washington: The Brookings Institute, 1995.

Macmillan, Harold. *Riding the Storm, 1956–1959.* London: Macmillan, 1971.

Maddox, Robert. *The Unknown War with Russia: Wilson and the Siberian Intervention.* San Rafel, CA: Presidio Press, 1977.

Manning, Charles. *The Siberian Fiasco.* New York: Library Publishing, 1952.

March, Peyton. *The Nation at War.* New York: Doubleday, Doran and Co., 1932.

Markey, Daniel. "Prestige and the Origins of War: Returning to Realism's Roots." American Political Science Association, Boston, 1998.

Martin, André. "The Military and Political Contradictions of the Suez Affair: A French Perspective." *The Suez-Sinai Crisis, 1956: Retrospective and Reappraisal.* Selwyn Ilan Troen and Moshe Shemesh, eds. London: Frank Cass, 1990: 54–59.

May, Larry and Jerome Kohn, eds. *Hannah Arendt: Twenty Years Later.* Cambridge, MA: MIT Press, 1996.

Mayer, Arno. *Political Origins of the New Diplomacy.* New Haven: Yale University Press, 1959.

McClure, Kirstie. "The Odor of Judgement: Exemplarity, Propriety, and Politics in the Company of Hannah Arendt." Manuscript. Baltimore: The Johns Hopkins University, 1995.

McElroy, Robert. *Morality and American Foreign Policy.* Princeton: Princeton University Press, 1992.

Mearshimer, John. "The False Promise of International Institutions" *International Security* 19 (1994/95): 5–49.

Meisler, Stanely. "From Guard to Enforcer: U. N. Peacekeepers in Somalia." *Foreign Service Journal* (February 1993): 21–24.

Menkhaus, Ken. "Getting Out vs. Getting Through: U. S. and U. N. Policies in Somalia." *Middle East Policy* 3 (1994): 146–62.

Menkhaus, Ken and John Pendergast. "The Stateless State." *Africa Report* 40 (May–June 1995): 22–25.

Meyer, Jean, et. al. *Histoire de la France coloniale: Des originesà 1914.* Paris: Armand Colin, 1991.

Mill, John Stuart. "A Few Words On Intervention." *The Collected Works of John S. Mill.* Vol. 21. Toronto: University of Toronto Publishing, 1988.

———. *On Liberty.* Ed. David Spitz. New York: Norton Publishing Co., 1975.

Millman, Brock. "The Problem with Generals: Military Observers and the Origins of the Intervention Russia and Persia, 1917–1918." *Journal of Contemporary History* 33 (2): 291–320.

Mollet, Guy. *Bilan et perspectives socialistes.* Paris: Librairie Plon, 1958.

Moncrieff, A. ed. *Suez: Ten Years After.* New York: Pantheon Books, 1966.

Morales, Waltraud Q. "U. S. Intervention and the New World Order: Lessons from Cold War and Post-Cold War Cases." *Third World Quarterly* 15 (March 1994): 77–101.

Morgenthau, Hans. "Fragment of an Intellectual Biography, 1904–1932." *Truth and Tragedy: A Tribute to Hans J. Morgenthau.* Aug. ed. Edited by Kenneth Thompson and Robert J. Meyers. New Brunswick: Transaction Books, 1984: 1–20.

———. *Politics Among Nations.* 6th ed. New York: Alfred Knopf Publishers, 1986.

———. *Politics in the Twentieth Century.* Chicago: University of Chicago Press, 1962. 3 vols.

———. *The Purpose of American Politics.* New York: Alfred Knopf Publishers, 1965.

————. "To Intervene or Not To Intervene." *A New Foreign Policy for the United States*. New York: Praeger Publishers, 1969: 111–56.

Morley, James William. *The Japanese Thrust into Siberia, 1918*. New York: Columbia University Press, 1957.

Morris, Benny. *Israel's Border Wars, 1949–1956: Arab Infiltration, Israeli Retaliation, and the Countdown to the Suez War*. Oxford: Clarendon Press, 1993.

Murphy, Agnes. *The Ideology of French Imperialism, 1871–1881*. New York: Howard Fertig, 1968.

Murphy, Robert. *Diplomat Among Warriors*. Garden City: Doubleday and Co., 1964.

Murray, Alastair. *Reconstructing Realism: Between Power Politics and Cosmopolitan Ethics*. Edinburgh: Keele University Press, 1997.

Napolean in Egypt: Al-Jabarti's Chronicle of the French Occupation, 1798. Trans. Shmuel Moreh, Intro. Robert Tignor. Princeton and New York: Markus Wiener Publishing, 1993.

Nardin, Terry. *Law, Morality and the Relations of States*. Princeton: Princeton University Press, 1983.

————, ed. *The Ethics of War and Peace: Religious and Secular Perspectives*. Princeton: Princeton University Press, 1996.

Nardin, Terry, and David Mapel, eds. *Traditions of International Ethics*. Cambridge: Cambridge University Press, 1992.

Ndegwa, Stephen. *The Two Faces of Civil Society: NGOs and Politics in Africa*. West Hartford: Kumanian Press, 1992

Neff, Donald. *Warriors at the Suez: Eisenhower Takes America into the Middle East*. New York: The Linden Press/Simon Schuster, 1981.

Nicolson, Harold. *Curzon: The Last Phase, 1919–1925: A Study in Post War Diplomacy*. New York: Harcourt Brace and Co., 1939.

————. *Diaries and Letters*. Volume III. The Later Years. Edited by Nigel Nicolson. New York: Athenaeum, 1968.

Nicolson, Nigel. *People and Parliament*. London: Weidenfeld and Nicolson, 1958.

Niebuhr, Reinhold. *Moral Man and Immoral Society*. New York: Charles Scribner's Sons, 1932.

Northedge, F. S. *British Foreign Policy: The Process of Readjustment, 1945–1961*. London: George Allen and Unwin, 1962.

Nutting, Anthony. *Nasser*. New York: E. P. Dutton Co., 1972.

————. *No End of a Lesson: The Story of Suez*. New York: Clarkson N. Potter, 1967.

Oberdorfer, Dan. "Bush Sends Forces to Help Somalia." *The Washington Post*. December 5, 1992.

————. "The Path to Intervention." *The Washington Post*. December 6, 1992.

Omar, Mohammed Osman. *The Road to Zero: Somalia's Self-Destruction.* London: Hoon Associates, 1992.

Oppenheim, L. *International Law: A Treatise,* 7th ed. H. Lauterpecht. London: Longmans and Green Co., 1948.

Our Global Neighborhood: The Report of the Commission on Global Governance. New York: Oxford University Press, 1995.

Palmer, Frederick. *Newton A. Baker: America at War.* New York: Dodd, Mead, and Co., 1931. 2 vols.

Pendergast, John. "Human Rights: The Forgotten Agenda in Somalia." *Review of African Political Economy* 59 (March 1994): 66–71.

Peres, Shimon. "The Road to Sevres: Franco-Israelis Strategic Cooperation." *The Suez-Sinai Crisis, 1956: Retrospective and Reappraisal.* Selwyn Ilan Troen and Moshe Shemesh, eds. London: Frank Cass, 1990: 140–61.

Perlez, Jane. "Deaths in Somalia Outpace Delivery of Food." *The New York Times.* July 19, 1992: A1.

———. "Somalia Self-Destructs and the World Looks on." *The New York Times.* December 29, 1991: 4.

Pershing, John J. *My Experiences in the World War.* New York: Frederick A. Stokes Co., 1931. 2 vols.

Pfaff, William. "A New Colonialism? Europe Must Go Back to Africa." *Foreign Affairs* 74 (Jan./Feb. 1995): 2–6.

Pineau, Christian. *1956/Suez.* Paris: Robert Laffont, 1976.

Plotke, A. J. *Imperial Spies.* New York: Greenwood Press, 1993.

Pocock, J. G. A. "Deconstructing Europe." *The London Review of Books.* December 19, 1991: 1–5.

Porter, A. N. and A. J. Stockwell, eds. *British Imperial Policy and Decolonization, 1938–1964.* London: Macmillan Press, 1989.

Reed, Laura W. and Carl Kaysen, eds. *Emerging Norms of Justified Intervention.* Cambridge: American Academy of Arts and Sciences, 1993.

Reich, Robert. "What is a Nation?" *Political Science Quarterly* 106 (Summer 1991): 193–210.

Rey-Goldzeiguer, Annie. "La France Coloniale de 1830 à 1870" in Jean Meyer, et. al. *Histoire de la France Colonial: Des Origines à 1914.* Paris, Armand Colin, 1991.

Rhodes, Benjamin. *The Anglo-American War with Russia, 1918–1919: A Diplomatic and Military Tragi-Comedy.* New York: Greenwood Press, 1988.

Rich, Adriene. *On Lies, Secrets and Silence: Selected Prose, 1966–1978.* New York: Norton, 1979.

Richburg, Keith. "Relations with Warlords and Disarmament." Learning from Operation RESTORE HOPE. Princeton University. April 21–22, 1995.

Ricouer, Paul. "Action, Story and History: On Reading the Human Condition" in Reuben Gardener, ed. *The Realm of Humanitas: Responses to the Writings of Hannah Arendt.* New York, Peter Long, 1990.

Rosenau, James N. "The Concept of Intervention." *Journal of International Affairs* 22 (1968): 165–76.

———. "Intervention as a Scientific Concept." *Journal of Conflict Resolution* 13 (1969): 149–71.

Rosenthal, Joel. *Righteous Realists—Political Realism, Responsible Power, and American Culture in the Nuclear Age.* Baton Rouge: Louisiana State University Press, 1991.

———, ed. *Ethics and International Affairs: A Reader.* Washington, DC: Georgetown University Press, 1995.

Rothchild, Donald and Naomi Chazan, eds. *The Precarious Balance: State and Society in Africa.* Boulder: Westview Press, 1988.

Rothwell, Victor. *Anthony Eden: A Political Biography, 1931–1957.* Manchester: Manchester University Press, 1992.

Ruggie, John, ed. *Multilateralism Matters.* New York: Columbia University Press, 1993.

Russell, Greg. *Hans J. Morgenthau and the Ethics of American Statecraft.* Baton Rouge: University of Louisiana Press, 1988.

Sahnoun, Mohammed. *Somalia: The Missed Opportunities.* Washington: The U. S. Institute of Peace Press, 1994.

———. "Mixed Intervention in Somalia and the Great Lakes." *Hard Choices: Moral Dilemmas in Humanitarian Intervention.* J. Moore, ed. Lanham: Rowman and Littlefield, 1998: 87–98.

Said, Edward. *Covering Islam: How the Media and the Experts Determine How We See the Rest of the World.* New York: Pantheon Books, 1981.

———. *Orientalism.* New York: Vintage Books, 1979.

Salamé, Ghassan. *Appels d'empire: Ingérences et résistances à l'âge de la mondialisation.* Paris: Fayard, 1996.

Sandel, Michael, ed. *Liberalism and Its Critics.* New York: New York University Press, 1984.

Schuckburgh, Evelyn. *Descent to Suez: Diaries, 1951–1956.* London: Weidenfeld and Nicolson, 1986.

Sciolino, Elaine. "CIA Warns Bush on Somalia Mission." *International Herald Tribune.* December 31, 1992.

Seymour, Charles, ed. *The Intimate Papers of Colonel House.* Boston: Houghton Mifflin Co., 1928. 4 vols.

Shamir, Shimon. "The Collapse of Project Alpha." *Suez 1956: The Crisis and Its Consequences.* William Roger Louis and Roger Owen, eds. Oxford: Clarendon Press, 1991: 73–100.

Shapiro, Michael, ed. *Language and Politics*. New York: New York University Press, 1984.

Sloyan, Patrick. "How the Warlords Outsmarted Clinton's Spooks." *The Washington Post*. April 3, 1994: C3.

Smith, Michael. "Ethics and Intervention." *Ethics and International Affairs* 3 (1989): 1–26.

———. "Humanitarian Intervention: An Overview of the Issues" *Ethics and International Affairs* 12 (1998): 63–80.

———. *Realist Thought from Weber to Kissinger*. Baton Rouge: University of Louisiana Press, 1986.

Sommer, John. *Hope Restored? Humanitarian Aid in Somalia 1990–1994*. Washington D. C.: Refugee Policy Group, 1994.

Spegele, Roger. *Political Realism in International Theory*. Cambridge: Cambridge University Press, 1996.

Spitz, David. "Politics and the Realms of Being" *Dissent* 6, 1 (1959): 56–65.

Steigerwald, David. "The Reclamation of Woodrow Wilson?" *Diplomatic History* 23, 1 (Winter 1999): 79–99.

Stern, Jacques. *The French Colonies: Past and Future*. New York: Dideir Pub. Co., 1944.

Stevenson, Jonathan. *Losing Mogadishu: Testing U. S. Policy in Somalia*. Annapolis: Naval Institute Press, 1995.

Strakhovsky, Leniod. *Intervention at Archangel: The Story of the Allied Intervention and Russian Counter-Revolution in Northern Russia, 1918–1920*. Princeton: Princeton University Press, 1944.

———. *The Origins of the American Intervention in North Russia*. Princeton: Princeton University Press, 1937.

The Suez Canal: A Selection of Documents Relating to the International Status of the Suez Canal and the Position of the Suez Canal Company. London: The International and Comparative Law Quarterly, 1956.

Tarrade, Jean. "De l'apogée économique à l'effrondment du domaine colonial (1763–1830)" in Jean Meyer, et. al., *Histoire de la France Coloniale: Des Origines à 1914*. Paris: Armand Colin, 1991.

Teson, Fernando. *Humanitarian Intervention: An Inquiry into Law and Morality*. Dobbs Ferry: Transnational Publishers, 1989.

Thobie, Jacques, et. al. *Histoire de la France coloniale: 1914–1990*. Paris: Armand Colin, 1990.

Thomas, Abel. *Comment Israël l fut sauvè: Les secrets l'expedition de Suez*. Paris: Albon Michael, 1978.

Thompson, John M. *Russia, Bolshevism, and the Versailles Peace*. Princeton: Princeton University Press, 1966.

Thompson, Kenneth and Robert J. Meyers, eds. *Truth and Tragedy: A Tribute to Hans J. Morgenthau.* Aug. ed. New Brunswick: Transaction Books, 1984.

Thornton, A. P. *The Imperial Idea and Its Enemies: A Study in British Power.* New York: St. Martins Press, 1966.

Thornton, Willis. *Newton D. Baker and His Books.* Cleveland: The Press of Western Reserve University, 1954.

Tignor, Robert, ed. *Napoleon in Egypt: Al–Jabarti's Chronicles of the French Occupation, 1798,* trans. by Shmuel Moreh. Princeton and New York: Markus Wiener Publishing, 1993.

Todorov, Tvzetan. *The Morals of History.* Trans. Alyson Waters. Minneapolis: University of Minnesota Press, 1995.

Tomes, Jason. *Balfour and Foreign Policy: The International Thought of a Conservative Statesman.* Cambridge: Cambridge University Press, 1997.

Troen, Selwyn Ilan and Moshe Shemesh, eds. *The Suez-Sinai Crisis, 1956: Retrospective and Reappraisal.* London: Frank Cass, 1990.

Ulman, Richard. *Britain and the Russian Civil War, Nov. 1918–Feb. 1920.* Princeton: Princeton University Press, 1968.

————. *Intervention and the War.* Princeton: Princeton University Press, 1961.

United States. Department of State. Selected Files from the Office of East European Affairs, Record Group 56. The National Archives, College Park, Maryland.

United States. Department of State. Selected Files on Soviet Union, Roll M316. The National Archives, College Park, Maryland.

United States. Department of State. *Papers Relating to the Foreign Relations of the United States: The Lansing Papers, 1914–1920.* Washington: GPO, 1939. 2 vols. (Cited as FRUS RLP in text.)

————. *Papers Relating to the Foreign Relations of the United States: 1918 Russia.* Washington: GPO, 1931–32. 3 vols. (Cited as FRUS Russia 1918 in text.)

————. *Papers Relating to the Foreign Relations of the United States: 1919 Russia.* Washington: GPO, 1937. (Cited as FRUS Russia 1919 in text.)

————. *Papers Relating to the Foreign Relations of the United States: 1920. Vol. III Russia.* Washington: GPO, 1936. (Cited as FRUS Russia 1920 in text.)

————. *Papers Relating to the Foreign Relations of the United States: The Paris Peace Conference.* Washington: GPO, 1945–47. 11 vols. (Cited as FRUS Paris Peace Conference in text.)

United States. Congress. *Congressional Record,* 1917–1919. Washington: GPO. (Cited as Congressional Record in text.)

United States Congress. House of Representatives. Subcommittee on African Affairs. "The Crisis and Chaos in Somalia." September 16, 1992. Washington: GPO, 1992.

―――. "The Horn of Africa: Changing Realities and U. S. Response." March 19, 1992. Washington: GPO, 1992.

―――. "Recent Developments in Somalia." February 17, 1993. Washington: GPO, 1993.

―――. "Recent Developments in Somalia." July 29, 1993. Washington: GPO, 1994.

―――. "A Review of U.S. Policy and Current Events in Kenya, Malawi, and Somalia." June 23, 1992. Washington: GPO, 1993.

―――. "Somalia: Prospects for Peace and Stability." March 16, 1994. Washington: GPO, 1995.

United States. Congress. House of Representatives. Committee on Foreign Affairs. "Withdrawal of U.S. Forces from Somalia." November 3, 1993. Washington: GPO, 1994.

United States. Congress. House of Representatives. Subcommittee on Government Operations. "United Nations Peacekeeping: The Effectiveness of the Legal Framework." March 3, 1994. Washington: GPO, 1994.

United States. Congress. House of Representatives. Select Committee on Hunger. 102nd Congress. "Humanitarian Tragedy in Somalia." January 30, 1992. Washington: GPO, 1992.

United States. Congress. Senate. Committee on Armed Services. "Joint Chiefs of Staff Briefing on Current Military Operations in Somalia, Iraq, and Yugoslavia." January 29, 1993. Washington: GPO, 1993.

―――. "Joint Chiefs of Staff Briefing on Current Military Operations in Somalia, Iraq, and Yugoslavia." June 24, 1993. Washington: GPO, 1994.

―――. "Operation Restore Hope: The Military Operation in Somalia." December 9, 1992. Washington: GPO, 1993.

United States. Congress. Senate. Committee on Foreign Affairs. "The Crisis in Somalia." December 17, 1992. Washington: GPO, 1993.

―――. "U. S. Participation in Somalia Peacekeeping." October 19–20, 1993. Washington: GPO, 1994.

United States. Congress. Senate. Joint Hearing before the Subcommittees on African Affairs and International Operations. "An Assessment of Recent Developments in the Horn of Africa." April 8, 1992. Washington: GPO, 1992.

United States. Department of State. *Foreign Relations of the United States, 1955–1957. Volume XVI. The Suez Crisis, July 26–December 31, 1956.*

Edited by Nina Nerring. Washington D. C.: Government Printing Office, 1990. (Cited as FRUS The Suez Crisis in text.)

United States. Department of State. Files, Egypt: Foreign Affairs, 1955–1959. Lanham, MD: University Publishers of the U.S.

United States. Government Accounting Office. Somalia: *Observations Regarding the Northern Conflict and Resulting Conditions.* Washington: GPO, 1989.

United States. Office of the President. Communication from the President to the 103rd Congress. "Humanitarian Aid to Somalia." January 5, 1993.

———. Communication from the President to the 103rd Congress. "Military Operations in Somalia." October 13, 1993.

———. Communication from the President to the 103rd Congress. "Progress on U. S. Efforts in Somalia." July 1993.

Unterberger, Betty, ed. *American Intervention in the Russian Civil War.* Lexington: D.C. Heath Co., 1969.

———. *America's Siberian Expedition, 1918–1920: A Study in National Policy.* Durham: Duke University Press, 1956.

———. *The United States, Revolutionary Russia, and the Rise of Czechoslovakia.* Chapel Hill: University of North Carolina Press, 1989.

Vaise, Maurice. "France and the Suez Crisis." *Suez 1956: The Crisis and Its Consequences.* William Roger Louis and Roger Owen, eds. Oxford: Clarendon Press, 1991: 131–43.

———. "Post-Suez France." *Suez 1956: The Crisis and Its Consequences.* William Roger Louis and Roger Owen, eds. Oxford: Clarendon Press, 1991: 335–40.

Vatikiotis, P. J. *The History of Modern Egypt: From Muhammed Ali to Mubarak,* 4th ed. Baltimore: The Johns Hopkins University Press, 1991.

Villa, Dana. *Arendt and Heidegger: The Fate of the Political.* Princeton: Princeton University Press, 1996.

Vincent, R. J. *Non-intervention and International Order.* Princeton: Princeton University Press, 1979.

Vivant Denon, Dominique. *Voyage dans la Basse et la Haute Égypte.* Paris: Editions Gallimard, 1998.

Walker, R. B. J. *Inside/Outside: International Relations as Political Theory.* Cambridge: University of Cambridge Press, 1993.

———. *One World, Many Worlds: Struggles for a Just World Peace.* Boulder: Lynne Rienner Publishers, 1988.

Walzer, Michael. *Just and Unjust Wars,* 2nd. ed. New York: Basic Books, 1992.

———. "The Moral Standing of States: A Response to Four Critics." *International Ethics.* Charles Betiz, et al. Princeton: Princeton University Press, 1985: 217–37.

———. "Liberalism and the Art of Separation." *Political Theory* 12 (1984): 315–30.

———. *Spheres of Justice: A Defense of Pluralism and Equality.* New York: Basic Books, 1983.

Waltz, Kenneth. *Theory of International Relations.* Reading: Addison-Wesley Press, 1979.

Warner, Daniel. *An Ethic of Responsibility in International Relations.* Boulder: Lynne Rienner Publishers, 1991.

Watt, D. C., ed. *Documents on the Suez Crisis: 26 July–6 November 1956.* London: Royal Institute of International Affairs, 1957.

Weber, Cynthia. *Simulating Sovereignty: Intervention, the State, and Symbolic Exchange.* Cambridge: Cambridge University Press, 1995.

Weil, Robert. "Somalia in Perspective." *Review of African Political Economy* 57 (July 1993): 103–19.

Weiss, Thomas. "Principles, Politics and Humanitarian Action." *Ethics and International Affairs* 13 (1999): 1–22.

Weiss, Thomas and Larry Minear. *Humanitarianism Across Borders: Sustaining Civilians in Times of War.* Boulder: Lynne Rienner Publishers, 1993.

Welch, David. *Justice and the Genesis of War.* Cambridge: Cambridge University Press, 1993.

Wendt, Alexander. "The Agent-Structure Problem in International Relations Theory" *International Organization* 41, 3 (1987): 335–70.

Wheeler, Nicholas. *Saving Strangers: Humanitarian Intervention in International Society.* Oxford: Oxford University Press, 2000.

White, John Albert. *The Siberian Intervention.* Princeton: Princeton University Press, 1950.

———. "On Constitution and Causation in International Relations." *Review of International Studies* 24 (1998): 101–18.

Wight, Martin. "Why is There no International Theory?" *Diplomatic Investigations.* Edited by Herbert Butterfield and Martin Wight. London: Allen and Unwin, 1966.

Williams, William A. "The American Intervention in Russia, 1917–1920." *Studies on the Left* 3 (1963): 24–48.

———. *American Russian Relations, 1781–1947.* New York: Octagon Books, 1971.

———. "Anarchy is What States Make of It." *International Organization* 46, 2 (1992): 391–425.

———. "Collective Identity Formation and the International State" *American Political Science Review* 88, 2 (1994): 384–96.

Wilson, Woodrow. *A History of the American People.* New York: Harper Brothers Publishing, 1902. 5 vols.

————. *An Old Man and Other Political Essays*. New York: Charles Scribner's Sons, 1893.

————. *The State*. Boston: D.C. Heath Co., 1918.

Winch, Peter. *The Idea of a Social Science and Its Relation to Philosophy*, 2nd ed. Atlantic Highlands: Humanities Press International, 1990.

Windsor, Philip. "Superpower Intervention." *Intervention in World Politics*. Ed. Hedley Bull. Oxford: Clarendon Press, 1984.

Wittgenstein, Ludwig. *Philosophical Investigations*, 3rd ed., trans. by G. E. M. Anscombe. New York: Macmillan Publishing Co., 1958.

Woodhouse, C. M. *British Foreign Policy Since the Second World War*. London: Hutchinson of London, 1961.

Wolf, Eric. *Europe and the People Without History*. Berkeley: The University of California Press, 1982.

Wolfers, Arnold. *Discord and Collaboration: Essays on International Politics*. Baltimore and London: The Johns Hopkins University Press, 1962.

Young, Crawford. "The African Colonial State and its Political Legacy." *The Precarious Balance: State and Society in Africa*, eds. Donald Rothchild and Naomi Chazan. Boulder: Westview Press, 1988: 25–66.

Young, Kenneth, ed. *The Diaries of Sir Robert Bruce Lockhart: Volume 1, 1915–1938*. London: Macmillan, 1973.

Young-Bruehl, Elisabeth. *Hannah Arendt: For Love of the World*. New Haven: Yale University Press, 1982.

Yousseff, Ahmed. *La Fascination de L Egypte: Du Rêve au Projet*. Paris: L Harmattan, 1998.

Zartman, I. William, ed. *Collapsed States: The Disintegration and Restoration of Legitimate Authority*. Boulder: Lynne Rienner, 1995.

Zorgbibe, Charles. *Le droit d'ingérence*. Paris: Presses Universitaires de France, 1994.

Index

SUNY series in Global Politics
James N. Rosenau, Editor

LIST OF TITLES

241

9423